PENGUIN BOOKS

HIGH-FLAVOR, LOW-FAT VEGETARIAN COOKING

Steven Raichlen's thirteen books include *High-Flavor, Low-Fat Cooking* (winner of a James Beard Award) and the Julia Child/IACP award-winning *Miami Spice*. In addition to the 1996 James Beard Award for Best Vegetarian Cookbook, *High-Flavor, Low-Fat Vegetarian Cooking* received the top honor from the Physicians' Committee for Responsible Medicine as well as a 1995–96 Critics' Choice Award. Raichlen is a cooking instructor and popular syndicated food columnist who has appeared on *Good Morning America*, the *Today* show, and CNN. He lives in Coconut Grove, Florida, with his wife, Barbara.

Steven Raichlen's

HIGH-FLAVOR, LOW-FAT VEGETARIAN COOKING

Photography by Greg Schneider

PENGUIN BOOKS

PENGUIN BOOKS
Published by the Penguin Group
Penguin Books USA Inc., 375 Hudson Street, New York, New York 10014, U.S.A.
Penguin Books Ltd, 27 Wrights Lane, London W8 5TZ, England
Penguin Books Australia Ltd, Ringwood, Victoria, Australia
Penguin Books Canada Ltd, 10 Alcorn Avenue,
Toronto, Ontario, Canada M4V 3B2
Penguin Books (N.Z.) Ltd, 182–190 Wairau Road,
Auckland 10, New Zealand

Penguin Books Ltd, Registered Offices: Harmondsworth, Middlesex, England

First published in the United States of America by Viking Penguin,
a division of Penguin Books USA Inc. 1995
Published in Penguin Books 1997

1 3 5 7 9 10 8 6 4 2

THE LIBRARY OF CONGRESS HAS CATALOGUED THE HARDCOVER AS FOLLOWS:
Raichlen, Steven.
[High-flavor, low-fat vegetarian cooking]
Steven Raichlen's high-flavor, low-fat vegetarian cooking/photography by Greg Schneider.
p.   cm.
Includes index.
ISBN 0-670-85782-3 (hc.)
ISBN 0 14 02.4124 8 (pbk.)
1. Vegetarian cookery.   2. Low-fat diet—Recipes.
I. Title.   II. Title: High-flavor, low-fat vegetarian cooking.
TX837.R25   1995
641.5´636—dc20   94–41220

Printed in the United States of America
Set in Goudy Old Style

to the next generation of vegetarians
Martha, Andy, Robby, and David
and to their parents
Linda and Marty Millison, Fred and Judy Raichlen
I love you one and all

ACKNOWLEDGMENTS

One of the most pleasurable tasks in writing a book is thanking the people who helped make it possible. This one had a great cast of characters.

First, I would like to thank my test-kitchen director, Didi Emmons, whose unerring taste buds are matched only by her wonderful disposition. Recipe testers Elida Proenza and Sharon Morrisson brought a Caribbean cheerfulness to what can be an exhausting and arduous process. Karen Brasel provided the nutritional analyses for all the recipes.

Greg Schneider brought my recipes alive with his energy and spectacular photographs. He was assisted by Michael Donnelly.

Dawn Drzal at Viking Penguin proved to be an editor extraordinaire. Theodora Rosenbaum and Patty O'Connell polished my manuscript with skillful copyediting. Designer Katy Riegel put the pieces together into the handsome volume you hold in your hands. I'd like to thank all my friends at Viking for their enthusiasm and support, including Barbara Grossman, Cathy Hemming, Norm Sheinman, and Paul Slovak.

From the first nervous day of media training to the last grueling stop on book tour, Lisa and Lou Ekus and Merrilyn Siciak have made public relations not only a necessity but a pleasure. I'd also like to thank Doe Coover of the Doe Coover Agency and my friends Howard and Susan White.

Finally, I'd like to thank my family for enduring those long months of recipe testing and a photo shoot in our living room. Daughter Betsy offered nutritional insights from Generation X; son Jake turned out to be a skilled recipe tester; while Marc Billings freed me up for writing by taking charge of Big Flavor Foods, Inc.

My parents, Sonny and Cecille Raichlen, instilled in me a love of fine food from an early age, a love that was fostered by my grandparents, Sarah Goldman and Sam and Ethel Raichlen, and great-aunts, Anette Farber and Rena Aronson. I greatly miss my grandfather, who did not live to see this book to its completion, but is with me in spirit, always.

Above all, I want to thank my wife, Barbara, whose wisdom, love, and devotion made this and all my endeavors possible. I love you, Pumpkin.

CONTENTS

INTRODUCTION

When I was growing up, vegetarians were the radicals of the food world, extremists who wore Earth Shoes and ate endless quantities of alfalfa sprouts, undercooked soybeans, and gluey brown rice; people who put the political correctness of food above its pleasure and taste.

My, how times have changed!

Today's vegetarians are just as likely to wear Cole Haan loafers as Birkenstocks, to work on Wall Street as at the Sierra Club. They delight in the fruits of the vine and the pleasures of the table every bit as much as any meat-eating foodie of the late twentieth century. They are, in short, just like us. And their numbers are growing.

According to a survey conducted by *Vegetarian Times* magazine and reported in the *Washington Post*, there are more than twelve million vegetarians in the United States. (In the last five years, the circulation of *Vegetarian Times* has skyrocketed from eighty thousand to three hundred thousand.) Nor do these individuals belong to a cultish minority. The American military has even developed shelf-stable vegetarian field rations.

Home cooks aren't the only ones turning to a vegetarian diet. Chicago chef Charlie Trotter has received national acclaim for his exquisite seven-course vegetable tasting menu, which is ordered by a full 25 percent of his customers. Celebrated Washington, D.C., chef Jean-Louis Palladin gets weekly requests for his special vegetarian *menu dégustation*. The cost? Fifty-five dollars for six courses.

As Americans become increasingly health-conscious, more and more people are turning to at least a partially vegetarian diet. I fit into this category. I am not a vegetarian. I do, however, try to eat meatless meals more often than not. My diet is high in beans, grains, vegetables, and soy products. And it's getting higher as I grow older—a trend reflected among my fellow baby boomers.

There are many reasons for the newfound popularity of vegetarian cooking. For starters, it's good for you. Vegetarian food is generally higher in vitamins, minerals, and fiber, and lower in fat (especially saturated fat), than the traditional meat and potatoes. Many people (including me) feel that a vegetarian diet is easier to digest.

A vegetarian diet is also better for the planet. A piece of land used to grow vegetables, grains, and beans will feed up to twenty times the number of people as the same-sized plot used to raise beef. Vegetarian cooking is also more economical than meat or fish cookery, which is no small advantage in these cost-conscious times.

Another reason for the vegetarian boom is the increasing danger of contamination associated with animal products. Researchers estimate that as much as 60 percent of the uncooked chicken sold in this country is infected with the salmonella bacteria. Beef is shot up with hormones. The "fresh" fish you buy at the supermarket may have languished in the hold of a fishing boat for two weeks. And even when seafood is truly fresh, who knows what pollutants have fouled the waters it swam in?

Given the worsening condition of the environment, is it any wonder that more and more people are turning to a vegetarian diet? What's surprising is that there are still individuals who haven't.

But this book isn't solely for vegetarians. After all, the author is an avowed omnivore. I hope that the following recipes will appeal to you wherever you fall on the food chain.

STRATEGIES FOR HIGH-FLAVOR, LOW-FAT VEGETARIAN COOKING

There is, of course, no shortage of vegetarian cookbooks. What makes this one different is its emphasis on high-flavor, low-fat cooking. When you're used to cooking with meat, eliminating it can represent a considerable challenge. Equally challenging is eliminating a major cooking technique and a whole class of ingredients that have long been mainstays of the vegetarian diet.

The technique to eliminate is deep-fat frying. For centuries, vegetarians have breaded or battered and deep-fried foods to give them a crisp-textured crust. Biting into this crust gives your mouth the same sort of satisfaction a carnivore feels when sinking his teeth into a charbroiled steak. The brittleness of a pie crust against the creaminess of a quiche filling gives you a similar pleasing contrast of textures.

Deep-fat frying is not a desirable method for the low-fat cook. Fortunately, there are several alternative techniques you can use to achieve this contrast of textures in low-fat vegetarian cooking. One such technique is creating crisp coatings with phyllo dough and bread crumbs instead of the old butter-laden pie crusts. Another is to wrap foods in crisp vegetables, such as lettuce or cabbage leaves, instead of deep-frying them in tortillas or egg-roll wrappers. Yet another is to make pie crusts with ground dried fruits instead of butter or shortening.

As you read through the recipes in this book, you will find these and other techniques as well.

The class of ingredients to be eliminated is dairy products.* (There are a few exceptions here, which we'll get to in a minute.) Traditional vegetarian cooking makes generous use of cheese to provide richness, flavor, and protein. Unfortunately, most types of cheese are high in fat. (Low- and no-fat cheese are discussed on pages 264–65.) The same is true of clarified butter, which is so beloved by Indian cooks, and heavy cream and sour cream, which are mainstays of European cooking.

For cooks like myself, brought up in the Euro-American tradition, eliminating fat-laden dairy products can be even more frustrating than doing without meat or seafood. Here, too, there are several alternative methods for adding flavor without fat. One is to use vegetable stock, instead of cream, to make casseroles and stews moist and creamy. Another is to substitute skim milk, nonfat yogurt, or no-fat sour cream, then bolster the overall flavor with extra spices and seasonings.

Eggs are another no-no for most low-fat diets. But most of the egg's fat and cholesterol reside in the yolk. Egg whites have the same jelling properties as whole eggs—without the fat. Egg whites are perfect for setting custards and pie fillings and firming up vegetable loaves and terrines. (Indeed, egg whites are the main ingredient in Egg Beaters and other low-fat egg substitutes.) When replacing whole eggs with whites, use two whites for every egg.

Nuts are another important ingredient in many vegetarian cookbooks. Nuts are a useful source of protein, but they're also high in fat. Freshly toasted bread crumbs can be used to add a nutty flavor and crunch to dishes without the fat. When I do use nuts, I roast them in the oven to intensify the flavor. Roasting makes a smaller quantity of nuts go a longer way.

*This is not an issue for vegans (vegetarians who eat no animal-based products).

This brings us to the central tenet of my high-flavor, low-fat philosophy: Make food tasty and satisfying by using flavorings instead of fat. You'll notice that my recipes abound with spices, fresh herbs, strong-flavored condiments, and aromatic vegetables. (I can't imagine cooking without the "holy trinity": onions, garlic, and peppers.)

This emphasis on these intense flavorings gives my recipes a different sort of richness. Flavorful? Yes. Fat-laden? No. Cook the high-flavor way, and you'll find that your food actually tastes fresher and cleaner without the artery-clogging cargo of fat.

I've also tried to stress cooking techniques—like pan roasting, smoking, and grilling—that bring out the maximum flavor of a particular ingredient. All three techniques (discussed in full later in this book) evaporate some of the water in the vegetables, concentrating the flavor. The dry heat of roasting and grilling caramelizes the sugars in the vegetables, intensifying their sweetness. Smoking and grilling impart a smoky flavor as well.

The list of low-fat flavorings available to the vegetarian cook includes fresh herbs, whole spices, capers, pickles, chilies, dried fruits, dried tomatoes, exotic mushrooms, exotic vinegars, miso, and soy sauce. Cheese does appear in some of the recipes in this book, but it's likely to be a strong-flavored cheese, like feta or romano. (Thanks to the strong flavor, you need to use only a little.) When I use a fat for sautéing or sauce-making, I make sure it's a flavorful fat, like sesame oil or extra-virgin olive oil.

Several valuable new low-fat products have come out since I wrote my last book, *High-Flavor, Low-Fat Cooking.* For me, as a French-trained cook, the most exciting is no-fat sour cream. (The brand I recommend is Land O' Lakes.) Here is a product that looks and tastes like sour cream, with a similar luxurious texture. Unlike regular sour cream, it won't curdle when you boil it. On the contrary, it actually thickens when boiled, so you can use it to give body to sauces. The invention of this product

has reintroduced into my repertory many of the cream-laden soups and casseroles I learned to prepare during my culinary training in Europe.

Note: No vegetarian cookbook would be complete without a few recipes for tofu. Unfortunately, tofu is quite high in fat (20 grams per 8-ounce serving). This is substantially higher than the limits I've tried to follow for the other recipes in this book. Nonetheless, I like tofu and believe that, eaten in moderation, it is compatible with a healthy diet.

First of all, the fat in tofu isn't as bad for you as, say, the fat in meat or cheese. (Tofu contains no saturated fat.) Second, tofu is quite rich in vitamins and minerals—especially calcium. Finally, as a source of protein, tofu is a lot more healthful for the planet than meat. After all, it takes a lot less farmland to grow the soybeans for a pound of tofu than it does to raise a steer for a pound of beef.

On pages 189 to 197 you'll find some of my favorite tofu recipes. One way to reduce the fat is to serve them as appetizers. Another way to reduce the fat is to use Mori-Nu Extra Firm Silken Tofu or a reduced-fat tofu (see Cook's Notes). These products can be found at natural foods stores and are becoming more widely available every day. Or do as I do at home, and serve tofu only occasionally as an entrée.

ABOUT THE RECIPES

Many of the recipes in this book contain a lot of ingredients. This doesn't make them more complicated (most can be made in thirty minutes or less). It does make them more tasty. My personal taste runs to big-flavored foods: lots of spices, garlic, and chilies. But you can certainly tone down the recipes (I often offer a range of quantities). The most important words in this book are "Season to taste." Your taste.

If I could give one bit of advice to the fledgling low-fat cook, it would be "Think flavor instead of fat." Why add water to a recipe when you can use a flavored liquid, like vegetable stock or tomato juice? That doesn't necessarily mean that you have to go out and make stock before you cook from this book. Of course, if you take the trouble to do so (there's an easy recipe on page 247), your food will taste richer and better. For further information on stock, please see page 270 of Cook's Notes.

The same goes for herbs and spices. For the best results, use fresh herbs in your cooking, even if they're not necessarily those called for in a particular recipe. If a recipe calls for fresh tarragon and I don't have any on hand, I'd much rather use fresh basil than dried tarragon. Use fresh herbs and plenty of them, and your food will taste flavorful—without fat.

Spices are another important ally in the fight for flavor without fat. Buy whole spices (preferably in bulk from an ethnic market or natural foods store) and grind them fresh in a spice mill. A good way to intensify the flavor of any spice is to roast it for a few minutes in a dry skillet over low heat. The resulting caramelization imparts a rich, smoky flavor.

Many of the recipes in this book are international in inspiration. There are several reasons for this. A number of Eastern countries, such as India and Cambodia, have long-established vegetarian traditions. Thus, many of their recipes are already geared toward the vegetarian cook. Other ethnic cuisines, like Thai and Middle Eastern, are by their nature high in flavor and low in fat. Recipes from these regions require less "tinkering" than dishes from the cream- and butter-loving West.

International recipes sometimes call for what some people might consider to be exotic ingredients. But most of these ingredients are available in gourmet shops, natural foods stores, and many well-stocked supermarkets. After all, we live in the age of the global village. Never before have distances seemed so short. Thanks to America's increasing cosmopolitanism—and air freight—you can find almost all of the ingredients you once would have tasted only in Tuscany or Bangkok at your local ethnic market or gourmet shop.

At the back of this book you'll find a Cook's Notes section: a complete guide to the less-familiar ingredients called for in my recipes. In many instances, I've tried to suggest alternative ingredients or substitutions. On page 276, you'll find a list of Mail-Order Sources.

I hope you'll think of high-flavor, low-fat vegetarian cooking as an exciting new culinary adventure. It's not about deprivation or sacrifice. Despite the restrictions imposed by vegetarian low-fat cooking, I found this book to be one of the most exciting and stimulating I've written. I love the challenge of using a fixed set of ingredients to create a bold new world of flavors. (Perhaps that's why some poets find the best outlet for their creativity to be the restrictive form of a sonnet.) I hope these recipes will give you some great new ideas about cooking and eating.

MENU PLANNING AND DIET

My first experience with vegetarian cooking came from a college roommate. It was anything but love at first bite. The experience of a steady diet of soybeans and brown rice turned me into a committed carnivore. And so I remained until the last few years, when nutritional, health, and even ecological concerns led me to reassess the vegetarian diet.

Many people worry that a vegetarian diet won't give them enough protein. This belief stems from the fact that animal foods contain all eight amino acids not manufactured by the human body, while plant foods may lack some of these essential amino acids.

To compensate, vegetarians were taught to "complement proteins," that is, to combine grains with beans or beans with dairy products to give the body all eight essential amino acids. That's what Mexicans do instinctively when they eat tortillas with bean dishes. Italians do the same when they combine pasta with beans in the classic *pasta e fagioli.*

The concept of complementary proteins guided vegetarian menu planning for several decades. Now there's new evidence to suggest that a varied diet provides all the essential amino acids without the necessity of eating beans and grains together at every meal. The World Health Organization recommends the following protein intake: 5 percent of all calories for men and women, 6 percent for pregnant women, and 6.7 percent for nursing women. "This quantity of protein is almost impossible to avoid if enough food is consumed to meet daily calorie needs," writes Dr. John McDougall, author of the intriguing book *The McDougall Plan.*

McDougall maintains that the importance of complementary proteins has been grossly exaggerated—a position echoed by *Vegetarian Times* magazine. My own belief is that if a meal is varied, well balanced, and aesthetically pleasing, it will probably be good for you, too.

Nonetheless, many vegetarians (or would-be vegetarians) feel more comfortable when they incorporate complementary proteins into their meal planning. A great many dishes in this book contain both beans and grains (or beans and dairy products). Thus, by themselves, they offer a complete set of proteins. For the others, add a side serving of pasta, tortillas, or bread, and you've got a meal that's guaranteed to be nutritious.

I bid you welcome to the exciting world of high-flavor, low-fat vegetarian cooking. I hope you enjoy cooking the recipes as much as I enjoyed creating them.

CULINARY MATH

The following numbers are given to help interpret the nutritional analysis included with each recipe.

	Per day for a 120-pound person	Per day for a 170-pound person
Calories	1,800	2,550
Protein	Min. 44 g	Min. 62 g
Fat*	Max. 60 g	Max. 85 g
Carbohydrate	Min. 248 g	Min. 351 g
Sodium†	Max. 6,000 mg	Max. 6,000 mg
Cholesterol	Max. 300 mg	Max. 300 mg

*An easy way to limit fat consumption to the recommended 30 percent of calories is to divide your ideal weight in half. The number is an estimate of the allowed fat in grams per day for a moderately active person. The above values are given as a reference only, since calories needed to maintain ideal body weight vary from person to person.
†There is no general consensus for healthy people to reduce sodium below this moderate level.

APPETIZERS

CHICKPEA CRUNCHIES

Chickpea Crunchies are a great, nutritious snack. The spicing is limited only by your imagination. Cajun crunchies could be made, for example, by using Cajun spices; Southwestern crunchies by using chili powder and cumin. The crunchies taste best served the same day. **Note:** *If you use canned chickpeas, reduce or omit the salt.*

2 cups cooked chickpeas (page 261), drained
    well and blotted dry
1 tablespoon extra-virgin olive oil
½ teaspoon of each of the following seasonings:
    salt, freshly ground black pepper, ground
    cumin, and ground coriander

¼ teaspoon cayenne pepper

1. Preheat the oven to 400° F.
2. Toss the chickpeas with the oil and salt, black pepper, cumin, coriander, and cayenne pepper. Spread them on a nonstick baking sheet and bake for 30 to 40 minutes, or until chickpeas are golden brown and crisp.

Makes about 1¼ cups (serves 4)

109 CALORIES PER SERVING: 4 G PROTEIN; 4 G FAT; 13 G CARBOHYDRATE; 242 MG SODIUM; 0 MG CHOLESTEROL

Jenny Chips
(Low-Fat Potato Chips)

*Here's a recipe from the college front—a low-fat twist on one of America's favorite snacks.
The recipe comes from our daughter's college roommate, Jen. Bake the chips on the back of the
baking sheet. That way, if any stick, it's easy to pry them loose with a knife.*
Note: *If you have a nonstick baking sheet, you can omit the spray oil.*

**2 large baking potatoes, thoroughly scrubbed
spray oil**

**2 teaspoons extra-virgin olive oil (or as needed)
salt and freshly ground black pepper**

1. Preheat the oven to 350° F.
2. Thinly slice the potatoes on a mandoline or in a food processor. They should be no more than ⅛ inch thick. Blot the potato slices dry.
3. Lightly spray the back of a baking sheet with spray oil. Arrange the potato slices on top of the sprayed surface in a single layer and lightly brush them with olive oil. Season the slices with salt and pepper.

4. Bake the chips until golden brown, 15 to 20 minutes. Transfer the chips to a cake rack to cool.

Note: In the unlikely event you have any chips left over the next day and they become soggy, simply re-bake them for a few minutes. They'll regain their crispness as they cool.

Makes about 80 chips, enough to serve 4

115 CALORIES PER SERVING: 2 G PROTEIN; 3 G FAT; 22 G CARBOHYDRATE; 5 MG SODIUM; 0 MG CHOLESTEROL

NOT CHOPPED LIVER

I first tasted this meatless chopped liver at the house of my wife's aunt Elsie Malschick.
I was astonished by how closely the combination of mushrooms and peas approximated the taste of liver.
Sieving the egg yolk gives it the delicate appearance of a mimosa flower.

2 eggs
1 tablespoon olive oil
1 small onion, finely chopped
1 clove garlic, finely chopped
5 ounces fresh mushrooms, finely chopped
    (about 2 cups before chopping)
1 cup cooked green peas (if using frozen peas,
    thaw them but don't cook)

approximately ¼ cup Basic Vegetable Stock
    (page 247) or water
1 to 2 tablespoons dried bread crumbs
salt, freshly ground black pepper, or cayenne
    pepper

1. Boil the eggs, starting with cold water, for 11 minutes. Rinse under cold water and peel. Halve the eggs and remove the yolks, reserving half of 1 yolk, discarding the remaining yolks. Coarsely chop the whites.

2. Heat the olive oil in a nonstick frying pan. Cook the onion and garlic over medium heat until soft but not brown, about 3 minutes. Increase the heat to high and add the mushrooms. Cook until most of the mushroom liquid has evaporated, about 5 minutes.

3. Stir in the peas and vegetable stock and simmer until most of the stock is absorbed, about 5 minutes. Stir in enough bread crumbs to hold the mixture together. Coarsely purée the mushroom mixture with the hard-cooked egg whites in the food processor and let cool. Correct the seasoning, adding salt, pepper, or cayenne to taste.

4. Transfer the mixture to a bowl or plate for serving. Push the reserved half egg yolk through a sieve over the Not Chopped Liver or finely chop it and sprinkle on top. Serve with saltine crackers, as Aunt Elsie does, or with Pita Chips (page 7).

Serves 4

103 CALORIES PER SERVING: 5 G PROTEIN; 4 G FAT; 11 G CARBOHYDRATE; 43 MG SODIUM; 27 MG CHOLESTEROL

COWBOY HUMMUS

The Middle East meets the Wild West in this recipe—a variation on Arabic hummus.
I like the smokiness imparted by chipotle chilies, but you may also use fresh or pickled jalapeño chilies.
Warning: *Chipotles are hotter than jalapeños, so don't use two unless you mean to.*

2 cups cooked red kidney beans (the beans should be quite soft; see page 261)
3 to 4 tablespoons lime juice
1 to 2 canned chipotle chili peppers (see Cook's Notes) or 1 to 2 fresh or pickled jalapeño chilies, seeded and minced (for hotter hummus, leave the seeds in)
2 cloves garlic, minced
2 scallions, minced

3 tablespoons minced fresh cilantro, plus a few whole sprigs for garnish
½ teaspoon ground cumin
2 tablespoons extra-virgin olive oil (optional)
a splash of your favorite hot sauce
salt, freshly ground black pepper, and cayenne pepper (to taste)
⅓ cup Basic Vegetable Stock (page 247) or as needed
Paleface Chips (see below) or nonfat tortilla chips

1. Purée the beans, lime juice, chilies, garlic, scallions, minced cilantro, cumin, olive oil, hot sauce, salt, pepper, and cayenne in the processor, adding enough stock to obtain a soft purée. Correct the seasoning, adding salt, chilies, or lime juice to taste. The mixture should be highly seasoned.

2. Transfer the hummus to a bowl and garnish with cilantro sprigs. (If you want to get fancy, make decorative lines on top with a wet spatula.) Serve the hummus with the Paleface Chips below.

Serves 8

60 CALORIES PER SERVING: 4 G PROTEIN; 0 G FAT; 11 G CARBOHYDRATE; 33 MG SODIUM; 0 MG CHOLESTEROL

PALEFACE CHIPS

White (wheat flour) tortillas make wonderful, crackling crisp chips without added fat or deep frying.

4 9- or 10-inch flour tortillas

Preheat the oven to 350° F. Cut each tortilla into 12 wedges. Arrange the wedges on baking sheets and bake until just beginning to brown,

about 8 minutes. The chips will crisp as they cool.

Makes 48 chips

8 CALORIES PER CHIP: 1 G PROTEIN; 0 G FAT; 9 G CARBOHYDRATE; 0 MG SODIUM; 0 MG CHOLESTEROL

EGGPLANT DIP WITH ASIAN SPICES

This tangy dip is an Asian takeoff on Middle Eastern baba ganooj. *Grilling gives the eggplant a distinctive smoky flavor, but it can also be baked. To serve the dip, you can use Oriental rice crackers or Pita Chips (page 7).*

2 pounds eggplant (2 medium eggplants—enough
  to make 2 cups cooked pulp)
1 to 2 cloves garlic, minced
2 teaspoons minced ginger
1 tablespoon minced scallion (white part only—
  reserve green for garnish, below)
2 tablespoons rice vinegar
4 to 5 teaspoons soy sauce
2 teaspoons sugar or honey

1 teaspoon Asian sesame oil
a splash of chili oil (optional)
a pinch of salt (optional)
3 tablespoons chopped cilantro leaves

FOR THE GARNISH
2 tablespoons minced scallion greens
1 teaspoon black sesame seeds or darkly toasted
  regular sesame seeds

1. Prick the eggplants in a few spots with a fork. (This keeps them from exploding.) Grill the eggplants over a medium flame, turning often, until the skin is charred on all sides (I mean really charred!) and the flesh is soft. Alternatively, the eggplant can be cooked on an open flame or electric burner on the stove (set the heat to medium), broiled, or baked in a 400° F. oven for about 1 hour. Let cool.

2. Using a paring knife, scrape the burnt skin off the eggplant. Purée the eggplant in the food processor, adding the garlic, ginger, minced white scallion, vinegar, soy sauce, sugar, sesame oil, chili oil (if using), and salt (if desired). Correct the seasoning, adding vinegar, soy sauce, or chili oil to taste. Stir in the cilantro leaves and transfer the dip to a serving bowl. Garnish with scallion greens and sesame seeds and serve.

Makes 2 cups, enough to serve 8

78 CALORIES PER SERVING: 2 G PROTEIN; 2 G FAT; 16 G CARBOHYDRATE; 349 MG SODIUM; 0 MG CHOLESTEROL

ARMENIAN POMEGRANATE PÂTÉ

This tangy dip is modeled on an Armenian dish called mohamarra. *I make it every September,
when fresh pomegranates are in season. Serve with Pita Chips for dipping.*

2 pomegranates
¼ cup chopped walnuts (1 ounce), lightly
   toasted
¾ to 1 cup fresh bread crumbs
2 cups finely chopped red bell pepper (1 very
   large or 2 small)
2 tablespoons lemon juice (or to taste)

½ to 1 teaspoon red pepper flakes, soaked in
   1 tablespoon hot water
1 teaspoon ground cumin
salt and freshly ground black pepper
3 tablespoons coarsely chopped fresh cilantro

Pita Chips for serving (recipe follows)

1. Cut one of the pomegranates in half and juice on a citrus reamer. You should have ¼ cup juice. Break the other pomegranate apart and extract the seeds. Reserve half these seeds for garnish.

2. Grind the walnuts and ¾ cup bread crumbs in a food processor. Grind in half the pomegranate seeds and the bell pepper, pomegranate juice, lemon juice, pepper flakes, cumin, salt, and pepper. The mixture should be the consistency of soft ice

cream; add bread crumbs as necessary. Correct the seasoning, adding salt, cumin, or lemon juice: The pâté should be highly seasoned.

3. Transfer the pâté to a bowl and sprinkle the top with cilantro and the remaining pomegranate seeds. Arrange the Pita Chips around the pâté and serve at once.

Makes about 2 cups, enough to serve 4 to 6

137 CALORIES PER SERVING: 4 G PROTEIN; 5 G FAT; 22 G CARBOHYDRATE; 50 MG SODIUM; 0 MG CHOLESTEROL

Analysis based on 4 servings

PITA CHIPS

Pita Chips are great for dipping (not to mention for using up leftover pita bread). The oil is optional.
For extra color, you could sprinkle the chips with white or black sesame seeds before baking.

3 large or 4 small pita breads
1 tablespoon extra-virgin olive oil (optional)

1. Preheat the oven to 350° F.
2. Separate the pita breads lengthwise into halves. Lightly brush each half with olive oil (if using). Cut each half into 8 wedges (6 for small breads).

3. Arrange the pita chips on a baking sheet and bake for 8 to 10 minutes, or until golden brown. Transfer the chips to a cake rack to cool.

Makes 48 chips

7 CALORIES PER CHIP: 0.2 G PROTEIN; 0 G FAT; 1 G CARBOHYDRATE; 13 MG SODIUM; 0 MG CHOLESTEROL

BRUSCHETTA (ITALIAN GRILLED BREAD) WITH THREE TOPPINGS

Bruschetta (pronounced bru-SKE-ta) is an Italian canapé, a grilled bread slice topped with a simple salad or pâté. Grilling gives the bread a distinctive smoky flavor, but you can also toast the bread under the broiler.

1 French- or Italian-style baguette
1 clove garlic, cut in half

1 or more of the following toppings
whole flat-leaf parsley leaves for garnish

1. Preheat the grill to medium. If using a fat loaf (3 inches in diameter), cut the bread widthwise into ¾-inch-thick slices. If using a skinny (2-inch) loaf, cut it on the diagonal into ¾-inch slices.

2. Grill the bread slices for 1 to 2 minutes per side, or until well browned. Let cool on a cake rack.

3. Just before serving, rub each bruschetta with cut garlic. Top each with a heaping tablespoon of one or more of the toppings. Garnish with parsley leaves and serve at once.

Makes 20 to 24 bruschette, enough to serve 6 to 8

98 CALORIES PER SERVING (WITHOUT TOPPING): 3 G PROTEIN; 1 G FAT; 18 G CARBOHYDRATE; 193 MG SODIUM; 0 MG CHOLESTEROL
Analysis based on 6 servings

RED AND YELLOW TOMATO TOPPING

I like to think of this colorful topping as Italian salsa. If yellow tomatoes aren't available, just use red. The most important thing is that they be ripe.

2 large or 3 medium ripe red tomatoes
1 large or 2 small yellow tomatoes
10 large fresh basil or flat-leaf parsley leaves, finely chopped
2 to 3 shallots, minced (about 3 tablespoons)

1 tablespoon capers, drained
2 tablespoons balsamic vinegar, or to taste
1 to 1½ tablespoons extra-virgin olive oil
salt and freshly ground black pepper

1. Cut the tomatoes in half widthwise and squeeze out the seeds and liquid over a strainer in a bowl. Reserve the liquid. Cut the tomatoes into ¼-inch dice.

2. Not more than 20 minutes before serving, combine the red and yellow tomatoes, basil or pars-ley, shallots, capers, vinegar, oil, salt, and pepper, adding enough strained tomato liquid to make the mixture moist but not wet. Correct the seasoning, adding vinegar or salt to taste.

Makes about 3 cups, enough to serve 6

50 CALORIES PER SERVING: 1 G PROTEIN; 3 G FAT; 7 G CARBOHYDRATE; 40 MG SODIUM; 0 MG CHOLESTEROL

ARTICHOKE AND PIMIENTO TOPPING

Here's another colorful topping. Purists may want to cook their own artichoke hearts and roast their own peppers from scratch. To prepare an artichoke heart, cut off the crown, tough leaves, and stem, rubbing heart with cut lemon to prevent browning. Scrape out the "choke"—the fibers—with a spoon or melon baller. Boil the artichoke hearts in salted water until tender, 10 to 15 minutes. But canned artichoke hearts work well for this recipe, too. Pepper roasting instructions are found on page 257. If you're in a hurry, use bottled pimientos and canned roasted peppers.

2 cups finely diced cooked artichoke hearts
1 cup finely diced pimientos or roasted red
peppers
1 to 1½ tablespoons extra-virgin olive oil

1 tablespoon sherry vinegar (or to taste)
⅛ teaspoon saffron soaked in 1 tablespoon warm
water
salt and freshly ground black pepper

Combine the artichoke hearts, pimientos, oil, vinegar, saffron, salt, and pepper in a mixing bowl and toss to mix. Correct the seasoning, adding more vinegar or salt to taste. The topping should be highly seasoned.

Note: The topping can be made ahead of time, but put it on the bruschetta just before serving.

Makes about 3 cups, enough to serve 6

56 CALORIES PER SERVING: 2 G PROTEIN; 3 G FAT; 8 G CARBOHYDRATE; 59 MG SODIUM; 0 MG CHOLESTEROL

BEAN AND PEPPER TOPPING

There are many candidates for this topping: Italian cannellini beans, pea beans, navy beans, or fava beans.
For a Latin American touch, you could even use black beans. Whichever beans you use, cook them until quite soft.

2 cups cooked beans, drained well (page 261)
½ small red onion, cut into ¼-inch dice (about ¼ cup)
½ red or yellow bell pepper, cored, seeded, and cut into ¼-inch dice (about ½ cup)
½ green bell pepper or 1 whole ancho chili, cored, seeded, and cut into ¼-inch dice (about ½ cup)

1 stalk celery, cut into ¼-inch dice
2 tablespoons finely chopped fresh tarragon, chervil, and/or basil
2 tablespoons finely chopped flat-leaf parsley
1½ tablespoons red wine vinegar (or to taste)
1½ tablespoons extra-virgin olive oil
salt and freshly ground black pepper

Combine the beans, onions, bell peppers, celery, herbs, parsley, vinegar, oil, salt, and pepper in a mixing bowl and toss to mix. Correct the seasoning, adding vinegar or salt to taste. Add a little water, if necessary, to make a mixture that is moist but not wet.

Makes about 3 cups, enough to serve 6

112 CALORIES PER SERVING: 5 G PROTEIN; 4 G FAT; 15 G CARBOHYDRATE; 11 MG SODIUM; 0 MG CHOLESTEROL

QUINOA CAVIAR

Quinoa (pronounced KEEN-wa), the wonder grain from the Andes, has a softly crunchy consistency that reminds me of caviar. That set me thinking about Russia's eggplant caviar, and I decided to combine the two. Tamari gives this "caviar" a briny quality, while the cilantro hints at the iodine tang of sturgeon roe.

1 small eggplant (10 to 12 ounces)
1 tablespoon extra-virgin olive oil
1 onion, finely chopped
1 cup quinoa
2 cups salted water
2 cloves garlic, minced

3 tablespoons minced fresh cilantro
3 tablespoons chopped parsley
4 to 5 teaspoons tamari or soy sauce (or to taste)
2 tablespoons fresh lemon juice (or to taste)
salt and freshly ground black pepper (to taste)

1. Preheat the oven to 350° F. Prick the eggplant in several spots with a fork. Roast the eggplant on a nonstick baking sheet for 40 minutes, or until soft. Let eggplant cool.

2. Heat the olive oil in a nonstick frying pan. Add the onion and cook over medium heat until soft but not brown, 3 to 4 minutes. Stir in the quinoa and lightly toast it for 1 minute. Stir in 2 cups water and salt to taste and bring to a boil. Reduce the heat, cover the pan, and gently simmer the quinoa for 15 minutes. Remove the pan from the heat and let stand for 10 minutes. Uncover the pan and fluff the quinoa with a fork. Transfer the quinoa to a mixing bowl and let cool.

3. Cut the eggplant in half lengthwise. Scrape out the flesh, taking care not to pierce the eggplant skin, and place it in a food processor with the garlic, cilantro, parsley, tamari, and lemon juice. Purée to a smooth paste. Stir the eggplant mixture into the quinoa. Correct the seasoning, adding tamari, pepper, or lemon juice to taste. Spoon the "caviar" back into the eggplant skins and serve it with toast points, Bruschetta (page 8), or Pita Chips (page 7), or on boiled new potatoes with no-fat sour cream.

Makes 4½ cups, enough to serve 8 to 10

100 CALORIES PER SERVING: 3 G PROTEIN; 3 G FAT; 16 G CARBOHYDRATE; 160 MG SODIUM; 0 MG CHOLESTEROL
Analysis based on 10 servings

CHINESE VEGETABLE LETTUCE ROLLS

One of the greatest challenges in low-fat vegetarian cooking is acquiring crisp textures without the use of deep-frying. In this version of a classic Chinese recipe, water chestnuts and bean sprouts provide crunch to the filling, while iceberg lettuce leaves make a crisp wrapping. Fresh water chestnuts can be found at Asian markets, but the canned variety is perfectly acceptable. For ease in preparation, you can chop the vegetables in a food processor.

6 to 8 dried Chinese black mushrooms
1 tablespoon cornstarch
1 head iceberg lettuce
1 cup very finely chopped napa (Chinese cabbage) or savoy cabbage
½ cup very finely chopped carrots
½ cup very finely diced water chestnuts (1 8-ounce can)
½ cup very finely chopped snow peas
½ cup bean sprouts
½ cup very finely diced bamboo shoots (1 8-ounce can), optional
¼ cup very finely chopped celery

FOR THE SAUCE
2 tablespoons soy sauce or tamari
2 tablespoons rice wine
1 tablespoon sugar or honey
a little salt (optional)

1 tablespoon canola oil
½ tablespoon dark sesame oil
2 cloves garlic, minced
2 scallions, minced
2 teaspoons finely chopped fresh ginger
3 tablespoons chopped fresh cilantro (optional)

¼ cup hoisin sauce, placed in a small bowl, with a spoon or scallion brush for serving

1. Soak the mushrooms in hot water to cover for 20 to 30 minutes, or until tender. Drain the mushrooms and squeeze out any liquid over a bowl. Dissolve the cornstarch in 2 tablespoons mushroom liquid in a small bowl and set aside. (Extra mushroom liquid can be reserved for soups and sauces.)

2. Cut the lettuce in half vertically (through the core). Cut the core out of each and peel off 20 large outer leaves, reserving the center leaves for salads. Pile 16 of the leaves in a bowl. Use the remaining leaves to line a platter.

3. Finely chop the mushrooms. Combine with the cabbage, carrots, water chestnuts, snow peas,

bean sprouts, bamboo shoots (if using), and celery and set aside.

4. Mix together the ingredients for the sauce—soy sauce, rice wine, sugar, and salt (if using)—in a small bowl and set aside.

5. Heat a wok over high heat almost to smoking. Swirl in the canola and sesame oils. Add the garlic, scallions, and ginger and stir-fry for 15 seconds, or until fragrant but not brown. Add the chopped vegetables and stir-fry until the vegetables lose their rawness, 2 to 3 minutes.

6. Add the sauce and continue stir-frying until the vegetables are crispy-tender, 2 to 3 minutes.

Restir the cornstarch and add it to the vegetables with the cilantro (if using). Bring the mixture just to a boil and remove the wok from the heat. Transfer the vegetable mixture to the platter lined with lettuce leaves.

7. To serve, have each guest take a lettuce leaf from the bowl and spread the inside with a little hoisin sauce. Place a spoonful of vegetable mixture inside and roll the lettuce leaf up like a blintz or an egg roll.

Makes 16 rolls, enough to serve 8 as an appetizer,
4 as a light main course

80 CALORIES PER SERVING: 2 G PROTEIN; 2 G FAT; 12 G CARBOHYDRATE; 298 MG SODIUM; 0 MG CHOLESTEROL

Analysis based on a 2-roll serving

VIETNAMESE-STYLE SPRING ROLLS

Every nation in Asia has its version of a spring roll or egg roll. My favorite is Vietnam's spring roll, a tangy, soft, chewy cylinder chock-full of noodles, herbs, and vegetables. The wrapper is rice paper, which is actually a type of noodle made from rice flour. Rice paper is available at Asian markets and many gourmet shops and supermarkets. Rice paper is cooked at the factory, so all you really need to do is rehydrate the sheets in cold water. (The fragile sheets often break, so I've called for a few more than you'll actually need.) Bean threads are thin noodles made from mung bean starch and sold in small net packages.
Note: *Spring rolls aren't difficult to make, but it may take a bit of practice before they come out perfectly. Don't be discouraged if you have to reroll your first few with fresh sheets of rice paper.)*

8 to 10 dried Chinese black mushrooms
2 1¾-ounce packages bean threads (also known as mung bean noodles or glass noodles) or rice vermicelli
salt
2 medium carrots, julienned (about 1 cup)
1 cup snow peas, stemmed, stringed, and very finely julienned
1 cup mung bean sprouts

16 to 18 9-inch round rice papers
24 mint leaves
3 scallions, cut into thin slivers
salt and freshly ground black pepper (to taste)
12 large basil leaves (Thai basil, if available)

lettuce leaves for garnish
1 or more dipping sauces (recipes follow)

1. Soak the black mushrooms in hot water to cover for 20 to 30 minutes. Stem the mushrooms, reserving the soaking water for soups. Cut the mushrooms into a fine julienne.

2. Soak the bean threads in cold water to cover for 20 to 30 minutes, or until tender. Drain well. Cook the noodles in 2 quarts lightly salted boiling water until al dente, about 1 minute. Transfer the noodles to a colander with a slotted spoon. Rinse the noodles with cold water and drain well.

3. Blanch the carrots in the boiling noodle water for 1 minute. Transfer the carrots to a colander with a slotted spoon. Rinse the carrots under cold water and drain well. Blanch, drain, and rinse the snow peas and bean sprouts the same way.
Note: Blanch the bean sprouts for only 30 seconds.

4. Fill a large shallow bowl with cold water.

Soak a sheet of rice paper in the water for 1 minute. Carefully transfer the rice paper to a clean dish towel on a cutting board and let sit for 1 to 2 minutes, or until pliable.

5. Assemble the rolls. Arrange 2 mint leaves in a row along the bottom third of the rice paper. Arrange ¹/₁₂ of the bean noodles, black mushrooms, carrots, scallions, and snow peas in a row on top. Lightly salt and pepper these ingredients. Roll up the rice paper to form a tight cylinder, folding in the side flaps halfway up, as you would to form an egg roll or a blintz. Once you complete 1 turn, add a basil leaf and continue rolling. The idea is to form a compact roll about 6 inches long. Assemble the remaining spring rolls the same way. Once assembled, the spring rolls will keep for up to 6 hours, covered, in the refrigerator.

6. To serve, cut each spring roll in half on the diagonal. Arrange the halves on platters covered with lettuce leaves. Serve with small bowls of the following dipping sauces.

Makes 12 rolls, enough to serve 6 as an appetizer, 3 to 4 as a light main course

112 CALORIES PER SERVING: 2 G PROTEIN; 0.2 G FAT; 36 G CARBOHYDRATE; 14 MG SODIUM; 0 MG CHOLESTEROL

Analysis based on a 2-roll serving

PEANUT DIPPING SAUCE

3 tablespoons chunky-style peanut butter
1 teaspoon minced fresh ginger
1 to 2 cloves garlic, minced
2 scallions, minced
⅓ cup Basic Vegetable Stock (page 247)
3 tablespoons soy sauce or tamari

2 tablespoons rice vinegar
2 to 3 teaspoons honey or sugar (or to taste)
3 tablespoons minced fresh cilantro
1 teaspoon Thai hot sauce or hot sauce of your choice

Combine all the ingredients in a mixing bowl and whisk until smooth. Correct the seasoning, adding soy sauce, vinegar, or honey to taste. The mixture should be a little sweet, sour, and salty.

Makes 1 cup

46 CALORIES PER SERVING: 2 G PROTEIN; 3 G FAT; 4 G CARBOHYDRATE; 418 MG SODIUM; 0 MG CHOLESTEROL

Analysis based on a 1-oz. serving

GINGER SOY DIPPING SAUCE

½ cup fresh lime juice
6 tablespoons tamari or soy sauce
¼ cup water
2 tablespoons honey
2 cloves garlic, minced

1 teaspoon fresh ginger, minced
2 scallions, minced
1 to 3 serrano, jalapeño, Thai, or other hot chilies, sliced crosswise as thinly as possible

Combine the lime juice, tamari or soy sauce, water, honey, garlic, ginger, and scallions in a mixing bowl and whisk to mix. If the sauce tastes too strong, add a little more water. Just before serving, transfer the sauce to a bowl and float the chili slices on top.

Makes 1 cup

31 CALORIES PER SERVING: 1.3 G PROTEIN; 0 G FAT; 7 G CARBOHYDRATE; 418 MG SODIUM; 0 MG CHOLESTEROL

Analysis based on a 1-oz. serving

CILANTRO DIPPING SAUCE

1 cup fresh cilantro leaves, finely chopped
3 tablespoons fresh lime juice (or to taste)
2 cloves garlic, minced
1 teaspoon minced fresh ginger
½ cup hot Basic Vegetable Stock (page 247) or
    hot water

3 tablespoons tofu (preferably silken)
1 to 2 teaspoons sugar or honey
salt and freshly ground black pepper (to taste)

Combine the cilantro, lime juice, garlic, ginger, vegetable stock, tofu, sugar, salt, and pepper in a blender and purée. Correct the seasoning, adding lime juice, salt, or sugar to taste.

Note: The sauce should be creamy, but not too thick. It will thicken as it sits. Add stock to thin it as necessary.

Makes 1 cup

14 CALORIES PER SERVING: 1 G PROTEIN; 0.5 G FAT; 1.6 G CARBOHYDRATE; 2 MG SODIUM; 0 MG CHOLESTEROL

Analysis based on a 1-oz. serving

BARLEY AND MINT STUFFED GRAPE LEAVES

Stuffed grape leaves are a popular snack throughout Greece and the Near East. I like the chewy texture the barley gives the filling. The grape leaves can be served cold as an appetizer or hot as an entrée.

24 grape leaves, thoroughly rinsed in cold water
2½ cups cooked barley (recipe follows), drained
   but not rinsed, so it remains slightly sticky
⅓ cup very finely chopped red onion
2 cloves garlic, minced
3 tablespoons chopped fresh mint, dill, or
   oregano (or to taste)

2 tablespoons lemon juice (or to taste)
2 teaspoons extra-virgin olive oil (optional)
2 tablespoons lightly toasted pine nuts (optional)
salt and freshly ground black pepper
approximately 1½ cups Basic Vegetable Stock
   (page 247) or water

1. Soak the grape leaves in a bowl with cold water to cover for 30 minutes, changing the water 2 or 3 times. Cook the barley, drain it, and cool it, but do not rinse. You want the barley to be a little sticky.

2. Combine the barley, onion, garlic, mint, lemon juice, olive oil and pine nuts (if using), salt, and pepper in a mixing bowl and mix well. Correct the seasoning, adding salt or lemon juice to taste: The mixture should be highly seasoned.

3. Rinse the grape leaves in a colander. Blanch the leaves, a few at a time, in a shallow pan of boiling water for 1 minute. Drain the grape leaves in a colander, rinse with cold water, and let cool. Blot dry.

4. Lay a grape leaf on your work surface, stem end toward you. Place a heaping tablespoon of filling in a row along the bottom third of the leaf. Roll up the leaf to form a tight cylinder, folding in the side flaps halfway up, as you would to form an egg roll or a blintz. The idea is to form a compact roll about 3 inches long and 1 inch thick. Assemble the remaining grape leaves the same way. The grape leaves can be assembled several hours ahead and stored, covered, in the refrigerator.

5. Place the stuffed grape leaves in a nonreactive baking dish with ½ inch vegetable stock or water. Cover the pan with foil. Bake the grape leaves for 30 minutes, or until tender. Drain off any extra cooking liquid before serving. Serve either hot or cold.

Note: If you serve the grape leaves hot, Sugo di Pomodoro (page 211) would make a great accompaniment; if you serve them cold, try the Lemon Garlic Dressing (page 206).

Makes 24, enough to serve 6 as an appetizer,
3 to 4 as an entrée

130 CALORIES PER SERVING: 4 G PROTEIN; 1 G FAT; 29 G CARBOHYDRATE; 7 MG SODIUM; 0 MG CHOLESTEROL

Analysis based on a 4-roll serving

To Cook Barley

My method for cooking barley differs from most in two ways. First, I like to presoak the grain in cold water to soften it.
Second, I cook barley (and other grains) in lots of boiling water, like pasta.
This eliminates the gluey consistency found in many barley recipes

1 cup pearl barley
4 quarts water
salt (optional)

1. Soak the barley in 4 cups cold water for at least 4 hours, preferably overnight. Drain the barley.
2. Bring 4 quarts water to a boil. Add the barley and boil, uncovered, for 30 to 40 minutes, or until soft. Add salt to taste (if using). Drain the barley well before serving.

Makes 2½ cups

176 CALORIES PER SERVING: 5 G PROTEIN; 1 G FAT; 39 G CARBOHYDRATE; 5 MG SODIUM; 0 MG CHOLESTEROL

Analysis based on 4 servings

SAR MOO SARS (BURMESE CURRY TURNOVERS)

*This dish is deeply rooted in nostalgia. I first tasted it at a funky Burmese restaurant in Boston called Mandalay.
I raved about the establishment in my restaurant reviews (some of the first I ever wrote). It wasn't long before
business boomed and the restaurant moved from its homey basement location on Huntington Avenue
to swank new digs in Cambridge. Unfortunately, the upscale décor did not bring commensurate
prosperity, and the restaurant eventually closed. I dedicate the following recipe to the memory
of the Mandalay and its owners, the Chin family.*

2½ tablespoons olive oil
1 small onion, finely chopped
2 cloves garlic, minced
2 teaspoons minced fresh ginger
1 to 2 jalapeño or other hot chilies, seeded and
    minced (for hotter turnovers, leave the
    seeds in)
1½ teaspoons curry powder

½ teaspoon cumin
1 cup cooked split peas (recipe follows)
1 medium potato, peeled and finely chopped,
approximately ⅔ cup Basic Vegetable Stock
    (page 247)
salt (optional)
15 sheets phyllo dough (each 14 x 18 inches)
¼ cup fine dry bread crumbs

1. Heat 1 tablespoon olive oil in a nonstick frying pan. Cook the onion, garlic, ginger, and chilies over medium heat until soft but not brown, 3 to 4 minutes, adding the curry powder and cumin after 2 minutes.

2. Stir in the peas, potatoes, and vegetable stock and simmer for 6 to 8 minutes, or until the potatoes are very tender and virtually all of the stock has been absorbed. If the stock evaporates before the potatoes are cooked, add a little more. Correct the seasoning, adding salt or curry powder. The mixture should be highly seasoned.

3. Unwrap 15 sheets of phyllo dough and cover with a slightly damp dish towel or plastic wrap. Lay one sheet of phyllo on the work surface, lightly brush it with some of the remaining 1½ tablespoons olive oil, and sprinkle with 1 teaspoon bread crumbs. Lay a second sheet of phyllo on top. Brush with more oil and sprinkle with bread

crumbs. Repeat with a third sheet of phyllo. Cut the sheets lengthwise into 3½-inch strips.

4. Place 1 generous tablespoon of filling 1 inch below the top of the strip. Fold over one corner to cover the filling, then fold the strip as you would a flag to form a neat triangle. Continue making sar moo sars in this fashion until all the filling and phyllo dough are used up. Brush the tops of the pastries with a little olive oil. The sar moo sars can be prepared several hours ahead to this stage and kept in the refrigerator.

5. Preheat the oven to 400° F. Bake the sar moo sars on a nonstick baking sheet until golden brown, about 15 minutes.

Makes 20 pieces

Note: as the name suggests, this is a dish of Indian extraction. In India, the dish would be called *samosa*.

112 CALORIES PER SERVING: 4 G PROTEIN; 2 G FAT; 21 G CARBOHYDRATE; 100 MG SODIUM; 0 MG CHOLESTEROL

Analysis per piece

To Cook Split Peas

½ cup split peas
2 quarts water
salt

Cook the peas in 2 quarts briskly simmering water in a large heavy pot for 30 minutes, or until tender. Add salt to taste during the last 3 minutes, Drain off any excess water in a strainer or colander.

Makes 1 cup

ROASTED VEGETABLE TERRINE

Terrines are the mosaics of the vegetarian artist, polychrome tableaux woven from asparagus greens, carrot oranges,
bell pepper reds and yellows. Polenta serves as the "mortar" that holds the vegetables together.
Oven-roasting the vegetables helps intensify their flavor. (Alternatively, the vegetables could be grilled.)
Feel free to vary the vegetables according to what's available and in season.

FOR THE ROASTED VEGETABLES
15 cloves garlic, peeled
2 leeks, trimmed, cut in half, and washed, or 2
    red onions, peeled and cut into 6 wedges
4 medium carrots, peeled
1 red bell pepper
1 yellow bell pepper
20 green beans
8 asparagus spears
2 cups mushrooms, stemmed
1½ tablespoons extra-virgin olive oil
salt and freshly ground black pepper

FOR THE POLENTA
1 cup yellow cornmeal (preferably stone-ground)
3½ cups Basic Vegetable Stock (page 247) or
    water
1 clove garlic, minced
¼ teaspoon minced fresh rosemary

10 savoy or green cabbage leaves

spray oil

1. Preheat the oven to 375° F. Place the garlic, leeks, carrots, bell peppers, green beans, asparagus, and mushrooms on a nonstick baking sheet and toss with the olive oil and salt and pepper. Roast the vegetables until soft and golden brown. The green beans and mushrooms will cook the quickest (15 to 20 minutes); the carrots and leeks will take the longest (40 to 50 minutes). Check the vegetables for doneness every 10 minutes; when cooked, a vegetable will feel soft. As soon as each is cooked, transfer it to a platter to cool. Reserve drippings, if any.

2. Meanwhile, prepare the polenta. In a mixing bowl, combine 1 cup cornmeal and 1 cup vegetable stock and whisk to a smooth paste. Bring the remaining stock to a boil in a heavy saucepan (preferably nonstick). Add the cornmeal mixture to the stock in a thin stream, whisking steadily. Boil the polenta for 3 minutes, whisking steadily. Reduce the heat; add the garlic, rosemary, and any drippings from the roasted vegetables.

3. Gently simmer the polenta for 30 to 40 minutes, or until the mixture thickens enough to pull away from the sides of the pan. It should be the consistency of soft ice cream. It's not necessary to whisk the polenta continuously, but you should give it a stir every 5 minutes. Season the polenta with salt and pepper: It should be highly seasoned and still warm when the terrine is assembled.

4. Meanwhile, cook the cabbage leaves in 3 quarts rapidly boiling, salted water for 2 minutes, or until tender. Drain the cabbage leaves and shock chill in ice water. Drain the cabbage leaves and blot dry on paper towels.

5. Assemble the terrine. Spray a 9-inch terrine mold or loaf pan (preferably nonstick) with oil. Line the mold with cabbage leaves, letting 2 inches of the leaves hang over the edge.

6. Spread ⅓ cup polenta in the bottom of the mold. Arrange a layer of vegetables on top, using polenta to fill in any gaps. Add more polenta, more vegetables, more polenta, more vegetables, etc.,

until all are used up. Press down firmly on the vegetables as you complete each layer. Vary the vegetables by shape and color to created a mosaic-like effect when the terrine is sliced. If using leeks, add them last. The final layer should be polenta.

7. Fold the cabbage leaves over the top of the terrine. Place a cutting board and a heavy weight on top of the terrine and let stand for 1 hour.

8. The terrine can be served hot or cold. (It's easier to slice cold.) To serve, invert the terrine onto a cutting board. Cut it widthwise into ¾-inch slices, using an electric knife, a serrated bread knife, or the sharpest, most slender carving knife you own. Press a spatula flat against the front of each slice to hold it steady as you cut it.

Serves 10 to 12 as an
appetizer, 5 to 6 as an entrée

Note: Many sauces would be great with this terrine, including Barbara's Chunky Tomato Sauce (page 212) or Cilantro Dipping Sauce (page 17).

123 CALORIES PER SERVING: 4 G PROTEIN; 3 G FAT; 23 G CARBOHYDRATE; 22 MG SODIUM; 0 MG CHOLESTEROL

Analysis based on 10 servings

SOUPS

PINEAPPLE GAZPACHO

Who says gazpacho has to be made from tomatoes? I first tasted this refreshing soup at the Lodge at Koele,
a luxurious manor-style hotel tucked on a mountainside on the Hawaiian island of Lanai.
Depending on the ripeness of the pineapple, you may want to add a little brown sugar or other sweetener.

1 ripe pineapple
1 cucumber, peeled and seeded
½ yellow bell pepper, cored and seeded
3 to 4 tablespoons diced Maui onion or other
    sweet onion
⅓ to ½ cup pineapple juice (preferably fresh)
2 to 3 teaspoons rice vinegar or cider vinegar
½ teaspoon Chinese chili paste or your favorite
    hot sauce (or to taste)
2 to 3 teaspoons brown sugar (optional)

salt (optional) and freshly ground black pepper

FOR THE GARNISH
¼ cup chopped fresh cilantro
¼ cup very finely diced red bell pepper (about
    ¼ pepper)
¼ cup very finely diced green bell pepper (about
    ¼ pepper)
¼ cup very finely diced, peeled, seeded cucumber
    (about ¼ cucumber)

1. Peel, core, and dice the pineapple, working over a bowl or slotted cutting board to catch the juice.

2. Purée the pineapple, cucumber, yellow pepper, and onion in the blender, working in several batches if necessary, adding enough pineapple juice to obtain a pourable consistency. Add vinegar, chili paste, sugar (if using), and salt and pepper to taste. The gazpacho can be prepared ahead to this stage, but you may need to add more pineapple juice or flavorings before serving.

3. Just before serving, stir the garnish into the gazpacho. Correct the seasoning and serve at once.

Makes about 1 quart, enough to serve 4

Note: If sweet onions are not available, soak a diced regular onion in a bowl of ice water for 30 minutes. Drain well before adding.

108 CALORIES PER SERVING: 1 G PROTEIN; 1 G FAT; 27 G CARBOHYDRATE; 7 MG SODIUM; 0 MG CHOLESTEROL

HUNGARIAN CHERRY SOUP

Cherry soup is one of the glories of Austro-Hungarian cooking. The traditional cherry is the sour, or amarelle, cherry (the yellow-white variety). As these are hard to find in many parts of the country, the following recipe calls for Bing cherries. (If you use sour cherries, you may need to add additional sweetener.) In the winter I make a similar soup with cranberries. Cookware shops sell mechanical cherry pitters, which make this recipe a snap. In a pinch you can use canned cherries, but the soup won't be quite as good.

2 pounds fresh Bing cherries (about 2 cups pitted)
2 cinnamon sticks
10 cloves
10 allspice berries
4 strips lemon zest
3 cups water

¾ to 1 cup sugar
1 tablespoon cornstarch or arrowroot
¾ cup dry red wine
½ cup no-fat sour cream, plus 2 tablespoons for garnish
6 sprigs mint for garnish

1. Pit the cherries, working over a bowl to catch the juices. Tie the cinnamon sticks, cloves, allspice berries, and lemon zest in a piece of cheesecloth or wrap them in a piece of foil and pierce the foil all over with a fork.

2. Combine the cherry juice, bag of spices, water, and ¾ cup sugar in a large saucepan and bring to a boil. Reduce the heat, add the cherries, and simmer, covered, for 10 minutes, or until very tender. Remove and discard the spice bag.

3. Combine the cornstarch with 2 tablespoons wine in a small bowl and whisk until dissolved. Whisk this mixture into the soup with the remaining wine and simmer for 30 seconds. Remove the

pan from the heat and whisk in the ½ cup sour cream. Correct the seasoning, adding sugar for sweetness or a little more wine for acidity as necessary. Let the soup cool to room temperature, then refrigerate until cold. The soup can be prepared up to 48 hours ahead to this stage.

4. Ladle the cherry soup into bowls or wineglasses. Garnish each with a dollop of sour cream and a sprig of mint.

Makes 4 cups, enough to serve 4 to 6

Note: To make chilled cranberry soup, substitute 1 12-ounce bag fresh or frozen cranberries for the cherries. Increase the sugar to 1 to 1¼ cups.

247 CALORIES PER SERVING: 2 G PROTEIN; 0 G FAT; 55 G CARBOHYDRATE; 54 MG SODIUM; 0 MG CHOLESTEROL

Analysis based on 4 servings

CUCUMBER DILL SOUP

Cucumber, onions, and dill are the ingredients of a classic Eastern European salad. Here, I've puréed them with yogurt to make a refreshing summer soup. **Note:** *To seed a cucumber, cut it in half lengthwise. Scrape out the seeds with a melon baller or spoon.*

3 medium cucumbers, peeled and seeded
2½ cups plain nonfat yogurt (or as needed)
1 to 2 cloves garlic, minced
3 tablespoons grated onion (or to taste)

3 tablespoons chopped fresh dill, plus 4 to 6
  whole sprigs for garnish
1 tablespoon fresh lemon juice (or to taste)
salt and freshly ground black pepper

1. Cut ½ cucumber into ¼-inch dice. Coarsely chop the remainder.

2. Combine the coarsely chopped cucumber, yogurt, garlic, onion, chopped dill, lemon juice, salt, and pepper in a blender and blend to a smooth purée. If the soup is too thick, add a little more yogurt. Chill the soup in the refrigerator until cold.

3. Correct the seasoning, adding salt, pepper, onion, or lemon juice to taste. Ladle the soup into bowls and sprinkle with the diced cucumber. Garnish each bowl with a sprig of dill before serving.

Serves 4 to 6

116 CALORIES PER SERVING: 10 G PROTEIN; 1 G FAT; 19 G CARBOHYDRATE; 115 MG SODIUM; 3 MG CHOLESTEROL

Analysis based on 4 servings

GRAIN SOUP

Zuppa di farro, grain soup, *is a specialty of Apulia in southern Italy. Farro,* a cousin of wheat, *is known as emmer in English.*
In this country, I use wheat berries. This recipe comes from the posh Melograno resort in the city of Monopoli on the Adriatic coast.
Note: *Because the recipe is somewhat time-consuming (although it involves very little actual cooking),*
I like to make this soup in large batches, freezing the excess for future use.

1 cup wheat berries
salt
2 zucchinis
2 tablespoons extra-virgin olive oil
1 onion, cut into fine dice
2 cloves garlic, minced
2 carrots, cut into fine dice
2 stalks celery, cut into fine dice
1 yellow bell pepper, cut into fine dice
1 red bell pepper, cut into fine dice
2 medium potatoes, preferably Yukon Golds, cut
    into fine dice

2 bay leaves
¼ teaspoon saffron threads, soaked in
    1 tablespoon hot water
1 teaspoon dried or fresh thyme
12 basil leaves, thinly slivered
¼ cup chopped flat-leaf (Italian) parsley
8 cups Basic Vegetable Stock (page 247), or as
    needed
freshly ground black pepper

1. Soak the wheat berries in a bowl with 4 cups warm water for at least 2 hours. **Note:** This step can be done the night before.

2. Transfer the wheat berries with their soaking liquid to a large saucepan. Simmer the wheat berries, covered, over medium heat for 1½ hours, or until tender. Add salt to taste after 1 hour and water as necessary to keep the grain covered by at least 1 inch. Drain the wheat berries and set aside. **Note:** The cooking time can be shortened to about 40 minutes by using a pressure cooker.

3. Meanwhile, cut the zucchinis in half lengthwise. Remove the core (the part with the seeds) with a melon baller or spoon. (Save the core for stock.) Cut the zucchini into fine dice.

4. Heat 1 tablespoon of the olive oil in a large, heavy pot. Add the onion, garlic, carrots, celery, diced zucchini, and yellow and red peppers and

cook over medium heat until soft but not brown, about 5 minutes, stirring occasionally with a wooden spoon.

5. Add the wheat berries, the potatoes, the bay leaves, the saffron, the thyme, half the basil, half the parsley, the stock, and the salt and pepper and bring the soup to a boil. Reduce the heat to medium and simmer the soup, uncovered, until it is well flavored and the vegetables are tender, about 20 minutes. Add stock as necessary—you may need another 1 to 2 cups.

6. Before serving, stir in the remaining tablespoon of the olive oil and correct the seasoning, adding salt, pepper, or thyme to taste. Garnish the soup with the remaining parsley and basil and serve at once.

Serves 8 to 10 as a first course, 6 as a main course

161 CALORIES PER SERVING: 4 G PROTEIN; 4 G FAT; 30 G CARBOHYDRATE; 22 G SODIUM; 0 MG CHOLESTEROL

Analysis based on 8 servings

MEXICAN PINTO BEAN SOUP

Tarasco, pinto bean soup, is a specialty of Michoacán in central Mexico. The chili of choice is the pasilla (literally, "raisin"), a large, elongated, wrinkled, black, dried chili with a rich, almost chocolaty flavor. It's a very flavorful chili, but it isn't particularly hot. Look for pasillas in gourmet shops or see Mail-Order Sources. Ancho chilies, dried New Mexican chilies, or even chili powder (2 to 3 tablespoons) will work in a pinch. For a great lunch, serve this soup with a Mango and Bell Pepper Salad (page 48) and Whole-Kernel Corn Muffins (page 73).

4 ripe tomatoes, stemmed but left whole
1 large onion, peeled and quartered
3 to 4 pasilla chilies
1 tablespoon olive oil
4 cloves garlic, finely chopped
3 cups cooked pinto beans (page 261)
4 to 5 cups Basic Vegetable Stock (page 247), or as needed (you can use water, but the soup won't be as rich)

salt and freshly ground black pepper
¼ cup finely chopped cilantro or flat-leaf parsley

FOR THE GARNISH
1 flour tortilla, cut in half, then into matchstick slivers
½ cup no-fat sour cream
3 tablespoons chopped chives or scallion greens

1. Preheat a barbecue grill or broiler to high heat.

2. Grill or broil the tomatoes and onion for 2 to 3 minutes per side, or until well browned. Grill or broil the chilies for 10 seconds per side, or until toasted and fragrant. They burn easily, so be careful. Stem and seed the chilies. (For a spicier soup, leave the seeds in.) Purée the onions, tomatoes, and chilies in a blender.

3. Heat the olive oil in a large saucepan over medium heat. Add the garlic and cook for 1 minute, or until soft but not brown. Add the vegetable-chili purée and cook it until thick and fragrant, about 3 minutes.

4. Stir in the beans, 4 cups vegetable stock, salt, and pepper. Simmer for 10 minutes, or until the beans are very soft. Purée the soup in a blender, adding additional stock if necessary to obtain a pourable consistency. Return the soup to the saucepan, adding salt and pepper to taste. Just before serving, stir in the cilantro.

5. Meanwhile, prepare the garnish. Preheat the oven to 400° F. Spread the tortilla strips on a non-stick baking sheet. Bake the strips until crisp and golden brown, about 5 minutes.

6. To serve the *tarasco*, ladle the soup into bowls or a tureen. Place a dollop of sour cream in the center and sprinkle the tortilla slivers around it. Sprinkle the chives on top of the sour cream and serve at once.

Makes about 8 cups, enough to serve 8 as a rich first course, 4 to 6 as a light main course

Note: If using canned beans, you'll need 2 15-ounce cans, drained well.

149 CALORIES PER SERVING: 7 G PROTEIN; 3 G FAT; 26 G CARBOHYDRATE; 33 MG SODIUM; 0 MG CHOLESTEROL

Analysis based on 8 servings

BLACK BEAN SOUP

*Every nation in Latin America has its version of black bean soup. I've omitted the bacon found in traditional recipes, adding flavor with extra spices and aromatic vegetables. The resulting soup will fill your kitchen with tropical warmth even on the coldest winter night. **Note:** Poblano chilies will give you a spicy soup; for a mild soup, use green bell pepper. Sofrito is the cornerstone of Hispanic cooking, a redolent blend of sautéed onions, garlic, and bell peppers used as a flavoring for soups, stews, and rice dishes. Think of it as Hispanic mirepoix.*

2 cups dried black beans
8 cups water

FOR THE *SOFRITO*
2 tablespoons extra-virgin olive oil
1 large onion, finely chopped
2 poblano chilies or 1 green bell pepper, cored, seeded, and finely chopped
1 red bell pepper, cored, seeded, and finely chopped
6 cloves garlic, minced
1½ teaspoons cumin

½ cup chopped fresh cilantro
1 Bouquet Garni of bay leaf, thyme, and parsley (page 263)
2 tomatoes, peeled, seeded, and chopped (about 1½ cups)
2 tablespoons tomato paste
1 to 2 tablespoons balsamic or wine vinegar (or to taste)
½ teaspoon Liquid Smoke (optional)
salt and freshly ground black pepper
¼ cup no-fat sour cream for garnish

1. Pick through the beans, discarding any pebbles. Soak the beans in 8 cups water in a large bowl for at least 4 hours, preferably overnight. **Note:** The soaking can be omitted, but you'll need to cook the soup an extra 40 to 50 minutes.

2. Prepare the *sofrito*. Heat the olive oil in a large nonstick frying pan. Add the onion, poblanos, red pepper, and garlic and cook over medium heat for 4 minutes, or until soft and fragrant but not brown. Stir in the cumin and half the cilantro, and cook the mixture for 2 minutes.

3. Transfer the beans with their soaking liquid to a large heavy pot. Stir in half the *sofrito* and the bouquet garni. Bring the beans to a boil, reduce the heat, and briskly simmer the soup, stirring occasionally, for 1 hour, or until beans are tender. The pot should be loosely covered. Add water as necessary to keep the beans submerged. Stir in the chopped tomatoes and tomato paste during the last 15 minutes.

4. Discard the bouquet garni. Stir in the remaining *sofrito*, and the vinegar, Liquid Smoke (if using), salt, and pepper. Simmer the soup, uncovered, for 10 minutes more, or until the beans are very soft. Correct the seasoning, adding salt, cumin, or vinegar to taste: The soup should be highly seasoned.

5. Transfer 2 cups beans and broth to a blender or food processor and purée. Return this mixture to the soup. (This step is optional, but it will give you a thicker, creamier soup.)

6. To serve, ladle the soup into bowls and sprinkle with the remaining cilantro. Place a dollop of sour cream in the center of each and serve at once.

Makes 8 to 10 cups, enough to serve 8 as an appetizer, 4 to 6 as a main course

Note: As in other recipes in this book, you can use canned beans instead of dried. Rinse the beans well to remove excess salt. Omit step 1, and cook the beans for only 10 minutes in step 3. Add the tomatoes and tomato paste with the *sofrito*.

209 CALORIES PER SERVING: 11 G PROTEIN; 4 G FAT; 33 G CARBOHYDRATE; 44 MG SODIUM; 0 MG CHOLESTEROL

Analysis based on 8 servings

CHINESE HOT AND SOUR SOUP

*This pungent soup could be called Chinese penicillin. It boasts a formidable arsenal for fighting a cold: ginger and pepper
for blasting open stuffed nasal passages; garlic as an antiviral agent; black mushrooms and wood ears (a
wrinkled black fungus prized by the Chinese for its chewy-crisp texture), to which the Chinese ascribe
prodigious healing properties. **Note:** This recipe may seem complicated because it contains lots of
ingredients. In fact, it's very simple and requires only 10 minutes of actual cooking.*

6 Chinese black mushrooms
5 large or 10 small wood ears
6 cups Asian Vegetable Stock (page 250) or
   Basic Vegetable Stock (page 247)
2 to 3 tablespoons soy sauce, or to taste
3 to 4 tablespoons rice vinegar or wine vinegar
   (or to taste)
2 teaspoons Pickapeppa sauce or vegetarian
   Worcestershire-style sauce
1 teaspoon Asian sesame oil
½ teaspoon sugar or maple syrup
2 to 3 teaspoons minced fresh ginger
2 to 3 cloves garlic, minced

3 scallions, white part minced, green part thinly
   sliced
½ pound tofu (preferably silken), cut into
   ½-inch dice
½ cup thinly slivered bamboo shoots
½ cup thinly slivered water chestnuts
½ red bell pepper, cored, seeded, and thinly
   slivered
salt
¼ to ½ teaspoon freshly ground black pepper
2 tablespoons cornstarch
3 tablespoons cold water
3 tablespoons chopped fresh cilantro (optional)

1. Soak the mushrooms and wood ears in 1 cup hot vegetable stock for 20 to 30 minutes, or until tender.

2. Strain the mushrooms and wood ears over a large heavy saucepan. Cut off and discard the mushroom stems. Thinly slice the mushrooms and wood ears.

3. Add the remaining stock to the saucepan and bring it to a boil. Stir in the mushrooms and wood ears, soy sauce, vinegar, Pickapeppa sauce, sesame oil, sugar, ginger, garlic, minced scallions, tofu, bamboo shoots, water chestnuts, bell pepper, salt, and pepper. Simmer the soup for 5 minutes.

4. Dissolve the cornstarch in the 3 tablespoons cold water. Stir this mixture into the soup and simmer for 1 minute. The soup should thicken. Correct the seasoning, adding salt, pepper, soy sauce, and vinegar to taste. The soup should be very spicy and a little sour. Sprinkle the top with scallion greens and cilantro (if using) and serve at once.

Serves 6 as an appetizer, 3 to 4 as a main course

Note: Black mushrooms, wood ears, bamboo shoots, and other Chinese ingredients are available at Asian markets, gourmet shops, and in the ethnic foods sections of some supermarkets. See Cook's Notes and Mail-Order Sources for further information.

81 CALORIES PER SERVING: 4 G PROTEIN; 2 G FAT; 12 G CARBOHYDRATE; 364 MG SODIUM; 0 MG CHOLESTEROL

Analysis based on 6 servings

SMOKED SQUASH SOUP

Gone are the days when smoked foods were limited to meats or seafood. Today, adventurous cooks can smoke everything from tomatoes to tofu. (A simple technique for stovetop smoking is outlined below.) This recipe comes from Gordon Hamersley of Hamersley's Bistro in Boston. **Note:** *If you're in a hurry, the recipe makes a perfectly delicious squash soup without the smoking.*

2 acorn squashes
2 tablespoons hardwood sawdust for smoking
1½ tablespoons olive oil
1 large onion or 2 leeks, finely chopped
4 stalks celery, finely chopped
4 cloves garlic, finely chopped
¼ cup Madeira or sherry
4 to 5 cups Basic Vegetable Stock (page 247)

1 cup no-fat sour cream
1 Bouquet Garni of bay leaf, thyme, and parsley (page 263)
salt and freshly ground black pepper
1 to 2 teaspoons brown sugar or honey (optional)
2 tablespoons finely chopped chives or scallion greens for garnish

1. Cut the squashes in half and scoop out the seeds. Smoke the squashes, cut side up, for 1 hour, or until tender, following the procedure outlined below. Let the squash cool, then peel off and discard the skin.

2. Heat the olive oil in a large saucepan. Cook the onion, celery, and garlic over medium heat until very soft but not brown, about 5 minutes. Add the squash and Madeira and cook over high heat for 1 minute. Add 4 cups vegetable stock, ¾ cup sour cream, the bouquet garni, salt, and pepper and simmer the soup for 30 minutes, or until all the vegetables are tender.

3. Remove the bouquet garni and purée the soup in a blender. Return it to the saucepan and thin, if necessary, with additional stock. Correct the seasoning, adding salt and pepper to taste. If a touch of sweetness is desired, add the sugar. To

serve, ladle the soup into bowls, garnish with dollops of the remaining sour cream, and sprinkle with chives.

Serves 8 as a first course, 4 to 6 as a main course

Note: To turn a wok or frying pan into a smoker, line it with foil and place the sawdust on the bottom in the center. Arrange the squash slices on a round wire cake rack over the chips. Place the wok on a burner over high heat until the first wisps of smoke begin to appear. Lower the heat to medium and tightly cover the wok. Seal any openings between the wok and the lid with strips of wet paper towel. Caution: Keep your stove exhaust fan on high when smoking. You may need to disconnect any nearby smoke alarms (be sure to reconnect them when you're done).

103 CALORIES PER SERVING: 3 G PROTEIN; 3 G FAT; 17 G CARBOHYDRATE; 44 MG SODIUM; 1 MG CHOLESTEROL
Analysis based on 8 servings

BARLEY AND BLACK MUSHROOM SOUP

*Here's a new twist on a vegetarian classic. Chinese black mushrooms add an intriguingly pungent,
smoky flavor. I actually prefer dried mushrooms to fresh shiitakes for this recipe,
as they have a stronger fragrance.*

⅓ cup pearl barley
10 dried Chinese black mushrooms (½ ounce, about ½ cup)
3 cups hot water
1½ tablespoons canola oil
6 to 8 shallots or 1 small onion (½ cup finely chopped)
4 scallions, white part minced, greens thinly sliced for garnish

4 cloves garlic, minced
3 to 4 cups Basic Vegetable Stock (page 247) or Mushroom Stock (page 251)
¼ cup dry white vermouth or dry sherry
salt and freshly ground black pepper
2 carrots, cut into ¼-inch dice (about 1 cup)

1. Soak the barley in 4 cups cold water for at least 4 hours, preferably overnight. Drain the barley.

2. Soak the mushrooms in 3 cups hot water for 20 to 30 minutes or until soft. Remove and discard the mushroom stems, reserving the soaking liquid. Thinly slice the mushroom caps.

3. Heat the oil in a large heavy saucepan. Cook the shallots, scallion whites, and garlic over medium heat until soft but not brown, 3 to 4 minutes.

4. Add the mushroom soaking liquid, 3 cups vegetable stock, the barley, the vermouth, and the salt and pepper and simmer the soup, covered, for 30 to 40 minutes, or until the barley is soft. Add the carrots during the last 15 minutes. Add stock as necessary to maintain a souplike consistency.

5. To serve, correct the seasoning, adding salt and pepper to taste. Ladle the soup into a tureen or bowls and sprinkle with the chopped scallion greens.

Serves 6 as a first course, 4 as a main course

110 CALORIES PER SERVING: 2 G PROTEIN; 4 G FAT; 16 G CARBOHYDRATE; 12 MG SODIUM; 0 MG CHOLESTEROL

Analysis based on 6 servings

GREEK LENTIL SOUP

This soup is lighter than most lentil soups. The reason? The flavor comes from fresh dill and lemon zest—a combination popular in Greek cooking—rather than the traditional sausage or ham hock. Unlike most beans, lentils don't require soaking before cooking, and so this soup is an ideal recipe when time is short.

2 tablespoons extra-virgin olive oil (preferably Greek)
1 medium onion, finely chopped
2 cloves garlic, minced
2 stalks celery, finely chopped
1½ cups lentils, picked through and rinsed
8 cups Basic Vegetable Stock (page 247) or water
1 teaspoon dried oregano (preferably Greek)

1 bay leaf
5 to 6 carrots, cut into ½-inch dice (1½ cups)
2 medium potatoes, cut into ½-inch dice (1½ cups)
½ teaspoon grated lemon zest (or to taste)
2 tablespoons fresh lemon juice (or to taste)
3 tablespoons finely chopped fresh dill
salt and freshly ground black pepper

1. Heat the olive oil in a large heavy saucepan. Add the onion, garlic, and celery and cook over medium heat until soft but not brown, about 4 minutes.

2. Add the lentils, vegetable stock, oregano, and bay leaf and bring to a boil. Reduce the heat and simmer the soup, loosely covered, for 20 minutes.

3. Stir in the carrots and potatoes and continue simmering the soup, uncovered, for 10 minutes, or until the lentils and vegetables are tender. During the last 3 minutes, stir in the lemon zest, lemon juice, dill, salt, and pepper. Just before serving, remove and discard the bay leaf. Correct the seasoning, adding salt, dill, or lemon juice to taste.

Serves 6 to 8

Note: For a thicker, creamier soup, you can purée ¼ to ½ of the soup in a blender and stir it back into the remainder.

266 CALORIES PER SERVING: 13 G PROTEIN; 5 G FAT; 44 G CARBOHYDRATE; 39 MG SODIUM; 0 MG CHOLESTEROL
Analysis based on 6 servings

BROCCO-LEEKIE SOUP

The hardest thing about making broccoli soup is keeping the broccoli green. To do this, I cook the broccoli in two stages:
the stems are boiled with the other vegetables. The florets are blanched in salted water, then shock-chilled to set
the bright green color, then added to the soup at the end.

1 bunch broccoli (about 5 cups when cut up)
1 tablespoon olive oil
1 leek, trimmed, washed, and finely chopped
4 cloves garlic, minced
4 cups Basic Vegetable Stock (page 247), or as
   needed

1 large potato (10 ounces), peeled and diced
1 Bouquet Garni of bay leaf, thyme, and parsley
   (page 263)
salt and freshly ground black pepper

1. Cut the florets (the green flowering part) off the broccoli and reserve. Trim the bottoms and any tough fibrous parts off the stems and discard. Finely chop the stems.

2. Heat the olive oil in a large saucepan. Cook the leek over medium heat for 3 to 4 minutes, or until soft but not brown, adding the garlic after 2 minutes. Stir in 4 cups stock, the potato, the bouquet garni, and the salt and pepper and simmer for 10 minutes. Add the chopped broccoli stems and cook for 5 minutes, or until soft.

3. Meanwhile, blanch the broccoli florets in rapidly boiling salted water until just tender, about

1 minute. Drain the florets in a colander and transfer to a bowl of ice water. Drain the florets and blot dry on paper towels, reserving 6 for garnish.

4. Discard the bouquet garni. Purée the soup with the blanched broccoli florets (minus the garnish) in a blender. Return the soup to the saucepan and heat thoroughly. If the soup is too thick, thin with more vegetable stock. Correct the seasoning, adding salt and pepper to taste. To serve, ladle the soup into bowls, garnishing each with a broccoli floret.

Serves 6

91 CALORIES PER SERVING: 5 G PROTEIN; 3 G FAT; 14 G CARBOHYDRATE; 43 MG SODIUM; 0 MG CHOLESTEROL

Brocco-Leekie Soup (left) and Cauliflower Cardamom Soup (right)

CAULIFLOWER CARDAMOM SOUP

For a spectacular presentation, serve this soup together with Brocco-Leekie Soup (page 39). (See photo on page 38.)
Use 2 ladles to transfer the soups to the bowls. Simultaneously pour this Cauliflower Cardamom Soup
from the right side, the Brocco-Leekie Soup from left. The two soups will meet in a clean line in the center.

1 head cauliflower (about 5 cups chopped)
1 tablespoon olive oil
1 onion, finely chopped
2 cloves garlic, minced
1 stalk celery, finely chopped
2 cups Basic Vegetable Stock (page 247)
2 to 3 cups skim milk

1 medium potato (10 ounces), peeled and diced
1 Bouquet Garni of bay leaf, thyme, and parsley
  (page 263)
½ teaspoon ground cardamom, or to taste
½ teaspoon ground coriander, or to taste
salt and freshly ground black pepper

1. Cut 6 florets (the flowering part) off the cauliflower and reserve. Trim the bottoms, leaves, and any tough fibrous parts off the remaining cauliflower and finely chop.

2. Heat the olive oil in a large saucepan. Cook the onion, garlic, and celery over medium heat for 3 to 4 minutes, or until soft but not brown. Stir in the chopped cauliflower, vegetable stock, 2 cups milk, potato, bouquet garni, cardamom, coriander, salt, and pepper and simmer for 15 minutes, or until the vegetables are very soft.

3. Meanwhile, cook the cauliflower florets in rapidly boiling salted water until crispy-tender, about 1 minute. Drain the florets in a colander and transfer to a bowl of ice water. Drain the florets and blot dry on paper towels.

4. Discard the bouquet garni. Purée the soup in a blender. Return the soup to the saucepan and heat thoroughly. If the soup is too thick, thin with a little more milk. Correct the seasoning, adding salt and pepper to taste. To serve, ladle the soup into bowls, garnishing each with a cauliflower floret.

Makes about 5 cups, enough to serve 4 to 6

159 CALORIES PER SERVING: 7 G PROTEIN; 4 G FAT; 26 G CARBOHYDRATE; 263 MG SODIUM; 2 MG CHOLESTEROL
Analysis based on 4 servings

ROASTED VEGETABLE SOUP

Here's a vegetable soup that's loaded with flavor. The secret? Roasting the vegetables caramelizes their sugars,
intensifying the sweetness. A grilled vegetable soup would have a wonderful smoky flavor and would
be prepared the same way. Feel free to vary the vegetables according to what's available and in season.

2 leeks
11 cloves garlic
2 carrots
1 large potato
1 red bell pepper
1 yellow bell pepper (or another red one)
1½ tablespoons extra-virgin olive oil
salt and freshly ground black pepper

¼ cup small tube-shaped pasta, like elbow
    macaroni, tubetti, or ditali
5 to 6 cups Basic Vegetable Stock (page 247)
¼ cup dry white vermouth
1 teaspoon sherry vinegar (or to taste)
2 teaspoons capers (optional)
1 cup cooked beans or chickpeas (optional)
¼ cup chopped fresh flat-leaf (Italian) parsley

1. Preheat the oven to 375° F. Trim and wash the leeks and cut them crosswise into ¼-inch slices. Peel the garlic. Mince 1 clove and set aside. Scrub or peel the carrots and cut into ½-inch dice. Scrub or peel the potato and cut into ½-inch dice. Core and seed the bell peppers and cut into ½-inch dice.

2. Place the leeks, whole garlic cloves, and diced potato and bell peppers in a roasting pan and toss with the olive oil, salt, and pepper. Roast the vegetables to a deep golden brown, 30 to 40 minutes.

3. Meanwhile, cook the pasta in 6 cups rapidly boiling salted water until al dente, 8 to 10 minutes. Drain the pasta in a colander.

4. Transfer the vegetables to a large saucepan and add 5 cups vegetable stock and the vermouth, vinegar, capers (if using), minced garlic clove, and salt and pepper. Simmer the soup for 10 minutes, or until all the vegetables are soft. Add the pasta, beans (if using), and half the parsley. Simmer for 2 minutes. If the soup is too thick, add the remaining 1 cup stock.

5. Correct the seasoning, adding salt, pepper, or vinegar to taste. The soup should be highly seasoned. Just before serving, sprinkle the soup with the remaining parsley.

Serves 8 as a first course, 4 to 6 as a main course

89 CALORIES PER SERVING: 2 G PROTEIN; 3 G FAT; 14 G CARBOHYDRATE; 13 MG SODIUM; 0 MG CHOLESTEROL

Analysis based on 8 servings

GRILLED CORN, FENNEL, AND PURPLE POTATO CHOWDER

This recipe is at once trendy and timeless, featuring three foods that were the mainstay of the Meso-American diet long before the arrival of Columbus: potatoes, chilies, and corn. The fennel provides a Mediterranean touch. Purple potatoes originated in Peru and can be found at specialty greengrocers'. But Yukon Golds or red potatoes will look and taste good, too. Grilling the corn adds an intriguing smoky flavor. Apartment-bound cooks could broil the corn.

3 ears fresh corn, shucked

5 teaspoons extra-virgin olive oil

salt and freshly ground black pepper

1 onion, finely chopped

6 to 8 shallots, finely chopped (about ½ cup)

3 cloves garlic, minced

2 poblano chilies or 1 large green bell pepper, cored and cut into ½-inch dice

2 stalks celery, finely diced

1 quart Basic Vegetable Stock (page 247) or water

1 Bouquet Garni of bay leaf, thyme, and parsley (page 263)

1 pound purple potatoes or regular potatoes, scrubbed and cut into ½-inch dice

1 small or ½ large fennel bulb, cut into ¼-inch dice, about 1 cup (optional)

1 cup no-fat sour cream (or to taste)

freshly grated nutmeg

2 tablespoons chopped fresh dill, flat-leaf (Italian) parsley, or fennel tops

1. Brush the corn with 2 teaspoons of the olive oil and sprinkle with salt and pepper. Grill the corn over medium heat, turning often, until golden brown on all sides, about 8 minutes. Transfer the corn to a plate to cool, then cut the kernels off the cobs, reserving the cobs. (The easiest way to do this is to lay the corn on its side on a cutting board. Make lengthwise cuts with the knife to remove the kernels.)

2. Heat the remaining 3 teaspoons olive oil in a large heavy saucepan. Add the onion, shallots, garlic, poblanos, and celery and cook over medium heat until soft but not brown, stirring often, about 5 minutes.

3. Stir in the vegetable stock, bouquet garni, potatoes, fennel, and corn cobs. Simmer the soup for 5 minutes. Stir in the corn kernels and continue simmering the chowder for 10 minutes, or until all the vegetables are soft but not mushy. Remove and discard the corn cobs and bouquet garni.

4. Whisk in the sour cream and salt, pepper, and nutmeg to taste and simmer the chowder for 2 minutes. Sprinkle the chowder with the dill and serve at once.

Makes about 8 cups, enough to serve 8 as a first course, 4 as a main course

143 CALORIES PER SERVING: 4 G PROTEIN; 3 G FAT; 26 G CARBOHYDRATE; 70 MG SODIUM; 0 MG CHOLESTEROL

Analysis based on 8 servings

CHINESE MUSHROOM SOUP

Black mushrooms give this soup a smoky flavor, while the straw mushrooms (slippery cone-shaped mushrooms), enokis (long, slender, white mushrooms), and wood ears (a chewy fungus) create an interesting play of textures. (A complete discussion of exotic mushrooms is found on page 267.) All four can be purchased at Asian markets and at gourmet shops and many supermarkets. Feel free to substitute or add other Asian or Western mushrooms that may be available. Note: Maggi may seem like a peculiar ingredient to include in this soup, but the Chinese seem to love it.

6 dried Chinese black mushrooms
5 cups Asian Vegetable Stock, Basic Vegetable
   Stock, or Mushroom Stock (pages 250, 247,
   or 251)
10 small or 5 large wood ears
1 cup drained straw mushrooms
1 3-ounce package fresh enoki mushrooms (or
   ½ cup canned)
1 tablespoon canola oil
2 cloves garlic, minced
2 teaspoons minced fresh ginger

2 scallions, white part minced, green part thinly
   sliced for garnish
½ cup julienned bamboo shoots
1 to 2 tablespoons soy sauce (or to taste)
1 tablespoon Maggi or other vegetable gravy base
¼ teaspoon freshly ground white pepper (or to
   taste)
1 tablespoon cornstarch
1 tablespoon Chinese rice wine or dry sherry
1 tablespoon chopped fresh cilantro

1. Soak the black mushrooms in 1 cup warm vegetable stock for 20 to 30 minutes, or until soft. Soak the wood ears in another cup warm vegetable stock for 30 minutes, or until soft. Cut the straw mushrooms in half lengthwise. Cut the bottom off the enokis and tease the mushrooms apart.

2. Drain the black mushrooms and wood ears, reserving the soaking liquid. Cut off and discard the black mushroom stems and thinly slice the caps. Thinly slice the wood ears.

3. Heat the oil in a large pot. Cook the garlic, ginger, and scallion whites until soft but not brown, 2 to 3 minutes. Stir in the remaining vegetable stock, and the reserved soaking liquid, the black

mushrooms, wood ears, straw mushrooms, enokis, bamboo shoots, soy sauce, Maggi, and white pepper. Gently simmer the soup for 5 to 8 minutes, or until the mushrooms and bamboo shoots are tender.

4. Dissolve the cornstarch in the rice wine. Stir this mixture into the soup and bring to a boil. The soup will thicken slightly. Correct the seasoning, adding soy sauce, rice wine, or white pepper to taste. The soup should be highly seasoned. Ladle the soup into soup bowls or a tureen and sprinkle with the scallion greens and cilantro.

Serves 4

90 CALORIES PER SERVING: 2–6 G PROTEIN; 4 G FAT; 13 G CARBOHYDRATE; 413 MG SODIUM; 0 MG CHOLESTEROL

SALADS

CAMBODIAN SALAD

The opening of the Elephant Walk restaurant in the Boston suburb of Somerville a few years ago brought a new galaxy of flavors to restaurant-goers. The merest bite of the Cambodian salad lit up my mouth like a Fourth of July sky. My vegetarian version uses soy sauce instead of fish sauce, but the vibrant seasonings are otherwise the same. Don't worry about the seemingly high proportion of oil: Most of it is discarded.

½ cup canola oil
4 cloves garlic, peeled and thinly sliced
2 cups bean sprouts
3 cups thinly shredded napa (Chinese cabbage) or savoy cabbage
3 carrots, shredded or coarsely grated
2 red bell peppers, cored, seeded, and sliced paper-thin into rings
1 small onion, sliced paper-thin
1 to 4 serrano or jalapeño chilies, sliced paper-thin into rings (do not seed unless you're a wimp)
½ cup basil leaves (preferably Asian basil, if available), cut into ½-inch strips

½ cup fresh mint leaves, cut into ¼-inch strips
½ cup fresh cilantro leaves

FOR THE DRESSING
4 to 5 tablespoons fresh lime juice (or to taste)
2 tablespoons soy sauce
2 tablespoons water
4 teaspoons sugar
1 clove garlic, minced
salt and freshly ground black pepper

3 tablespoons finely chopped dry-roasted peanuts

1. Heat the oil to 350° F. in a small skillet. Fry the garlic slices until a light golden brown, about 20 seconds. Transfer the garlic with a wire skimmer to paper towels to drain. Blot dry with paper towels. Discard the oil (or save it for use in other recipes).

2. Blanch the bean sprouts in boiling water for 30 seconds. Refresh under cold water and drain.

3. Combine the cabbage, carrots, bell peppers, onion, chilies, basil, mint, cilantro, and fried garlic in a salad bowl, reserving a few red pepper rings, chili slices, and fried garlic chips for garnish.

4. For the dressing, combine the lime juice, soy sauce, water, sugar, minced garlic, salt, and pepper in a bowl and whisk until the sugar is dissolved. Toss the vegetables with the dressing. Garnish the salad with pepper and chili rings, the remaining fried garlic, and the chopped peanuts. Serve at once.

Serves 4 very generously, 6 as a side dish salad

175 CALORIES PER SERVING: 7 G PROTEIN; 7 G FAT; 26 G CARBOHYDRATE; 675 MG SODIUM; 0 MG CHOLESTEROL

Analysis based on 4 servings

WHEAT BERRY SALAD WITH CHILIES AND CORN

Wheat berries are one of my favorite grains, kernels of whole wheat with a firm consistency that makes them a pleasure to bite into. I like to roast the corn on the grill to give it a smoky flavor (see page 252). But if you're in a hurry—and who isn't these days?—you can use frozen or canned corn kernels.

1 cup wheat berries
salt
2 ears corn (enough to make 1 cup kernels)
4 to 5 teaspoons extra-virgin olive oil
freshly ground black pepper
1 poblano chili or ½ green bell pepper
½ red bell pepper
½ yellow bell pepper
1 clove garlic, minced

1 to 2 jalapeño chilies, cored, seeded, and minced (optional) (for a spicier salad, leave the seeds in)
½ cup finely chopped fresh cilantro, mint, or flat-leaf parsley
4 scallions, very finely chopped
4 to 5 tablespoons fresh lime juice
½ teaspoon of your favorite hot sauce, or to taste (optional)

1. Rinse the wheat berries and soak in 6 cups cold water for at least 4 hours, preferably overnight. Drain well.

2. Briskly simmer the wheat berries in 1 quart lightly salted water for 1½ hours, or until tender but not soft. Drain the wheat berries in a colander, rinse with cold water, and drain again. **Note:** You can omit the soaking, but increase the cooking time to 2½ hours. The wheat berries can also be cooked in a pressure cooker, following the manufacturer's instructions. This will take about 30 minutes.

3. Meanwhile, brush the corn with 1 teaspoon olive oil and sprinkle with salt and pepper. Grill the ears over a medium flame on a barbecue (or under the broiler) until nicely browned, 2 to 3 minutes per side. Let the corn cool and cut the kernels off the cob.

4. Core and seed the poblano chili and red and yellow bell peppers. Cut each into strips 1 inch long and ¼ inch wide.

5. Combine the wheat berries, corn, poblano chili, bell peppers, garlic, jalapeños (if using), cilantro, scallions, remaining 3 to 4 teaspoons olive oil, lime juice, and hot sauce (if using) in a mixing bowl and toss well to mix. Correct the seasoning, adding salt, lime juice, or hot sauce to taste. The salad can be prepared ahead of time, but adjust the seasonings at the last minute.

Serves 4 to 6

244 CALORIES PER SERVING: 7 G PROTEIN; 7 G FAT; 44 G CARBOHYDRATE; 13 MG SODIUM; 0 MG CHOLESTEROL
Analysis based on 4 servings

MANGO AND BELL PEPPER SALAD

Part salsa, part salad, this dish makes a great summer refresher, especially when prepared with the large juicy Tommy Atkins or Keitt mangoes that grow in my home state of Florida. Most mangoes turn orange or red when ripe, but some varieties stay green. The best test for ripeness is to check the smell and feel. A ripe mango will smell very fragrant and be softly yielding when squeezed. Let mangoes ripen at room temperature.

1 large ripe mango
½ red bell pepper, cored, seeded, and julienned
½ green bell pepper, cored, seeded, and julienned
¼ red onion, thinly sliced
3 tablespoons chopped fresh cilantro or mint
    leaves

1½ to 2 tablespoons wine vinegar (or to taste)
1 tablespoon brown sugar (or to taste)
1 tablespoon extra-virgin olive oil (optional)
salt and freshly ground black pepper

1. Pare the skin off the mango. (You may want to wear rubber gloves if you have sensitive skin: Some people are allergic to mango sap.) Cut the flesh off the seed in large, broad swaths. Cut each swath into ¼-inch-wide strips.

2. Combine the mango, red and green bell peppers, onion, cilantro, wine vinegar, brown sugar, oil, salt, and pepper for the salad in a mixing bowl and toss just to mix. Correct the seasoning, adding vinegar, sugar, or salt to taste.

Serves 4 as a side dish

56 CALORIES PER SERVING: 1 G PROTEIN; 0 G FAT; 15 G CARBOHYDRATE; 3 MG SODIUM; 0 MG CHOLESTEROL

QUINOA TABOULI

Quinoa (pronounced "KEEN-wa") is a South American grain that contains more calcium than milk, twice as much protein as rice, and three times the phosphorus found in bananas. To these nutritional benefits, add a striking nutty flavor and a softly crunchy consistency, and you'll understand my enthusiasm for a food so prized by the Incas that they called it "mother grain." Tabouli, of course, is a Middle Eastern salad, whose flavorings go well with quinoa.
Note: *For extra flavor, you could cook the quinoa in vegetable stock.*

4 cups water
1 teaspoon salt (optional)
2 cups quinoa
½ cup chopped flat-leaf parsley
6 tablespoons chopped fresh mint (or to taste)

6 scallions, very finely chopped
5 tablespoons lemon juice, or to taste
1 to 1½ tablespoons extra-virgin olive oil
1 ripe tomato, cut into ¼-inch dice

1. Bring 4 cups water (or vegetable stock) and the salt to a boil in a large shallow pan. Stir in the quinoa and bring to a boil. Reduce the heat, cover the pan, and gently simmer the quinoa for 20 minutes, or until tender. Transfer the quinoa to a mixing bowl and let cool completely.

2. Fluff the quinoa with a fork. Stir in the parsley, mint, scallions, lemon juice, oil, and tomato. Correct the seasoning, adding salt or lemon juice to taste.

Serves 4

358 CALORIES PER SERVING: 12 G PROTEIN; 8 G FAT; 61 G CARBOHYDRATE; 22 MG SODIUM; 0 MG CHOLESTEROL

A TRIO OF SLAWS

When I was growing up, coleslaw meant a cabbage salad choked with artery-clogging doses of mayonnaise. Today's slaws are light, healthful, salsa-like accompaniments that derive their flavor from herbs and spices, not fat. Herewith, a trio of slaws that would do any picnic proud.

SANTA FE SLAW

Cilantro, lime juice, and jalapeño chilies lend this colorful slaw a Southwestern accent. If jicama isn't available, you could use julienned daikon radish. Santa Fe slaw would make a nice accompaniment to Black Bean Burritos (page 167).

3 cups thinly shredded green or savoy cabbage (about ⅓ whole cabbage)
½ red bell pepper, cored, seeded, and cut into ¼-inch dice
½ yellow bell pepper, cored, seeded, and cut into ¼-inch dice
1 poblano chili, cored, seeded, and cut into ¼-inch dice
½ cup jicama, cut into a fine julienne

2 scallions, finely chopped
¼ cup chopped fresh cilantro
1 to 3 fresh or pickled jalapeño chilies, minced or thinly sliced (for a milder slaw, seed the chilies)
1 clove garlic, minced
1 to 2 teaspoons sugar
3 tablespoons fresh lime juice (or to taste)
salt and freshly ground black pepper

Combine the cabbage, red and yellow bell peppers, poblano chili, jicama, scallions, cilantro, jalapeños, garlic, sugar, lime juice, salt, and pepper in a nonreactive bowl and toss to mix. Correct the seasoning, adding salt, sugar, or lime juice to taste. This slaw will keep for several days, but reseason it before serving.

Makes 4 cups, enough to serve 4 to 6

44 CALORIES PER SERVING: 2 G PROTEIN; 0 G FAT; 10 G CARBOHYDRATE; 15 MG SODIUM; 0 MG CHOLESTEROL
Analysis based on 4 servings

(clockwise) Shanghai Slaw, Santa Fe Slaw, and Slavic Slaw

SHANGHAI SLAW

Coleslaw originated in America, of course, but bean sprouts, napa (Chinese cabbage), and other Asian ingredients make a delectable variation. Serve with Peking Tacos (page 175).

3 cups thinly shredded napa or savoy cabbage
   (about ½ whole napa or ⅓ savoy cabbage)
½ cup mung bean sprouts
½ red bell pepper, very thinly sliced
3 scallions, white part minced, green part thinly
   sliced lengthwise
½ cup snow peas, snapped and julienned
3 tablespoons chopped cilantro
1 to 4 serrano, jalapeño, or Thai chilies, minced
   (for a milder slaw, remove the seeds)

1 clove garlic, minced
1 teaspoon minced fresh ginger
2 teaspoons black sesame seeds
3 to 4 tablespoons rice vinegar
2 teaspoons sesame oil (or to taste)
1 teaspoon sugar (or to taste)
salt and freshly ground black pepper

Combine the cabbage, bean sprouts, bell pepper, scallions, snow peas, cilantro, chilies, garlic, ginger, sesame seeds, rice vinegar, sesame oil, sugar, salt, and pepper in a nonreactive bowl and toss to mix.

Correct the seasoning, adding salt, sugar, or vinegar to taste. This slaw tastes best served within a few hours of making.

Makes 3 cups, enough to serve 4

64 CALORIES PER SERVING: 3 G PROTEIN; 3 G FAT; 9 G CARBOHYDRATE; 18 MG SODIUM; 0 MG CHOLESTEROL

SLAVIC SLAW

This slaw takes advantage of the new no-fat sour creams to create a creamy but healthful dressing.
Poppy seeds, onion, and fresh dill are typical Eastern European flavorings.

3 tablespoons no-fat sour cream
4 to 5 teaspoons red wine vinegar
½ teaspoon sugar or honey (optional)
salt and freshly ground black pepper
3 cups thinly shredded savoy or green cabbage
   (⅓ whole cabbage)

½ small red onion, thinly sliced lengthwise
1 tablespoon poppy seeds
1 tablespoon chopped fresh dill

In a salad bowl or large mixing bowl, whisk together the sour cream, vinegar, sugar, salt, and pepper. Stir in the cabbage, onion, poppy seeds, and dill. Correct the seasoning, adding salt, vinegar, or sugar to taste.

Makes 3 cups, enough to serve 4 to 6

40 CALORIES PER SERVING: 2 G PROTEIN; 1 G FAT; 7 G CARBOHYDRATE; 25 MG SODIUM; 0 MG CHOLESTEROL
Analysis based on 4 servings

FOUR HOTS BEAN SALAD

This salad is not for the timid, featuring four tongue-tingling members of the radish family: radish sprouts, radish roots, arugula (a peppery salad green), and freshly grated horseradish. It's just the ticket for warming up a meal on a cold winter night. I like to use a small white bean, like a navy or Great Northern. Radish sprouts are sold at natural foods stores and many supermarkets.

1 bunch radishes
1 bunch arugula, washed
½ cup radish sprouts

FOR THE DRESSING
2 tablespoons no-fat sour cream
2 teaspoons extra-virgin olive oil

1 to 2 tablespoons freshly grated or prepared
    white horseradish
2 teaspoons white wine vinegar or distilled
    vinegar (or to taste)
salt and freshly ground black pepper
2 cups cooked white beans (page 261)

1. Thinly slice most of the radishes, saving 4 or 5 whole ones for garnish. Make radish roses with the latter. (To do so, make shallow vertical cuts around the circumference of the root end of each radish and soak in ice water for 1 hour, or until the roses "bloom.") Use 6 to 8 large arugula leaves to line a salad bowl or platter. Cut the remaining arugula leaves crosswise into ½-inch slivers.

2. For the dressing, combine the sour cream, oil, horseradish, vinegar, salt, and pepper in a mixing bowl and whisk until smooth. Add the beans, the sliced radishes, half the radish sprouts, and the sliced arugula and toss just to mix. Correct the seasoning, adding horseradish, vinegar, or salt to taste: The dressing should be highly seasoned. Spoon the salad into the serving bowl. Garnish with the radish roses and remaining radish sprouts and serve at once.

Serves 4

Note: The salad ingredients and dressing can be prepared up to 4 hours ahead of time, but add the radishes, sprouts, arugula, and garnish not more than 10 minutes before serving.

146 CALORIES PER SERVING: 9 G PROTEIN; 3 G FAT; 23 G CARBOHYDRATE; 59 MG SODIUM; 0 MG CHOLESTEROL

ITALIAN FLAG SALAD
(ORZO, GREEN BEANS, AND DRIED TOMATOES)

Orzo is a tiny pasta that looks like grains of rice. Add haricots verts (skinny French green beans, available at specialty greengrocers' and many supermarkets) and dried tomatoes, and you've got a salad that's as colorful as the Italian flag. Sometimes I make this salad with barley instead of orzo.

10 homemade Dried Tomatoes (page 255) or
   store-bought dried tomatoes
1 cup orzo
salt
1½ tablespoons extra-virgin olive oil
8 ounces *haricots verts* or the skinniest green
   beans you can find
12 basil leaves, plus a small sprig of basil for
   garnish

¼ cup finely chopped flat-leaf parsley
1½ tablespoons tarragon vinegar or rice
   vinegar
1 tablespoon fresh lemon juice
½ teaspoon freshly grated lemon zest
1 clove garlic, minced
salt and lots of freshly ground black pepper

1. If using homemade dried tomatoes, cut them into ¼-inch slivers. If using packaged dried tomatoes, plump in very hot water to cover for 20 minutes.

2. Cook the orzo in 1 quart rapidly boiling salted water until al dente, about 8 minutes. Drain the orzo in a colander, refresh under cold water, and drain well. Transfer the orzo to a mixing bowl and toss with the olive oil.

3. Cut the *haricots verts* into 1-inch pieces. Blanch them in 1 quart boiling salted water until al dente, 2 to 3 minutes. Drain the beans in a colander and transfer to a bowl of ice water. (The ice helps set the bright green color.) Drain the beans, blot dry on paper towels, and add them to the salad.

4. Just before serving, cut the basil leaves crosswise into ¼-inch strips. Add the basil, parsley, vinegar, lemon juice, lemon zest, garlic, salt, and pepper to the salad and toss to mix. Correct the seasoning, adding salt or vinegar to taste. The salad should be highly seasoned.

5. Add most of the dried tomatoes and mix as gently as possible: Overmixing will cause the tomatoes to redden the salad. Garnish the salad with the basil sprig and remaining tomatoes and serve at once.

Serves 4

180 CALORIES PER SERVING: 6 G PROTEIN; 6 G FAT; 30 G CARBOHYDRATE; 14 MG SODIUM; 0 MG CHOLESTEROL

CARROT PEAR SALAD

This recipe is almost embarrassing in its simplicity, but the net result is luscious.
The tartness of the balsamic vinegar offsets the sweetness of the pears and honey.

1 pound carrots, peeled
2 ripe pears, peeled and cored
2 tablespoons balsamic vinegar

1 to 2 tablespoons brown sugar or honey
salt and freshly ground black pepper
½ cup dried currants

1. Julienne the carrots and pears, using the julienne disk of a food processor, a mandoline, or a sharp knife. The strips should be 2 to 3 inches long.

2. Combine the vinegar, brown sugar, salt, and pepper in a mixing bowl and whisk until smooth.

Stir in the currants, carrots, and pears. Correct the seasoning, adding salt, vinegar, or honey to taste: The salad should be a little sweet and a little sour.

Serves 4

147 CALORIES PER SERVING: 2 G PROTEIN; 1 G FAT; 37 G CARBOHYDRATE; 42 MG SODIUM; 0 MG CHOLESTEROL

PICKLED BEET SALAD WITH MINT

This tangy salad turns up at trattorias throughout southern Italy. The mint provides a nice counterpoint to the earthiness of the beets.
The combination will make converts of people who don't think they like beets. **Note:** *For an unusual presentation,*
serve the Pickled Beet Salad on a bed of steamed beet greens.

1 pound fresh beets, peeled and cut into ½-inch
  chunks
½ cup cider vinegar
2 teaspoons salt
½ clove garlic, minced

1 tablespoon extra-virgin olive oil
8 to 10 fresh mint leaves, preferably spearmint,
  coarsely chopped
freshly ground black pepper

1. Combine the beets, vinegar, 1½ cups water, and salt in a large, heavy, nonreactive saucepan and bring to a boil over high heat. Reduce the heat to medium and simmer the beets until al dente, 10 to 15 minutes. Let the beets cool in their cooking liquid.

2. Transfer the beets to a bowl with a slotted spoon. Mix in the garlic, olive oil, mint, and pepper. Correct the seasoning, adding salt or pepper to taste.

Makes 3 cups, enough to serve 4

55 CALORIES PER SERVING: 1 G PROTEIN; 3 G FAT; 6 G CARBOHYDRATE; 106 MG SODIUM; 0 MG CHOLESTEROL

MILLET SALAD WITH NORTH AFRICAN SPICES

Millet is not well known in this country, but this tiny yellow grain is a staple throughout Africa and India. This salad features spices characteristic of North African cooking. **Note**: *For a prettier presentation, serve the salad in radicchio or lettuce-leaf cups.*

1 tablespoon extra-virgin olive oil
1 cup millet
1 teaspoon ground cumin
1 teaspoon ground coriander
1 teaspoon turmeric
2¼ cups boiling water
salt and freshly ground black pepper
½ cucumber, peeled, seeded, and diced
½ cup cooked corn kernels

½ cup cooked peas
½ cup diced celery
1 small red bell pepper, cored, seeded, and finely
  diced (about ½ cup)
½ red onion, finely chopped
3 to 4 tablespoons fresh lemon juice (or to taste)
¼ cup nonfat yogurt (or to taste)
¼ cup chopped fresh cilantro

1. Heat the olive oil in a large saucepan over medium-high heat. Add the millet, cumin, coriander, and turmeric and cook for 2 minutes, or until lightly toasted. The grains should just start to turn golden brown.

2. Add the boiling water and salt and pepper. Stand back: the mixture will sputter. Bring the millet to a boil, stirring with a wooden spoon. Reduce the heat, cover the pan, and gently simmer the millet for 25 to 30 minutes, or until it is tender and all the liquid is absorbed. Fluff the millet with a fork and let cool completely. Fluff again with a fork.

3. Combine the cucumber, corn, peas, celery, bell pepper, onion, lemon juice, yogurt, and ½ the cilantro with the millet in a mixing bowl and toss to mix. Correct the seasoning, adding salt, spices, or lemon juice to taste: the salad should be highly seasoned. Sprinkle the salad with the remaining cilantro and serve at once.

Makes about 5 cups, enough to serve 4 to 6

190 CALORIES PER SERVING: 6 G PROTEIN; 4 G FAT; 34 G CARBOHYDRATE; 21 MG SODIUM; 0 MG CHOLESTEROL

Analysis based on 6 servings

INDIAN POTATO SALAD

I first tasted this unusual potato salad at a Boston Indian restaurant called Bombay Club. Garam masala is a roasted spice mix. You can buy it already made at Indian markets and gourmet shops. Or follow the simplified recipe on page 59 or the full recipe in my previous book, Steven Raichlen's High-Flavor, Low-Fat Cooking.

1½ pounds red or new potatoes, scrubbed and
    cut into ½-inch dice
½ teaspoon toasted cumin seeds
1 tablespoon garam masala (recipe follows)
⅔ cup nonfat yogurt
3 to 4 tablespoons fresh lemon juice

1 tomato, seeded and cut into ½-inch dice
½ small red onion, finely chopped
salt and freshly ground black pepper
3 tablespoons coarsely chopped fresh cilantro
1 tablespoon chopped fresh mint (optional)

1. Place the potatoes in a large saucepan with cold water to cover. Bring to a boil, reduce the heat, and simmer the potatoes until tender but not soft, 8 to 10 minutes. Drain the potatoes in a colander, then transfer to a mixing bowl.

2. Lightly toast the cumin seeds in a dry skillet over medium heat until fragrant and lightly browned, about 3 minutes. Set aside.

3. Stir the garam masala, ½ cup of the yogurt, and the lemon juice into the potatoes and let cool completely. Shortly before serving, stir in the tomato, onion, salt, pepper, half the cilantro, and mint (if using). Correct the seasoning, adding salt, lemon juice, or garam masala to taste.

4. Transfer the salad to a platter or bowl for serving. Spoon the remaining yogurt in the center and sprinkle the salad with the remaining cilantro and the cumin seeds.

Makes 4 cups, enough to serve 4 to 6

189 CALORIES PER SERVING: 6 G PROTEIN; 1 G FAT; 41 G CARBOHYDRATE; 278 MG SODIUM; 1 MG CHOLESTEROL
Analysis based on 4 servings

QUICK GARAM MASALA

Here's a simplified version of one of India's most popular spice mixes.

1 teaspoon cumin seeds
1 teaspoon coriander seeds
¼ teaspoon each sesame seeds and black
   peppercorns

½ teaspoon kosher salt
1 cardamom pod

Place the cumin, coriander, sesame seeds, peppercorns, salt, and cardamom pod in a dry skillet and roast lightly over medium heat until lightly browned and very fragrant, about 2 minutes. Grind the mixture in a spice mill or coffee grinder, or pulverize with a mortar and pestle.

Makes 1 tablespoon

19 CALORIES PER SERVING: 1 G PROTEIN; 1 G FAT; 2 G CARBOHYDRATE; 945 MG SODIUM; 0 MG CHOLESTEROL

FISHLESS CAESAR SALAD

Caesar salad was the first "gourmet dish" I ever learned to prepare. I would watch, enraptured, as a venerable waiter named Mr. Louis would combine and mix the ingredients with grave ceremony at the late Restaurant 3900 in Baltimore. I wonder what he'd think of my vegetarian version, which uses dried tomatoes and olives to create the salty tang of the anchovies and no-fat sour cream to achieve the creaminess of a dressing once made with coddled egg. For a novel presentation, use only the hearts of the romaine lettuce and leave the leaves whole.

FOR THE CROUTONS
4 ½-inch-thick slices of French bread
1 teaspoon extra-virgin olive oil
1 clove garlic, cut in half

FOR THE DRESSING
1 homemade Dried Tomato (page 255) or store-bought dried tomato (about 1 tablespoon minced)
2 kalamata or other black olives, pitted and minced
½ to 1 teaspoon Dijon-style mustard

2 tablespoons no-fat sour cream
1 tablespoon extra-virgin olive oil
1 tablespoon fresh lemon juice
1 teaspoon red wine vinegar
2 teaspoons Pickapeppa sauce or vegetarian Worcestershire-style sauce
salt and freshly ground black pepper

TO FINISH THE SALAD
2 hearts of romaine lettuce (or 1 whole head)
1 ounce thinly shaved or freshly grated Romano cheese

1. Preheat the grill or broiler to medium-high. Prepare the croutons. Lightly brush the bread slices with olive oil. Grill or broil until golden brown, 1 to 2 minutes per side. Let the bread slices cool, rub with cut garlic, then cut into quarters. Mince the garlic that remains for the dressing.

2. Prepare the dressing. If using a store-bought dried tomato, plump it in hot water for 30 minutes. (If using oil-packed dried tomatoes, drain well.) Mince the tomato and combine with the olives, minced garlic, mustard, sour cream, and olive oil in a large salad bowl and whisk to a smooth paste. Whisk in the lemon juice, vinegar, Pickapeppa

sauce, salt, and pepper. Correct the seasoning, adding salt, lemon juice, or Pickapeppa sauce to taste: The dressing should be highly seasoned.

3. Break apart the lettuce leaves, discarding any blemished or wilted leaves. Wash and dry the leaves. If using hearts of romaine lettuce, leave the leaves whole. If using a whole head of romaine, tear each leaf into 2-inch pieces.

4. Just before serving, add the lettuce and croutons to the dressing and gently toss to mix. Shave or sprinkle the cheese over the salad and serve at once.

Serves 4

195 CALORIES PER SERVING: 8 G PROTEIN; 8 G FAT; 23 G CARBOHYDRATE; 335 MG SODIUM; 0 MG CHOLESTEROL

KOREAN RADISH SALAD

Daikon is a long, cylindrical, crisp, white-fleshed radish sold at Asian markets, natural foods stores, and many supermarkets. This spicy dish makes a great cold-weather salad.

1½ pounds daikon radish

FOR THE DRESSING
2 tablespoons rice vinegar (or to taste)
1 tablespoon tomato paste
2 teaspoons sugar or honey (or to taste)
salt

6 scallions, finely chopped
6 cloves garlic, minced
1 teaspoon minced ginger
1 to 2 tablespoons hot paprika or 1 teaspoon cayenne
1 to 2 teaspoons Korean, Chinese, or Thai chili paste

1. Peel the daikon and cut it into ½-inch dice.

2. Combine the vinegar and tomato paste in a salad bowl and whisk until the latter is dissolved. Whisk in the sugar, salt, scallions, garlic, ginger, paprika, and chili paste, adding sugar, salt, vinegar, or chili paste to taste: The dressing should be highly seasoned.

3. Stir in the daikon. The salad can be served at once but will improve if it sits for a couple of hours. You may need to adjust the seasonings before serving.

Makes 4 cups, enough to serve 4 to 6

55 CALORIES PER SERVING: 2 G PROTEIN; 1 G FAT; 12 G CARBOHYDRATE; 92 MG SODIUM; 0 MG CHOLESTEROL

Analysis based on 4 servings

ROASTED PEPPER SALAD

When I was growing up, peppers meant green bell peppers. These days, cooks have a rainbow selection of peppers to choose from: red, yellow, orange, purple, and green bell peppers, not to mention pale green cubanelles. Grilling imparts a wonderful smoky flavor to the peppers, but a similar effect can be achieved by the apartment-bound cook by broiling the peppers or roasting them over a high heat on the stove. The important thing is to really char the peppers well. This is the one dish you can get away with burning!

2 red bell peppers
2 yellow bell peppers
2 green bell peppers

FOR THE DRESSING
1 tablespoon balsamic vinegar (or to taste)
1 teaspoon lemon juice (or to taste)
salt and freshly ground black pepper

1 tablespoon extra-virgin olive oil
1½ teaspoons capers, drained
2 tablespoons chopped fresh herbs (including flat-leaf parsley, basil, oregano, marjoram, and/or chives)

a sprig of fresh basil (or any of the above herbs) for garnish

1. Preheat the grill or broiler.

2. Grill the peppers over high heat, turning as necessary, until all are thoroughly charred. This will take 6 to 8 minutes. Alternatively, the peppers can be broiled, baked on a hot baking sheet, or even charred directly on a gas or electric stove burner.

3. Wrap the roasted peppers in wet paper towels or place them in a sealed paper bag and set aside to cool. (This helps loosen the skin.) Transfer the peppers to a plate. Scrape off the charred skin with the side of a knife. Cut each pepper in half, core, and seed, reserving the juices. Cut each half lengthwise in half or thirds and arrange the pepper pieces, alternating color, on a round platter.

4. Combine the vinegar, lemon juice, and salt and pepper to taste in a mixing bowl. Whisk until the salt crystals are dissolved. Whisk in the olive oil, capers, herbs, and any juices from the peppers. Correct the seasoning, adding vinegar or salt to taste. Spoon the dressing over the salad and garnish with a basil sprig in the center. Serve at once.

Serves 4 to 6

64 CALORIES PER SERVING: 1 G PROTEIN; 4 G FAT; 8 G CARBOHYDRATE; 26 MG SODIUM; 0 MG CHOLESTEROL
Analysis based on 4 servings

SESAME SPINACH SALAD

Dine at any Korean restaurant and you're apt to find this refreshing, chilled, sesame-scented spinach salad.
For the best results, use the young, tender, fresh spinach leaves sold in bunches.

1 pound flat-leaf spinach, stemmed and washed
salt
1½ tablespoons sesame seeds

2 teaspoons sesame oil (or to taste)
2 teaspoons soy sauce (or to taste)
½ to 1 teaspoon sugar or honey

1. Cook the spinach in a large pot of boiling salted water for 30 seconds, or until just tender. Drain the spinach in a colander and rinse with ice water. Blot the spinach leaves dry on paper towels or a dish towel.

2. Lightly toast the sesame seeds in a dry skillet over medium heat for 2 minutes. Combine half the sesame seeds and the sesame oil, soy sauce, and sugar in a bowl. Whisk until the sugar is dissolved. Add the spinach and toss well. Correct the seasoning, adding soy sauce or sugar to taste: The salad should be a little sweet and a little salty. Sprinkle the spinach with the remaining sesame seeds and serve at room temperature or chilled.

Serves 4

62 CALORIES PER SERVING: 4 G PROTEIN; 4 G FAT; 4 G CARBOHYDRATE; 234 MG SODIUM; 0 MG CHOLESTEROL

GRILLED BREAD AND VEGETABLE SALAD

You don't need a degree in restaurant-going to know that grill fever has reached epidemic proportions. Here's a summery salad featuring smoky grilled vegetables and bread. City-bound cooks can "grill" the ingredients under a broiler.
Note: *When you cut the onion into wedges, leave the root end intact. It will help hold the onion together. You can cut it off afterward.*

1 clove garlic, minced
1½ tablespoons extra-virgin olive oil
4 1-inch-thick slices of French bread, cut on the diagonal
2 zucchinis, cut on the diagonal into ¼-inch slices
2 yellow squash, cut on the diagonal into ¼-inch slices
1 onion, cut into ½-inch wedges

4 plum tomatoes, cut lengthwise in half
2 yellow or red bell peppers, cored, seeded, and quartered
1 to 2 tablespoons fresh lemon juice
1 to 2 tablespoons balsamic vinegar
2 tablespoons chopped fresh basil, plus 4 sprigs for garnish
salt and freshly ground black pepper

1. Preheat the grill to high. Mix the garlic with the oil and let it sit for 10 minutes.

2. Lightly brush the bread slices with a little garlic oil and grill them for 30 seconds per side or until golden brown. Take care not to let them burn. Transfer the bread slices to a cake rack to cool. Lightly brush the zucchini and squash slices with garlic oil and grill for 2 minutes per side or until a dark golden brown. Cook the onion slices, tomatoes, and peppers the same way. Set all the vegetables aside to cool to room temperature. Cut into 1-inch pieces.

3. Combine the grilled vegetables in a large bowl with any remaining garlic oil and the lemon juice, vinegar, chopped basil, and salt and pepper. Toss well. Correct the seasoning, adding salt or vinegar to taste. Place a grilled bread slice in the center of a salad plate and spoon a quarter of the grilled vegetables on top. Repeat with the remaining portions. Garnish each salad with a basil sprig and serve at once.

Serves 4

309 CALORIES PER SERVING: 10 G PROTEIN; 8 G FAT; 51 G CARBOHYDRATE; 401 MG SODIUM; 0 MG CHOLESTEROL

UNCOOKED VEGETABLE SALAD

*There's a small but significant segment of the vegetarian community that believes not only in eliminating animal foods from one's diet
but in actually eliminating cooking. While this is an impractical philosophy for someone who writes cookbooks for a living,
I'm intrigued by the notion of cuisine without cooking. I've certainly sampled enough raw dishes to know that no-cook
cuisine can be both tasty and sophisticated. (For an example, see the Uncooked Apple Pie on page 233.)
Here's a crisp summer salad that takes advantage of the natural sweetness of uncooked zucchini, squash,
and corn and will leave your teeth feeling squeaky clean, to boot!*

2 medium zucchinis
1 yellow summer squash (like a crookneck or
    yellow zucchini)
1 ear of corn
4 okras (optional)
1 jalapeño chili, seeded and minced (for a hotter
    salad, leave the seeds in)
3 tablespoons chopped fresh cilantro or fresh
    mint

3 scallions, finely chopped
2 to 3 tablespoons fresh lime juice
1 tablespoon extra-virgin olive oil
salt and freshly ground black pepper

4 large radicchio or Boston lettuce leaves for
    garnish

1. Wash the zucchini and squash and cut off the ends. Cut each into ¼-inch dice. Cut the kernels off the corn cob. The easiest way to do this is to lay the corn on its side on a cutting board and make lengthwise cuts. Cut the okras (if using) into ¼-inch dice.

2. Combine the zucchini, squash, corn, okra (if using), jalapeño, cilantro, scallions, lime juice, olive oil, salt, and pepper in a mixing bowl and toss to mix. Correct the seasoning, adding salt or lime juice to taste: The salad should be highly seasoned. Spoon the salad onto the radicchio or lettuce leaves and serve at once.

Serves 4

74 CALORIES PER SERVING: 3 G PROTEIN; 4 G FAT; 10 G CARBOHYDRATE; 10 MG SODIUM; 0 MG CHOLESTEROL

JICAMA AND GREEN BEAN SALAD WITH BLACK SESAME VINAIGRETTE

This colorful salad is pretty enough for framing. It requires a few special ingredients, which can be found at a well-stocked gourmet shop or natural foods store. Jicama (pronounced HEE-kim-a) is a crisp, white-fleshed, Mexican root vegetable whose flavor lies midway between apple and potato. My favorite green bean for this recipe is the haricot vert (a skinny French string bean), but any slender green bean or even snow peas will do. Mirin, a sweet rice wine, and black sesame seeds are used extensively in Japanese cooking (see Cook's Notes).

1 small or ½ large jicama (about 1 pound)
½ pound *haricots verts* or the skinniest green
    beans you can find
salt

FOR THE DRESSING
2 tablespoons mirin (sweet rice wine)

1½ tablespoons rice vinegar
1 teaspoon dark sesame oil
freshly ground black pepper

2 teaspoons black sesame seeds (or darkly
    toasted sesame seeds)

1. Peel the jicama with a paring knife and cut it into sticks the size of the *haricots verts*. Set aside. Snap the stem ends off the *haricots verts* and cook the beans in rapidly boiling salted water until al dente, 3 to 4 minutes. Drain the beans in a colander, refresh under cold water, and blot dry.

2. Just before serving, combine the mirin, rice vinegar, sesame oil, pepper, and salt to taste in a salad bowl. Whisk until the salt is dissolved. Add the jicama and *haricots verts* and toss to mix. Correct the seasoning, adding salt, vinegar, or mirin to taste. Sprinkle the salad with black sesame seeds and serve at once.

Serves 4

89 CALORIES PER SERVING: 3 G PROTEIN; 2 G FAT; 15 G CARBOHYDRATE; 9 MG SODIUM; 0 MG CHOLESTEROL

FAVA BEAN SALAD

*Fava beans are broad, flat beans with a rich, earthy flavor. Popular throughout the Mediterranean basin, they're available fresh for a few weeks in spring and dried year-round at Italian markets and specialty greengrocers'. If they are unavailable, you could use lima beans or any other type of bean. **Note:** The Spanish olive oil and sherry vinegar give this salad a Spanish touch. But you can certainly use Italian or French oil and red wine vinegar instead.*

3 cups cooked fava beans or lima beans (page 261)

3 pimientos or 1 roasted red bell pepper, cut into 1 × ¼-inch strips

½ small red onion, cut into ¼-inch dice

1 clove garlic, minced

1 to 2 jalapeño chilies, seeded and minced

3 tablespoons finely chopped flat-leaf parsley

3 tablespoons finely chopped fresh mint

1½ tablespoons extra-virgin olive oil (preferably Spanish)

4 teaspoons sherry vinegar or red wine vinegar (or to taste)

salt and freshly ground black pepper

Combine the beans, pimientos, onion, garlic, jalapeños, parsley, mint, oil, vinegar, salt, and pepper in a large salad bowl. Toss well, adding salt or vinegar to taste: The salad should be highly seasoned.

Makes 4 cups, enough to serve 4 to 6

217 CALORIES PER SERVING: 11 G PROTEIN; 6 G FAT; 32 G CARBOHYDRATE; 8 MG SODIUM; 0 MG CHOLESTEROL

Analysis based on 4 servings

LAND AND SEA SALAD

*Here's a picture-pretty salad made with purple cabbage, green avocado, and black hijiki seaweed. The latter is a curly, tube-shaped, dried seaweed from Japan. Rich in phosphorus, iodine, and calcium (one tablespoon of hijiki contains more calcium than one cup of milk), hijiki is widely available at natural foods stores and Japanese markets. **Note:** If possible, use Florida avocados, which contain a third less fat than California avocados. The salad is equally attractive made with green cabbage or napa.*

½ cup dried hijiki seaweed
1 avocado
1 tablespoon lemon or lime juice
3 cups shredded red cabbage (⅓ whole cabbage)

FOR THE DRESSING
¼ cup rice vinegar (or to taste)
3 tablespoons mirin (see Cook's Notes) or cream sherry

1 teaspoon sesame oil
1 clove garlic, minced
1 teaspoon minced fresh ginger
2 scallions, minced
1 serrano or jalapeño chili, seeded and minced (optional)
salt and freshly ground black pepper

1. Soak the hijiki in 4 cups cold water for 20 minutes, or until soft. Transfer the hijiki to a colander, rinse with cold water, and drain well.

2. Cut the avocado in half lengthwise to the pit. Twist the halves in opposite directions and pull them apart. Remove the pit. Scoop out the flesh with a large spoon and cut into ½-inch dice. Toss the avocado with lemon juice to prevent discoloration. Shred the cabbage.

3. For the dressing, combine the vinegar, mirin, sesame oil, garlic, ginger, scallions, chili, salt, and pepper in a salad bowl and whisk until the salt crystals are dissolved. Add the hijiki, avocado, and cabbage and gently toss to mix. Correct the seasoning, adding salt, mirin, or vinegar to taste.

Serves 4 to 6

129 CALORIES PER SERVING: 3 G PROTEIN; 8 G FAT; 15 G CARBOHYDRATE; 76 MG SODIUM; 0 MG CHOLESTEROL

Analysis based on 4 servings

SAINT BARTS LENTIL SALAD

Lentil salad is a specialty of the beachfront restaurant Taiwana in Saint Barthélemy, French West Indies, where it costs as much as an entire meal would in most places. (The astronomical price seems to make it all the more popular!) The owner won't part with the recipe, so here's my version. For the best results, use the Le Puy lentil from France, a tiny, dark-green legume that has a rich meaty flavor. Le Puy lentils are available at many gourmet shops and by mail order from Dean & Deluca, but other types of lentils work well, too.

1½ cups lentils (preferably Le Puy lentils)
1 cup radishes, cut into matchstick slivers, plus 8 whole radishes for garnish
2 tomatoes, peeled, seeded, and cut into ¼-inch dice
2 carrots, peeled and cut into ¼-inch dice
1 stalk celery, cut into ¼-inch dice
½ small red onion, cut into ¼-inch dice (about ¼ cup)
¼ cup finely chopped flat-leaf parsley
3 tablespoons finely chopped fresh tarragon (or other fresh herb or more parsley)

½ Scotch bonnet chili or 1 jalapeño chili, seeded and minced
½ teaspoon Caribbean hot sauce or Tabasco (or to taste)
1 clove garlic, minced
3 tablespoons fresh lime juice (or to taste)
2 tablespoons tarragon vinegar, rice vinegar, or red wine vinegar (or to taste)
2 tablespoons extra-virgin olive oil
salt and freshly ground black pepper
8 large Boston lettuce leaves

1. Cook the lentils in 6 cups boiling water until tender but not soft, about 25 minutes. Drain the lentils in a colander, reserving ½ cup of the cooking liquid. Refresh the lentils under cold water and drain well.

2. Cut 8 of the radishes into "roses." To do so, make shallow vertical cuts around the circumference of the root end of each radish and soak in ice water for 1 hour or until the roses "bloom."

3. In a mixing or salad bowl combine the lentils, radish slivers, tomatoes, carrots, celery, onion, parsley, tarragon, chili, hot sauce, garlic, lime juice, vinegar, oil, salt, and pepper and toss well. Correct the seasoning, adding lime juice, hot sauce, or salt to taste: The salad should be highly seasoned. Place a lettuce leaf on each plate and mound the lentil salad on top. Garnish each salad with a radish rose and serve at once.

Makes about 4 cups, enough to serve 8 as an appetizer, 4 as a light main course

185 CALORIES PER SERVING: 11 G PROTEIN; 4 G FAT; 28 G CARBOHYDRATE; 21 MG SODIUM; 0 MG CHOLESTEROL
Analysis based on 8 servings

MUFFINS AND BREADS

VANILLA BUTTERMILK PANCAKES

Vanilla and low-fat buttermilk give these pancakes plenty of flavor, while using egg whites instead of whole eggs and a nonstick frying pan to cook the pancakes dramatically reduces the fat. For moister, crustier pancakes, use 1 to 2 teaspoons canola oil instead of the spray oil for oiling the pan. Diced fresh fruit or fresh berries can be added as desired.

1 cup all-purpose unbleached white flour
1 teaspoon sugar, honey, or other sweetener
½ teaspoon baking powder
½ teaspoon baking soda
½ teaspoon salt

½ teaspoon vanilla extract
2 egg whites or 1 whole egg, lightly beaten
1 tablespoon canola or other vegetable oil
approximately 1 cup low-fat buttermilk
spray oil

1. Sift the dry ingredients—flour, sugar, baking powder, baking soda, and salt—into a mixing bowl and make a well in the center. Gently whisk in the wet ingredients—vanilla, egg whites, oil, and buttermilk—to obtain a smooth batter. (Whisk as little as possible, or the pancakes will be rubbery.) If the batter seems too thick, add a little more buttermilk or water.

2. Lightly spray a nonstick frying pan with oil. (This isn't necessary for all the pancakes, but it helps with the first batch.) Heat the pan over a medium flame. Spoon in dollops of batter to form 3-inch pancakes.

3. Cook the pancakes for 1 to 2 minutes, or until bubbles begin to form on the top. Turn the pancakes with a spatula and cook for 1 minute, or until both sides are golden brown, lowering the flame if the pancakes brown too quickly.

4. Continue frying the pancakes in this fashion until all the batter is used up. Respray the pan with oil if necessary. Serve the pancakes with maple syrup.

Makes 20 pancakes

37 CALORIES PER SERVING: 1 G PROTEIN; 1 G FAT; 6 G CARBOHYDRATE; 101 MG SODIUM; 0 MG CHOLESTEROL

Analysis per pancake (analysis does not include syrup)

PUMPKIN SPICE MUFFINS

Here's a Halloween twist on ordinary muffins. To make pumpkin purée from scratch, bake half a seeded pumpkin, cut side down, on a nonstick baking sheet at 350° F. for 1 hour, or until tender. Let the pumpkin cool, peel off the skin, and purée the flesh in a food processor. But canned pumpkin or squash works fine, too.

½ cup raisins
½ cup warm apple cider or other fruit juice
2 tablespoons vegetable oil (optional)
4 egg whites
1 cup sugar or Sucanat (see Cook's Notes), plus
  2 tablespoons for sprinkling on top
½ teaspoon ground cinnamon
½ teaspoon ground ginger

¼ teaspoon freshly ground nutmeg
⅛ teaspoon ground cloves
a pinch of salt (optional)
1½ cups pumpkin or squash purée
2 cups all-purpose flour
2 teaspoons baking powder
1 teaspoon baking soda
spray oil

1. Soak the raisins in the cider for 20 minutes. Stir in the oil (if using). Preheat the oven to 350° F.

2. Combine the egg whites, 1 cup sugar, cinnamon, ginger, nutmeg, cloves, and salt (if using) in a mixer and beat until smooth, about 3 minutes. Beat in the pumpkin purée. Sift together the flour, baking powder, and baking soda. Gradually stir the flour into the pumpkin mixture, alternating with the raisins, cider, and oil. Stir just to mix.

3. Grease muffin tins with spray oil and spoon in the batter, filling each cup to the rim. Sprinkle the tops with the remaining sugar. Bake the muffins for 25 to 30 minutes, or until puffed and firm. When done, an inserted skewer or toothpick will come out clean. Let the muffins cool in their tins for 5 minutes, then turn onto a cake rack to cool.

Makes 6 large or 8 to 9 small muffins

Note: Like all baked goods made with fruit or vegetable purées, these muffins keep well. (The purée keeps them moist.) Store the muffins in a Ziploc bag or tightly sealed container.

369 CALORIES PER SERVING: 8 G PROTEIN; 1 G FAT; 86 G CARBOHYDRATE; 290 MG SODIUM; 0 MG CHOLESTEROL

Analysis per large muffin

WHOLE-KERNEL CORN MUFFINS

This recipe uses skim milk and low-fat buttermilk in place of most of the oil, butter, or bacon fat found in traditional corn breads and muffins. For even more flavor, you could use Grilled Corn kernels (page 253). Cumin gives these muffins a Southwestern accent. Vanilla would add a touch of sweetness. (Use less salt if using vanilla.)
Note: *The finer the cornmeal, the more delicate the muffins will be. I make mine with stone-ground cornmeal.*

1 cup cornmeal (preferably stone-ground)
½ cup unbleached all-purpose flour
1 tablespoon sugar, honey, or Sucanat
1½ teaspoons baking powder
1 teaspoon baking soda
1 teaspoon salt
½ teaspoon cumin or vanilla

¼ to ½ teaspoon freshly ground black pepper
1 cup low-fat buttermilk
½ cup skim milk
3 egg whites
2 tablespoons canola oil
1 cup cooked corn kernels
spray oil

1. Preheat the oven to 425° F. Sift the dry ingredients—cornmeal, flour, sugar (if using honey, add it with the wet ingredients), baking powder, baking soda, salt, cumin, and pepper—into a mixing bowl. Combine the wet ingredients—buttermilk, milk, egg whites, and oil—and corn in a separate bowl and whisk to mix.

2. Add the dry ingredients to the wet and stir just to mix. Stir the batter as little as possible to keep the muffins tender.

3. Spoon the batter into muffin tins greased with spray oil, filling each cup almost to the top. Bake the muffins for 15 to 20 minutes, or until puffed and firm. When the muffins are done, an inserted skewer or toothpick will come out clean. Let the muffins cool in their tins for 5 minutes, then turn onto a cake rack to cool. Chipotle Apple Jelly (page 215) makes a great accompaniment.

Makes about 10 small muffins

Note: To make corn bread, bake the batter in a 9-inch-square pan.

136 CALORIES PER SERVING: 5 G PROTEIN; 3 G FAT; 22 G CARBOHYDRATE; 395 MG SODIUM; 1 MG CHOLESTEROL

Analysis per muffin

CRANBERRY SCONES

Scones are British tea pastries, of course. The notion of a low-fat scone first came from my friend (and Eating Well *magazine test kitchen director) Patricia Jamieson. My own test kitchen director, Didi Emmons, came up with the idea of using oat flour to increase the moistness of the scones. If cranberries aren't in season, use dried cherries or other dried fruit.* **Note:** *For even less fat, replace the egg with 2 whites.*

1¼ cups quick-cook oatmeal
approximately 1⅛ cups all-purpose unbleached
   white flour, plus flour for rolling the dough
¼ cup sugar
½ teaspoon baking soda
2 teaspoons baking powder
¼ teaspoon salt

2 tablespoons butter
⅓ cup nonfat yogurt
1 egg, beaten
1 tablespoon canola oil
⅓ cup cranberries or dried cherries
¼ cup raisins

1. Preheat the oven to 400° F.

2. Grind the oats to a fine powder in a food processor fitted with a metal chopping blade. Grind in the flour, 3 tablespoons of the sugar, and the baking powder, baking soda, and salt. Cut in the butter.

3. In a separate mixing bowl combine the yogurt, egg, oil, cranberries, and raisins. Add the oat mixture to the wet ingredients and stir just to mix. (Overstirring will make the scones tough.) The dough should be the consistency of biscuit dough. Add flour as necessary.

4. Turn the dough onto a lightly floured work surface and roll it into a rectangle 12 inches long, 6 inches wide, and about 1½ inches thick. Cut the dough into nine 4 × 2-inch rectangles and transfer to a nonstick baking sheet. (Alternatively, you can make round scones.) Sprinkle the scones with the remaining 1 tablespoon sugar.

5. Bake the scones for 12 to 15 minutes, or until firm and lightly browned on top. Transfer the scones to a cake rack to cool.

Makes 9 scones

184 CALORIES PER SERVING: 5 G PROTEIN; 6 G FAT; 29 G CARBOHYDRATE; 218 MG SODIUM; 31 MG CHOLESTEROL

Analysis per scone

APPLE CARROT MUFFINS

Here's a breakfast twist on a classic American carrot cake. For the best results, use a firm, tart apple, like a Granny Smith,
and leave the skins intact. The cereal helps create the crunchy texture of nuts, without the fat.
Note: *For even less fat, you can omit the canola oil, but the muffins won't be quite as moist.*

1½ cups cored, grated apples (1 large or 2 small fruits)
1½ cups grated carrots (3 medium carrots)
3 egg whites, lightly beaten
2 tablespoons canola oil
¼ cup applesauce
½ cup dark brown sugar
1 teaspoon vanilla
¾ cup unbleached all-purpose flour
1½ teaspoons baking soda

1½ teaspoons baking powder
½ teaspoon cinnamon
½ teaspoon cardamom
½ teaspoon ground cloves
pinch of salt (optional)
⅓ cup quick-cook oatmeal
⅔ cup raisins
½ cup Grape-Nuts or other crunchy cereal

spray oil

1. Preheat the oven to 350° F.
2. Combine the apple, carrots, egg whites, oil, applesauce, sugar, and vanilla in a mixing bowl and mix well with a wooden spoon. Sift the flour, baking soda, baking powder, cinnamon, cardamom, cloves, and salt (if using) into the apple mixture. Add the oatmeal, raisins, and Grape-Nuts and stir just to mix. Grease a muffin tin with spray oil.

3. Spoon the batter into the muffin tins, filling each cup to the top. Bake the muffins for 35 minutes, or until firm to the touch and an inserted toothpick comes out clean. Let muffins cool completely in the tins before unmolding.

Makes 8 medium or 10 small muffins

237 CALORIES PER SERVING: 5 G PROTEIN; 4 G FAT; 48 G CARBOHYDRATE; 300 MG SODIUM; 0 MG CHOLESTEROL
Analysis per muffin

DRIED TOMATO AND BASIL FOCACCIA

Ten years ago, few Americans had ever heard of focaccia (pronounced fo-KA-cha). Today, we can't seem to live without it!
Thicker than a pizza but flatter than a conventional loaf, this classic Italian bread makes a great snack,
hors d'oeuvre, soup or salad accompaniment, or enhancement to a bread basket.
Complete instructions for making Dried Tomatoes are found on page 255.

1 envelope (2¼ teaspoons) dry yeast or 0.6
   ounce compressed yeast
2 teaspoons sugar
1½ cups warm water
2 teaspoons salt
4 teaspoons extra-virgin olive oil
4½ to 5 cups unbleached white flour
12 dried tomatoes

2 tablespoons cornmeal
12 basil leaves
½ teaspoon kosher salt for sprinkling
½ teaspoon cracked black peppercorns for
   sprinkling
spray oil or a little extra olive oil for greasing the
   bowl

1. Combine the yeast, the sugar, and 5 tablespoons of the warm water in the bottom of a large mixing bowl. Let stand for 6 to 8 minutes, or until the mixture is foamy like a head of beer.

2. Stir in the remaining water, the 2 teaspoons salt, and 2 teaspoons of the olive oil. Stir in the flour, ½ cup at a time, to form a dough that is stiff enough to come away from the sides of the bowl. Turn it out onto a lightly floured work surface. Wash and lightly oil the bowl. Knead the dough until smooth and elastic, 6 to 8 minutes, adding flour as necessary. **Note:** The dough can be mixed and kneaded in a food processor fitted with a plastic dough blade or an electric mixer fitted with a dough hook.

3. Place the dough in the oiled bowl, cover with plastic wrap and a dish towel, and let rise in a warm place until doubled in bulk, 1 to 2 hours. If using store-bought dried tomatoes, plump them in hot water (place in a bowl with hot water just to cover) for 15 minutes. If using homemade dried tomatoes, drain well.

4. Punch the dough down and roll it out into 1 large or 2 small ovals, each ½ inch thick. Transfer the oval(s) to a baker's peel (wooden baker's paddle), cookie sheet, or tart pan bottom liberally sprinkled with cornmeal. Cover the focaccia with a clean cloth and let rise until doubled in height (30 to 60 minutes). Place a baking stone or sheet pan in the oven on the middle shelf and preheat to 375° F.

5. Poke your fingers over the surface of the focaccia to decoratively dimple the surface. Arrange the tomato halves (cut side down) and basil leaves in an attractive pattern on top. Brush the top with 1 teaspoon olive oil and sprinkle with kosher salt and black peppercorns.

6. Slide the focaccia onto the baking stone and bake until crisp and golden brown, 20 to 30 minutes. Let cool slightly before serving. Just before serving, drizzle focaccia with the remaining olive oil. Cut into wedges and serve.

Serves 6 to 8

300 CALORIES PER SERVING: 9.5 G PROTEIN; 3 G FAT; 60 G CARBOHYDRATE; 656 MG SODIUM; 0 MG CHOLESTEROL

Analysis based on 8 servings

FIVE-GRAIN BREAD

Rustic and rich is this five-grain bread, which is loaded with nutrients and fiber. Feel free to substitute any cooked grains or beans for the ones called for below. As in the Curried Onion Bread (page 81), we use a sponge (intermediary rising of part of the dough) to give the bread extra lift and flavor.

1 package dried yeast (2¼ teaspoons) or 0.6
 ounce compressed yeast
1 tablespoon honey
¼ cup warm water

FOR THE SPONGE
2¾ cups warm water
2 tablespoons honey
2 tablespoons molasses
2 cups all-purpose white flour
1 cup whole wheat flour

TO FINISH THE BREAD
½ cup rye flour
½ cup cooked wheat berries
½ cup cooked barley
½ cup rolled oats
4 teaspoons salt
1 cup whole wheat flour
approximately 2 cups white flour (or as needed)
spray oil

1. Combine the yeast, the honey, and the ¼ cup warm water in a small bowl and stir to mix. Let stand for 6 to 8 minutes: It should foam like a head of beer.

2. Prepare the sponge. Transfer the yeast mixture to a large mixing bowl. Stir in the 2¾ cups warm water, 2 tablespoons honey, 2 tablespoons molasses, 2 cups white flour, and 1 cup whole wheat flour. Let this mixture sit for 1 to 2 hours, or until it bubbles and starts to rise.

3. To finish the bread, stir the rye flour, wheat berries, barley, oats, salt, and remaining whole wheat flour and white flour into the sponge, adding white flour until the dough becomes too stiff to stir: It should be dry enough to come away from the sides of the bowl, but soft enough to knead. Turn the dough out onto a lightly floured work surface. Wash the bowl and lightly oil it with the spray oil.

4. Knead the dough for 6 to 8 minutes, or until smooth and elastic. If the dough is too sticky to knead, work in a little more flour. **Note:** The dough can be mixed and kneaded in a heavy-duty mixer fitted with a dough hook or a large food processor fitted with a plastic dough blade.

5. Return the dough to the oiled bowl and cover with plastic wrap and a dish towel. Place it in a warm, draft-free spot and let rise for 1½ to 2 hours, or until doubled in bulk. (The dough can be allowed to rise at lower temperatures—even in the refrigerator—but the rising time will be longer.)

6. Punch down the dough. To make one large round loaf, oil a large (12-inch), shallow, round-bottomed bowl. Place the dough in it. To make 2 rectangular loaves, cut the dough in half. Pat each half into an 8-inch-long oval. Plump the ovals in the center and drop them into 2 oiled 9-inch nonstick loaf pans, seam side down. Cover the loaves with dish towels and let the dough rise again until doubled in bulk.

7. Preheat the oven to 375° F. If making a round loaf, invert the dough onto an oiled nonstick baking sheet. If making rectangular loaves, leave them in the pans. Lightly sprinkle the tops of the loaves with flour. Using a razor blade, make a series of decorative slashes, ¼ to ½ inch deep.

8. Bake the loaves for 40 to 50 minutes, or until firm and nicely browned. (Rectangular loaves may

need a little less baking time.) The standard test for doneness is to tap the bottom of the loaf: If it sounds hollow, the bread is cooked. You can also test for doneness with an instant-read thermometer: The internal temperature should be about 190° F.

9. Transfer the bread to a cake rack to cool. If making rectangular loaves, turn them onto the cake rack. Let the bread(s) cool slightly or completely. (Bread piping hot out of the oven is very hard to slice.) Cut into slices for serving.

Makes two 9-inch loaves (24 slices)

145 CALORIES PER SERVING: 4 G PROTEIN; 1 G FAT; 31 G CARBOHYDRATE; 357 MG SODIUM; 0 MG CHOLESTEROL
Analysis per slice

CURRIED ONION BREAD

Caramelized curried onions give this bread a rich flavor, while chickpeas provide extra protein and a pleasing contrast in textures. The sponge (intermediary rising of part of the dough) gives the bread extra lift and flavor.

2 tablespoons olive oil, plus oil for the bowl
2 large onions, thinly sliced (6 cups thinly sliced)
2 cups cooked chickpeas (page 261)
5 teaspoons curry powder
1 envelope (2¼ teaspoons) dried yeast or
  0.6 ounce compressed yeast
1 tablespoon sugar or honey

2½ cups warm water
2 tablespoons honey
4 teaspoons sea salt
7 to 8 cups unbleached white flour
1 egg white, beaten, for glaze

spray oil

1. Heat the olive oil in a large nonstick skillet. Cook the onions over medium-low heat until a light golden brown, about 10 minutes, stirring occasionally. Stir in the chickpeas and curry powder and continue sautéing the onions until a deep golden brown, about 3 minutes.

2. Combine the yeast, sugar, and ¼ cup warm water in a small mixing bowl and stir to mix. Let stand for 6 to 8 minutes: It should foam like a head of beer.

3. Prepare the sponge: Stir 2 tablespoons warm water into the yeast mixture. Stir in 1 cup flour or enough to obtain a moist but shapable dough. Roll the dough into a ball and drop it into a deep bowl filled with warm water. It will sink to the bottom. After 5 to 10 minutes, it will rise to the surface. The sponge is now activated and ready to use.

4. Transfer the sponge to a large mixing bowl. Stir in the remaining water, the 2 tablespoons honey, the salt, and the onion-chickpea mixture. Stir in the flour, one cup at a time. Add flour until the dough becomes too stiff to stir: It should be dry enough to come away from the sides of the bowl but soft enough to knead. Turn the dough out onto a lightly floured work surface. Wash the bowl and lightly oil it with spray oil.

5. Knead the dough for 6 to 8 minutes, or until smooth and elastic. If the dough is too sticky to knead, work in a little more flour. **Note:** The dough can be mixed and kneaded in a heavy-duty mixer fitted with a dough hook or a large food processor fitted with a dough blade.

6. Return the dough to the oiled bowl and cover with plastic wrap. Place it in a warm, draft-free spot and let it rise for 1½ to 2 hours, or until doubled in bulk. (The dough can be allowed to rise at lower temperatures—even in the refrigerator—but the rising time will be longer.)

7. Punch the dough down and cut in half. Pat each half into an 8-inch-long oval. Plump the ovals in the center and drop them, seam side down, into two 9-inch loaf pans greased with spray oil.

8. Cover the loaves with dish towels and let the dough rise again until doubled in bulk. Preheat the oven to 375° F. Brush the top of each loaf with beaten egg white or water and, using a sharp knife or razor blade, make a series of parallel diagonal slashes, ¼ to ½ inch deep.

9. Bake the loaves for about 35 to 40 minutes,

or until firm and nicely browned. The standard test for doneness is to tap the bottom of the loaf: If it sounds hollow, the bread is cooked. You can also test for doneness with an instant-read thermometer: The internal temperature should be about 190° F.

10. Let the breads cool for 5 minutes in the loaf pans, then turn them out onto a cake rack. Let cool slightly or completely. (Bread piping hot out of the oven is very hard to slice.)

Makes 2 loaves (24 slices)

123 CALORIES PER SERVING: 4 G PROTEIN; 2 G FAT; 23 G CARBOHYDRATE; 416 MG SODIUM; 0 MG CHOLESTEROL

Analysis per slice

CRANBERRY CURRANT BREAD

Each fall, the marshy lowlands around Plymouth, Massachusetts, and Cape Cod become crimson seas of fresh cranberries. Applesauce replaces the oil in my low-fat version of a classic New England tea bread. Sucanat, freeze-dried sugar cane juice, is discussed in Cook's Notes.

2 cups unbleached white flour
1 cup sugar or Sucanat
2 teaspoons baking soda
1½ teaspoons baking powder
1 teaspoon cinnamon
½ teaspoon ground cardamom
½ teaspoon salt (optional)
2 tablespoons lemon juice
1 cup low-fat buttermilk

½ cup applesauce
2 egg whites, lightly beaten
1½ teaspoons grated orange zest
1½ teaspoons grated lemon zest
1 cup cranberries, picked over and washed
½ cup currants, plumped in hot water for
   15 minutes, then drained

spray oil

1. Preheat the oven to 350° F. Sift the flour, sugar, baking soda, baking powder, cinnamon, cardamom, and salt (if using) into a mixing bowl. Combine the lemon juice, buttermilk, applesauce, egg whites, and orange and lemon zest in another mixing bowl and whisk to mix. Stir the wet ingredients into the dry ones and whisk just to mix. Stir in the cranberries and currants.

2. Spray a loaf pan with spray oil. Spoon in the batter. Bake the cranberry bread for 40 to 50 minutes, or until an inserted skewer comes out clean. Let the bread cool in the pan for 5 minutes, then invert it onto a cake rack. Let cool completely. Cut the cranberry bread into slices for serving.

Makes 1 loaf (12 slices)

175 CALORIES PER SERVING: 4 G PROTEIN; 1 G FAT; 40 G CARBOHYDRATE; 210 MG SODIUM; 1 MG CHOLESTEROL
Analysis per slice

SPICED FIG BREAD

Applesauce and nonfat yogurt replace the butter in this fragrant fig bread, while the tiny fig seeds provide an interesting crunch.
If you have the willpower to wait, the bread tastes even better the second day.

⅓ cup fresh orange juice
¼ cup rum
12 ounces dried figs, stemmed
1⅓ cups brown sugar
1 cup applesauce
½ cup nonfat yogurt
2 tablespoons canola oil
4 egg whites, lightly beaten
2 cups flour, plus flour for the loaf pan
1 teaspoon baking soda

½ teaspoon baking powder
1½ teaspoons cinnamon
1 teaspoon ground ginger
¼ teaspoon freshly grated nutmeg
¼ teaspoon ground cardamom
⅛ teaspoon ground cloves
a pinch of salt

spray oil

1. Preheat the oven to 350° F. Gently warm the orange juice and rum in a saucepan over low heat. Remove the pan from the heat, add the figs, and let soften for 20 minutes.

2. Remove any stems or hard ends from the figs. Purée the figs with their soaking liquid in a food processor. Grind in the brown sugar, applesauce, yogurt, oil, and egg whites.

3. Sift the dry ingredients—2 cups flour, baking soda, baking powder, cinnamon, ginger, nutmeg, cardamom, cloves, and salt—into a mixing bowl. Fold in the wet ingredients and stir just to mix. Spoon the batter into two 9-inch loaf pans (preferably nonstick), sprayed with spray oil and lightly floured. Bake the breads for 50 minutes, or until an inserted skewer comes out clean. Let the breads cool for 10 minutes, then invert onto cake racks. Let cool completely before serving.

Makes two 9-inch loaves (24 slices)

147 CALORIES PER SERVING: 2 G PROTEIN; 2 G FAT; 31 G CARBOHYDRATE; 67 MG SODIUM; 0 MG CHOLESTEROL

Analysis per slice

Pizzas, Pies, and Sandwiches

Basic Pizza Dough

Pizza may have originated in Naples, but the best I've ever tasted was in the neighboring town of Sorrento at the Ristorante Vela Bianca (the White Sail). Its creator was a short, affable pizzaiolo (pizza maker) named Amadeo Cinque. To me Signore Cinque's recipe seemed as revolutionary (it uses milk instead of water) as his technique for leavening the dough (in four successive risings). He uses a mixture of Italian and American flours: The former is made from a softer wheat than ours. To achieve a similar effect, I combine regular flour and cake flour.

4 teaspoons dried yeast (a little less than 2 packages)
2 teaspoons sugar
3 tablespoons warm water
7 cups all-purpose unbleached white flour, plus flour for rolling and stretching the dough

1 cup cake flour
4 teaspoons salt
2 cups skim milk
approximately ¼ cup cornmeal for sprinkling

pizza topping (see below)

1. Dissolve the yeast and sugar in 3 tablespoons warm water in a small bowl. Let stand for 6 to 8 minutes: The mixture should foam like a head of beer.

2. Combine the white flour, cake flour, and salt in a large mixing bowl and whisk well to mix. Make a well in the center and add the yeast mixture and milk. Working with your fingertips, gradually mix the flour into milk mixture. Add flour or milk as necessary to obtain a soft pliable dough.

3. Turn the dough onto a lightly floured work surface and knead until smooth, about 5 minutes. The dough can also be made in a mixer with a dough hook or a food processor. **Note:** If using the latter, add the flours and salt and process to mix. Work in the yeast mixture and milk, running the machine in bursts until the dough comes away from the sides of the processor bowl. If you make the dough in the food processor, you should still turn it

out onto a floured work surface and knead it a little by hand.

4. Place the dough in a lightly oiled bowl and cover with plastic wrap. Let the dough rise for 30 minutes in a warm place. (It won't rise very much.)

5. Punch down the dough. Let it rise for another 30 minutes. Punch it down again and let it rise for another 30 minutes.

6. Punch down the dough one final time. Divide it into 4 equal parts and roll them into balls. Place the balls on a lightly floured work surface and cover with a damp cloth. Let the dough rise for 2 hours, or until doubled in bulk.

7. Preheat the oven to 450° F. If you have a baking stone, preheat it as well. If you don't, preheat a heavy baking sheet.

8. Lightly sprinkle your work surface with flour and roll each ball out to form a 9-inch circle. Gently stretch each circle with the palms of your hands to

form a 13-inch circle. Pleat the edge of each circle to wind up with an 11-inch pizza with a decorative edge. Transfer the pizza(s) to a peel (baker's paddle) or large tart-pan bottom or sideless cookie sheet generously sprinkled with cornmeal. Garnish the pizzas with one of the toppings in the recipes on pages 87–91.

9. Slide the pizzas onto the baking stone or preheated baking sheet. Bake until the crust is puffed and nicely browned, 10 to 15 minutes, rotating as necessary to ensure even cooking.

Makes four 11-inch pizzas

Note: If you're in a hurry, you can get away with two risings. Let the dough double in bulk during the first rising, then punch it down. Divide it into the 4 balls and let them rise until doubled in bulk again.

247 CALORIES PER SERVING: 8 G PROTEIN; 1 G FAT; 51 G CARBOHYDRATE; 550 MG SODIUM; 1 MG CHOLESTEROL

Analysis based on serving of ¼ pizza

WHITE BEAN, TOMATO, AND GOAT CHEESE PIZZA

This offbeat pizza was invented by my assistant, Didi Emmons. It would also be good with a sheep milk cheese, like feta. I like Barbara's Chunky Tomato Sauce (page 212) for this recipe, but any tomato sauce will work.

2 teaspoons olive oil
1 clove garlic, minced
1 cup cooked white beans, such as Great
  Northern beans or navy beans (page 261)
3 tablespoons coarsely chopped fresh cilantro or
  flat-leaf parsley

salt and freshly ground black pepper
¼ batch of Basic Pizza Dough (page 85)
1½ cup Barbara's Chunky Tomato Sauce (page
  212) or your favorite tomato sauce
2 ounces goat cheese, cut or crumbled into
  ½-inch pieces

1. Heat the olive oil in a nonstick skillet. Add the garlic and cook over medium heat for 1 minute, or until fragrant but not brown. Stir in the beans, half the cilantro, and salt and pepper to taste. Cook the beans for 3 minutes or until well flavored.

2. Roll out the pizza dough to form an 11-inch circle and pleat the edges. Spread the tomato sauce on top. Top the pizza with the beans and goat cheese and sprinkle with the remaining cilantro.

3. Bake the pizza for 10 to 15 minutes, or until nicely browned. Cut into wedges and serve.

Serves 4 to 6 as a first course, 2 to 3 as a main course

403 CALORIES PER SERVING: 16 G PROTEIN; 8 G FAT; 68 G CARBOHYDRATE; 1182 MG SODIUM; 11 MG CHOLESTEROL
Analysis based on 4 servings

ZUCCHINI, SQUASH, AND TOMATO PIZZA WITH FRIED GARLIC

I love this colorful pizza, made with smokily grilled zucchini and squash. Don't be overly concerned about the oil used for frying the garlic. Most of it is discarded. The garlic provides so much flavor, you don't even need cheese. For a striking presentation, roll the dough into a rectangle, as pictured on page 88. There are several possibilities for tomato sauce, including Barbara's Chunky Tomato Sauce (page 212), Sugo di Pomodoro (page 211), or another sauce you may prefer.

2 tablespoons of olive oil
4 cloves garlic, minced
2 8-inch zucchinis, cut lengthwise into ¼-inch strips
2 yellow squashes or yellow zucchinis, cut lengthwise into ¼-inch strips
salt and freshly ground black pepper

¼ batch of Basic Pizza Dough (page 85)
1 cup tomato sauce (see headnote above for suggestions)
3 plum tomatoes, cut lengthwise into ¼-inch slices
½ teaspoon finely chopped fresh rosemary (optional)

1. Heat the oil in a small skillet. Fry the garlic over medium heat for 1 minute or until golden brown. Drain the garlic in a strainer over a bowl, reserving the oil. Blot the garlic pieces dry on a paper towel.

2. Preheat the barbecue grill or broiler to high heat. Lightly brush the zucchini and squash strips with garlic oil (you'll only need 1 to 2 teaspoons) and sprinkle with salt and pepper. Grill these vegetables over high heat until lightly browned, 1 to 2 minutes per side. Transfer to a platter and let cool.

3. Preheat the oven to 450° F. Roll out the pizza dough, pleating the edges to form a 9 × 13-inch rectangle. Spread the tomato sauce on top. Arrange the zucchini, squash, and tomato slices in rows, alternating colors. Sprinkle the pizza with the rosemary (if using), the fried garlic, and salt and pepper to taste.

4. Bake the pizza for 10 to 15 minutes, or until nicely browned. Cut into squares and serve.

Serves 4 to 6 as a first course,
2 to 3 as a main course

361 CALORIES PER SERVING: 11 G PROTEIN; 8 G FAT; 63 G CARBOHYDRATE; 930 MG SODIUM; 1 MG CHOLESTEROL
Analysis based on 4 servings

POTATO PIZZA

Here's what happens when you cross Neapolitan pizza with good old American home fries. Actually, onion-potato pies are popular in many parts of Europe, especially in Alsace in eastern France.

1½ tablespoons olive oil
5 to 6 onions (3 cups thinly sliced)
2 cloves garlic, minced
2 teaspoons balsamic vinegar
1 teaspoon fresh thyme, or ½ teaspoon dried

1 large baking potato (12 ounces), peeled and cut
   into ¼-inch dice
salt and freshly ground black pepper
¼ batch of Basic Pizza Dough (page 85)

1. Heat the olive oil in a large nonstick frying pan. Cook the onions and garlic over medium-low heat until a rich golden brown, about 10 minutes. Add the balsamic vinegar and thyme and bring to a boil.

2. Meanwhile, place the potatoes in cold salted water to cover. Bring to a boil, reduce the heat, and simmer the potatoes for 8 to 10 minutes, or until tender. Drain the potatoes in a colander.

3. Stir the potatoes into the onion mixture and cook until soft, about 5 minutes. Add salt and pepper to taste.

4. Preheat the oven to 450° F. Roll out the pizza dough, pleating the edges to form an 11-inch circle. Spread the potato mixture on top.

5. Bake the pizza for 10 to 15 minutes, or until nicely browned. Cut into wedges and serve.

Serves 4 to 6 as a first course, 2 to 3 as a main course

457 CALORIES PER SERVING: 12 G PROTEIN; 6 G FAT; 89 G CARBOHYDRATE; 563 MG SODIUM; 1 MG CHOLESTEROL

Analysis based on 4 servings

ROASTED SQUASH AND GARLIC CALZONE

The last time I ate a store-bought calzone, I suffered from heartburn and butterfat burnout. I vowed that the next time I ate one,
I would rid this Italo-American favorite of the lion's share of its fat. This version features a savory filling of
roasted squash and garlic devised by my assistant, Didi Emmons.

½ batch of Basic Pizza Dough (page 85)

FOR THE FILLING
2 cups butternut squash, peeled and cut into
  ½-inch dice
2 onions, peeled and cut into ½-inch dice
12 cloves garlic, peeled
2 teaspoons olive oil
¼ teaspoon dried sage

salt and freshly ground black pepper
⅓ cup low-fat ricotta
2 tablespoons Parmesan cheese (optional)
approximately ¼ cup fine, dry bread crumbs

spray oil
½ egg white, beaten with a pinch of salt, for
  glaze

1. Prepare the dough through the third rising, as described on page 85. Divide the dough in half and form two balls. Let the balls rise, covered, until doubled in bulk.

2. Meanwhile, preheat the oven to 350° F. For the filling, place the diced squash, onions, and garlic on a baking sheet and toss with the olive oil, sage, salt, and pepper. Roast the vegetables until soft and golden brown, 30 to 40 minutes, stirring occasionally.

3. Transfer the vegetables to a mixing bowl and let cool. Stir in the ricotta, Parmesan (if using), and enough bread crumbs to obtain a dry but soft filling. Increase the oven temperature to 450° F.

4. Roll out each dough ball to form a 9-inch circle. Brush the outer edge of each circle with water. Mound the filling in the centers. Fold the circles in half to form half-moon-shaped turnovers. Pleat the edges together to wind up with two 7-inch calzones. Transfer the calzones to a nonstick baking sheet lightly oiled with spray oil. Brush the tops with egg-white glaze.

5. Bake the calzones for 15 to 20 minutes, or until crusty and golden brown. Let cool slightly, then serve.

Serves 4 as an appetizer, 2 as a hearty main course

644 CALORIES PER SERVING: 21 G PROTEIN; 6 G FAT; 126 G CARBOHYDRATE; 1185 MG SODIUM; 7 MG CHOLESTEROL
Analysis based on 4 servings

BRIKS (TUNISIAN TURNOVERS)

Briks are Tunisian turnovers filled with spiced vegetables or meats. This recipe uses lentils, with capers for spice and piquancy.
The combination of cumin, coriander, and caraway seed is very characteristic of Tunisian cooking. Traditionally,
briks would be deep-fried, but a crisp crust can be obtained using baked phyllo dough.

2 teaspoons extra-virgin olive oil, plus 2
    tablespoons for brushing the phyllo
3 shallots, minced (about ¼ cup)
2 cloves garlic, minced
½ teaspoon ground cumin
½ teaspoon ground coriander
½ teaspoon caraway seeds
¼ to ½ teaspoon hot pepper flakes (optional)
1 small potato, cut into ¼-inch dice (about ¾ cup)
1 carrot, cut into ⅛-inch dice (about ½ cup)

1 tomato, cut into ¼-inch dice (about ¾ cup
    with juices)
¾ cup cooked lentils (recipe follows)
1 teaspoon drained capers
1½ cups Basic Vegetable Stock (page 247), or as
    needed
salt and freshly ground black pepper
9 sheets phyllo dough
½ cup bread crumbs toasted in the oven on a
    baking sheet

1. Heat 2 teaspoons olive oil in a nonstick frying pan. Add the shallots and garlic and cook over medium heat for 2 minutes, or until soft but not brown. Stir in the cumin, coriander, caraway, and pepper flakes (if using) and cook for 1 minute, or until fragrant.

2. Stir in the potato, carrot, tomato, lentils, capers, and vegetable stock and bring to boil. Reduce the heat and gently simmer the mixture, uncovered, until the vegetables are very tender and most of the stock is absorbed. Add stock as necessary to keep the vegetables from drying out. The cooking time will be about 20 minutes. Correct the seasoning, adding salt, pepper, or spices to taste: The mixture should be highly seasoned. Let it cool.

3. Unwrap 9 sheets of phyllo dough and cover with a dish towel. Lay one sheet of phyllo dough on the work surface, long side facing you. Lightly brush it with olive oil and sprinkle with a spoonful of bread crumbs. Lay a second sheet of phyllo on top. Brush with more oil and sprinkle with bread crumbs. Repeat with a third sheet of phyllo. Cut the sheets lengthwise (i.e., parallel to the long edge) into 3½-inch strips.

4. Place a generous tablespoon of filling 1 inch below the top of the strip. Fold over one corner to cover the filling, then fold the strip as you would a flag to form a neat triangle. Continue making briks in this fashion until all the filling and phyllo dough are used up. Brush the tops of the briks with a little olive oil. The briks can be prepared several hours ahead to this stage and kept in the refrigerator.

5. Preheat the oven to 400° F. Bake the briks on a nonstick baking sheet until golden brown, about 15 minutes.

Makes 12 triangles

Note: For even more flavor, use whole spices and roast them in a dry skillet over medium heat until fragrant. Grind the spices in a spice mill before using.

133 CALORIES PER SERVING: 4 G PROTEIN; 3 G FAT; 23 G CARBOHYDRATE; 114 MG SODIUM; 0 MG CHOLESTEROL

Analysis per brik

To Cook Lentils

⅓ cup lentils
1 clove garlic

8 cups water
salt

1. Spread the lentils on a baking sheet and pick through them, removing any twigs or stones. Rinse well in a colander.

2. Place the lentils and garlic in a pot with 8 cups water. Bring the lentils to a boil, reduce the heat, loosely cover the pot, and simmer for 20 to 30 minutes, or until the lentils are tender. Add water as necessary to keep the lentils submerged. Add salt to taste the last 3 minutes.

Note: The cooking time can be shortened to about 8 minutes in a pressure cooker.

WILD RICE, MUSHROOM, AND CHEDDAR TART

One of the greatest challenges for the health-conscious cook is to come up with a low-fat pie crust. My version uses paper-thin layers of phyllo dough, which I brush with olive oil instead of butter. I sprinkle the phyllo layers with toasted bread crumbs to provide extra crunch and lift. I like the zing that cheddar cheese gives to this tart, and the new low-fat cheeses have acceptable flavors and levels of fat. You could also use a sharp tangy cheese, like feta, or omit the cheese entirely and add ¼ cup chopped fresh herbs instead. **Note**: *This recipe is somewhat time-consuming, but it never fails to fetch raves when I make it.*

FOR THE FILLING
1 tablespoon olive oil
1 large onion, finely chopped
2 cloves garlic
1 pound mushrooms, thinly sliced
salt and freshly ground black pepper
a pinch of cayenne pepper
3 carrots, cut into ⅛-inch dice
2 cups cooked Basic Wild Rice (page 259)
1½ cups coarsely grated no- or low-fat cheddar cheese (6 ounces)
3 tablespoons no-fat sour cream

2 teaspoons fresh lemon juice (or to taste)
3 tablespoons finely chopped flat-leaf parsley or 1 tablespoon chopped fresh dill
¼ cup bread crumbs

spray oil

FOR THE CRUST
6 sheets of phyllo dough
1 to 2 tablespoons extra-virgin olive oil
½ cup lightly toasted fresh bread crumbs

1. Prepare the filling first. Heat the oil in a large nonstick skillet. Cook the onion and garlic over medium heat until golden brown, about 5 minutes. Add the mushrooms and increase the heat to high. Cook the mushrooms over high heat until all the liquid has evaporated. You may need to add the mushrooms in several batches. Season the mushrooms with salt, pepper, and cayenne.

2. Blanch the diced carrots in boiling salted water until al dente, about 1 minute. Drain in a colander, refresh under cold water, and drain again well.

3. Combine the mushroom mixture, carrots, wild rice, cheese, sour cream, lemon juice, parsley, and bread crumbs in a mixing bowl and mix well. Add salt, pepper, and cayenne to taste: The filling should be highly seasoned.

4. Preheat the oven to 400° F. Lightly oil a 9-inch springform pan with spray oil.

5. To prepare the crust, unwrap the sheets of phyllo dough and cover with a dish towel. Lay one sheet of phyllo dough on the work surface, lightly brush it with olive oil, and sprinkle with a spoonful of bread crumbs. Drape the phyllo over the spring-form pan, easing the dough into the bottom and side of the mold, letting the excess hang over the edge.

6. Brush another sheet of phyllo with oil, sprinkle with crumbs, and lower it into the mold, perpendicular to the first. Brush and sprinkle a third sheet of phyllo. Lower it into the mold at a 45° angle to the second sheet. Brush and sprinkle a fourth sheet of phyllo and lower it into the mold perpendicular to the third. Repeat with the fifth and sixth sheets of phyllo. Spoon the filling into the pan and gather the overhanging phyllo at the edge as pictured on page 94.

7. Bake the tart until the filling is thoroughly heated and the phyllo on top is crusty and brown, about 50 minutes. Let cool slightly, then remove the sides of the pan. The tart can be served warm or at room temperature. Cut into wedges for serving.

Serves 12 as an appetizer, 8 as a light main course

253 CALORIES PER SERVING: 13 G PROTEIN; 8 G FAT; 35 G CARBOHYDRATE; 185 MG SODIUM; 10 MG CHOLESTEROL

Analysis based on 8 servings

PIROGI POCKETS

Pirogi are turnovers from Russia and Poland. This recipe features a traditional mushroom, potato, and onion filling served in pita bread instead of pastry dough.

1 tablespoon extra-virgin olive oil
1 onion, finely chopped
1 clove garlic, finely chopped
12 ounces mushrooms, trimmed and thinly sliced
1 large potato, peeled and coarsely grated
1 cup Basic Vegetable Stock (page 247)

¼ cup no-fat sour cream
1 tablespoon chopped fresh dill
salt, freshly ground black pepper, and cayenne pepper

6 small pita breads

1. Heat the oil in a large nonstick skillet. Lightly brown the onion and garlic over medium heat. Stir in the mushrooms, potato, and vegetable stock.

2. Cook the mixture, stirring often, until most of the liquid has evaporated and the vegetables are soft, 8 to 10 minutes. Stir in the sour cream and bring to a boil. Stir in the dill and salt, black pepper, and cayenne to taste: The mixture should be highly seasoned.

3. Spoon the hot filling into the pita breads and serve at once.

Makes 6 pockets

145 CALORIES PER SERVING: 5 G PROTEIN; 3 G FAT; 25 G CARBOHYDRATE; 166 MG SODIUM; 0 MG CHOLESTEROL

Analysis per pocket

FRENCH COUNTRY TOURTE

A tourte is a deep-dish covered pie. This one features a rustic filling of cabbage, potatoes, and goat cheese, and pays homage to what the French would call le goût du terroir ("the taste of the earth"). The crust is a simple yeast dough that provides a satisfying texture and crunch with a minimum of fat.
***Note**: This recipe is a little higher in fat than most in this book.*
Serve it as an appetizer or for special occasions.

FOR THE DOUGH
2 teaspoons dry yeast (a little less than a
   package)
1 tablespoon sugar or honey
2 tablespoons warm water
1 teaspoon extra-virgin olive oil
1½ cups unbleached all-purpose white flour
¾ teaspoon salt
1 egg white, beaten with a pinch of salt, for glaze
approximately ½ cup warm water

FOR THE FILLING
1 tablespoon olive oil
2 onions, finely chopped

3 cloves garlic, minced
1 teaspoon chopped fresh rosemary or
   ½ teaspoon dried
4 cups coarsely chopped green or savoy cabbage
   (about ⅓ head of cabbage)
1 large or 2 small potatoes (about 12 ounces),
   peeled and cut into ¼-inch dice
2 tablespoons flour
1 cup low- or no-fat ricotta cheese
1 egg white, lightly beaten
salt and freshly ground black pepper
a pinch of cayenne pepper
spray oil
2 to 4 ounces goat cheese

1. Prepare the crust. Dissolve the yeast and sugar in 2 tablespoons warm water in a small bowl. Let stand for 6 to 8 minutes: the mixture should foam like a head of beer.

2. Combine the yeast mixture, olive oil, flour, and salt in a food processor fitted with a chopping blade or a mixer with a dough hook. Pulse the machine to mix these ingredients. Add the egg white and water and run the processor in bursts until the ingredients come together to form a dough that is soft but not too sticky. Add a little water if the mixture seems too dry. Knead the dough in the food processor for 2 to 3 minutes or by hand on a lightly floured work surface for 5 minutes, or until smooth. You can also make the dough in a heavy-duty mixer fitted with a dough hook.

3. Transfer the dough to a lightly oiled bowl and cover with plastic wrap. Let the dough rise in a warm, draft-free spot until doubled in bulk, about 1 hour. Punch down the dough and refrigerate it until using. The dough can be made the day before.

4. Meanwhile, prepare the filling: Heat the olive oil in a large nonstick frying pan or sauté pan. Add the onion and ⅔ of the minced garlic and cook over medium heat until soft and lightly browned, about 4 minutes.

5. Reduce the heat slightly and stir in the rosemary, cabbage, and potatoes. (Depending on the size of the pan, you may need to add the cabbage gradually.) Cook the mixture, covered, for 15 minutes, stirring occasionally. Uncover the pan and continue cooking the vegetables for 5 to 10 minutes, or until they are very tender and all the pan juices have evaporated, stirring often. Stir in the flour.

6. Stir in the ricotta. Cook the mixture until thick and creamy, about 2 minutes. Remove the pan

from the heat, let cool for 2 minutes, and stir in the egg white. Correct the seasoning, adding salt, pepper, and cayenne to taste: The mixture should be highly seasoned. Remove the pan from the heat and let cool. Stir in the remaining 1 clove garlic.

7. Roll out ½ of the dough and use it to line a 7 × 11-inch tart pan or baking dish, or a 9-inch springform pan, lightly oiled with spray oil. Let at least 1 inch of dough hang over the edge. Arrange all of the potatoes in a layer on the bottom. Spoon the cabbage mixture on top. Crumble the goat cheese over the cabbage. Brush the top of the overhanging dough with a little of the egg-white glaze.

8. Roll out the remaining dough. Use most of the dough to form a cover for the *tourte*, leaving enough for a 1-inch overlap. Place the cover over the filling and pleat the top and bottom edges to form a tight seal. Brush the top with egg-white glaze. Cut any leftover dough into fanciful shapes, like leaves and berries, and use them to decorate the top of the *tourte*. Brush these shapes with glaze. Preheat the oven to 350° F.

9. Using a sharp knife or razor blade, cut 5 or 6 slits in the top crust to allow any steam to escape. Bake the *tourte* on the bottom rack of the oven for 40 to 50 minutes, or until the crust is a rich golden brown. Transfer the *tourte* to a cake rack to cool for 5 minutes. Unmold the *tourte* and cut into wedges or rectangles for serving.

Serves 8 as an appetizer, 4 as an entrée

290 CALORIES PER SERVING: 12 G PROTEIN; 9 G FAT; 42 G CARBOHYDRATE; 376 MG SODIUM; 15 MG CHOLESTEROL

Analysis based on 8 servings

VEGETABLE STRUDEL

*This recipe is dedicated to my Hungarian aunt, Judy Raichlen. Paprika, of course, is Hungary's national seasoning (for the best results, use imported), while caraway seed is a popular flavoring throughout Eastern Europe. **Note**: This dish is a little higher in fat than most of the recipes in this book, but I like it so much, I couldn't resist including it. Serve it as an appetizer or for special occasions.*

FOR THE FILLING
1 tablespoon olive oil
1 onion, thinly sliced
¼ green cabbage, thinly sliced
2 to 3 teaspoons Hungarian sweet paprika
½ teaspoon caraway seeds
1 medium potato (preferably Yukon Gold), cut into ¼-inch dice
½ cup dry white wine
salt and freshly ground black pepper
½ cup no-fat sour cream

2 teaspoons vinegar, preferably balsamic (optional)

TO FINISH THE STRUDEL
1 tablespoon butter, melted
1 tablespoon olive oil
5 sheets phyllo dough
3 tablespoons dried bread crumbs

spray oil

1. Prepare the filling. Heat the oil in a large non-stick skillet. Lightly brown the onion over medium heat. Stir in the cabbage, paprika, and caraway seeds and cook until the cabbage is tender. Stir in the potato, wine, salt, and pepper.

2. Cover the pan and cook the vegetables over medium heat, stirring occasionally, until tender, about 15 minutes. Uncover the pan the last few minutes to let any excess liquid evaporate. Stir in the sour cream and vinegar, if using, and bring to a boil. Let the mixture cool to room temperature, then refrigerate until cold.

3. Preheat the oven to 400° F. To finish the strudel, combine the butter and olive oil in a small bowl. Lay one sheet of phyllo dough on a dry dish towel on a work surface, long edge toward you. Lightly brush it with the butter mixture and sprinkle a spoonful of bread crumbs on top. Lay another sheet of phyllo on top, brush with the butter mixture, and sprinkle with crumbs. Repeat with the remaining phyllo, butter mixture, and bread crumbs, reserving a little butter mixture and crumbs for garnish.

4. Mound the filling along the long edge of the phyllo closest to you. Roll the phyllo rectangle up lengthwise, halfway, using the dish towel to help with rolling. Tuck in the side ends and continue rolling the strudel. The idea is to create what looks like a giant egg roll. Carefully transfer the strudel to a cookie sheet or inverted baking sheet lightly sprayed with spray oil.

5. Brush the top of the strudel with the remaining butter mixture and sprinkle with the remaining crumbs. Lightly score the top of the strudel with a sharp knife. Bake the strudel for 30 to 40 minutes, or until nicely browned. Let it cool for 5 minutes, then cut into diagonal slices. Serve at once.

Serves 6 to 8 as an appetizer, 3 or 4 as a main course

Note: A dollop of no-fat sour cream topped with a sprig of dill would make an appropriate garnish.

200 CALORIES PER SERVING: 5 G PROTEIN; 7 G FAT; 28 G CARBOHYDRATE; 165 MG SODIUM; 5 MG CHOLESTEROL

Analysis based on 6 servings

CAPRESE SANDWICH

This sandwich takes its inspiration from a famous salad from the isle of Capri. For the best results, use fresh buffalo milk or cow milk mozzarella—the sort that's still dripping with whey. Such cheese can be found at Italian markets, gourmet shops, and an increasing number of supermarkets.

1 long, slender, freshly baked baguette
1 clove garlic, cut in half
2 very ripe tomatoes, thinly sliced, the slices cut in half
24 fresh basil leaves

4 ounces fresh mozzarella, drained and cut into ½-inch dice
2 to 3 teaspoons extra-virgin olive oil
2 teaspoons drained capers
kosher salt and freshly ground black pepper

1. Lay the baguette on a cutting board. Make a lengthwise cut down the middle, starting on the top of the loaf and cutting to but not through the bottom. (A serrated knife works best for cutting.) Gently pry open the loaf to make a V-shaped cavity.

2. Rub the sides of the cavity with the cut garlic. Arrange tomato slices down each side of the cavity, followed by the basil leaves.

3. Gently mix the cheese, olive oil, capers, salt, and pepper in a mixing bowl. Spoon this mixture into the loaf, between the rows of tomato and basil. Cut the sandwich crosswise into 6-inch lengths and serve.

Makes 4 sandwiches

291 CALORIES PER SERVING: 16 G PROTEIN; 8 G FAT; 39 G CARBOHYDRATE; 611 MG SODIUM; 10 MG CHOLESTEROL
Analysis per sandwich

ARUGULA AND HERBED CHEESE TEA SANDWICHES

Watercress and tomato sandwiches are requisite accompaniments to an English high tea. But arugula has more zip, and so does the low-fat Boursin-style cheese I use in place of the traditional mayonnaise or butter. (The original Boursin is an herb-flavored but butterfat-laden cheese from France.) In keeping with the tea theme, this recipe calls for thin-sliced sandwich bread, but you could also pile the ingredients onto a crusty baguette.

FOR THE HERBED CHEESE
3 ounces low-fat cream cheese, at room temperature
⅓ cup dry-curd low-fat cottage cheese
1 to 2 cloves garlic, minced
3 tablespoons chopped fresh herbs, including tarragon, basil, parsley, chives or scallion greens, chervil, and/or dill (try to use at least 3 different herbs)

a few drops of fresh lemon juice
salt and freshly ground black pepper

16 very thin slices white bread (such as Pepperidge Farm thin-sliced bread) or light whole wheat bread
1 bunch arugula, stemmed, washed, and dried (use a salad spinner)
1 tomato, very thinly sliced

1. Prepare the cheese: Place the cream cheese, cottage cheese, and garlic in a food processor and purée until smooth. You'll need to scrape down the sides of the processor bowl with a spatula several times. Transfer the mixture to a bowl and stir in the herbs, lemon juice, and salt and pepper to taste.

2. Arrange 8 bread slices on a work surface. Lightly spread them with half the cheese mixture.

Cover half the sandwiches with arugula leaves, the other half with sliced tomatoes. Spread the remaining bread slices with the remaining cheese mixture and place them, spread side down, on top. Cut the crusts off the sandwiches (this is, after all, high tea). Cut the sandwiches in quarters and transfer to doily-lined platters.

Serves 4 to 8

299 CALORIES PER SERVING: 12 G PROTEIN; 7 G FAT; 46 G CARBOHYDRATE; 642 MG SODIUM; 8 MG CHOLESTEROL
Analysis based on 4 servings

PASTA AND NOODLE DISHES

SPAGHETTI ALLA PUGLIANESE
(WITH POTATOES AND ZUCCHINI)

One of the most remarkable aspects of contemporary Italian cuisine is the reverence that even the most celebrated chefs have for the cooking of their peasant ancestors. Consider this pasta from Italy's southeasternmost province, Apulia. Although it contains just three main and exceedingly humble ingredients—spaghetti, potatoes, and zucchini—I tasted it not at a farmhouse but at a celebrated Michelin two-star restaurant, Bacco, in Barletta. Ricotta salata is a hard, piquant cousin of the soft cheese we fill cannoli with. It's available at Italian markets and cheese shops, or you can use Pecorino Romano or Parmigiano-Reggiano.

salt
2 potatoes (about 1 pound), preferably Yukon
  Golds or Finnish yellow potatoes, cut into
  ¼-inch dice
6 ounces of spaghetti, broken into 1-inch pieces
2 small zucchini (about 10 ounces in all), cut
  into ¼-inch dice

1 to 2 teaspoons extra-virgin olive oil
1 tablespoon chopped flat-leaf parsley
freshly ground black pepper
½ to 1 ounce ricotta salata or other grating
  cheese

1. Bring 1 quart water to a boil with salt to taste in a large heavy saucepan. Add the potatoes and briskly simmer over medium heat until they lose their rawness, about 3 minutes. Add the spaghetti and cook until almost al dente, about 3 minutes. Add the zucchini and cook for 2 to 4 minutes or until all the vegetables and pasta are tender.

2. Drain the ingredients in a colander over a bowl, reserving a little of the cooking liquid. Transfer the ingredients to a serving bowl or individual bowls. Stir in the olive oil, parsley, and pepper, and 1 to 2 tablespoons cooking liquid. Correct the seasoning, adding salt and pepper to taste. Grate a little cheese on top and serve at once.

Serves 2 as a light main course

580 CALORIES PER SERVING: 19 G PROTEIN; 6 G FAT; 113 G CARBOHYDRATE; 155 MG SODIUM; 6 MG CHOLESTEROL

Spaghetti alla Puglianese (with Potatoes and Zucchini)

THREE Cs STEW
(CAVATELLI, CANNELLINI, AND CARROTS)

Dishes that combine pasta and beans are an ancient Italian tradition. Like the bean and rice dishes of Central America, they serve an important nutritional end: providing a cheap, tasty, healthful, complete form of protein. Cavatelli are small pasta shells shaped like cowry shells. Cannellini are small white beans. Both can be found at Italian and specialty markets. But this dish could be made with any type of pasta shell and bean.

2 cups cooked cannellini beans or other white
    beans (page 261)
1 cup cavatelli
salt
½ pound baby carrots or large carrots cut into
    2 × ½-inch pieces
1½ tablespoons olive oil
1 small onion, finely chopped
1 stalk celery, finely chopped

2 cloves garlic, minced
2 ripe tomatoes, peeled, seeded, and chopped
¼ cup finely chopped flat-leaf parsley
½ to 1 cup Basic Vegetable Stock (page 247) or
    cooking water from the pasta
1 tablespoon tomato paste
¼ teaspoon chopped fresh rosemary (or to taste)
salt and freshly ground black pepper

1. If using canned beans, rinse and drain well.

2. Cook the cavatelli in a large pot in 4 quarts rapidly boiling salted water until al dente, about 8 minutes. Transfer the cavatelli with a slotted spoon to a colander to drain, reserving the cooking water.

3. Cook the carrots in the rapidly boiling pasta water until al dente, about 5 minutes. Transfer the carrots with a slotted spoon to the colander to drain, reserving the cooking water.

4. Meanwhile, heat the oil in a large saucepan. Cook the onion, celery, and garlic over medium-low heat until lightly browned, stirring often, about

5 minutes. Stir in the chopped tomato and half the parsley and continue cooking until the tomato has lost its rawness, about 2 minutes.

5. Stir in the beans, pasta, carrots, vegetable stock, tomato paste, and rosemary, and salt and pepper to taste. Cook the mixture for a couple of minutes to blend the flavors. The stew should be moist but not soupy. If too dry, stir in a little more stock or cooking water. Correct the seasoning, adding salt, pepper, or rosemary to taste. Sprinkle with the remaining parsley and serve at once.

Serves 4

310 CALORIES PER SERVING: 13 G PROTEIN; 6 G FAT; 53 G CARBOHYDRATE; 90 MG SODIUM; 0 MG CHOLESTEROL

SHIITAKE MACARONI AND CHEESE

The Italo-American classic, macaroni and cheese, would hardly seem like a candidate for a low-fat makeover.
This version uses shiitake mushrooms and garlic to compensate for the reduced amount of cheese.
***Note**: Shiitake mushrooms are available fresh at gourmet shops and most supermarkets.*
You could also make this dish with portobello or button mushrooms.

2 cups elbow macaroni (8 ounces)
salt
1 tablespoon extra-virgin olive oil
3 cloves garlic, minced
½ pound fresh shiitake mushrooms, stemmed and cut into ¼-inch strips
3 tablespoons flour
3 cups skim milk
1 tablespoon Dijon-style mustard

¼ cup chopped flat-leaf parsley
salt and freshly ground black pepper
a pinch each freshly grated nutmeg and cayenne pepper
¼ cup freshly grated Parmigiano-Reggiano or low-fat cheddar cheese
spray oil
½ cup dried bread crumbs

1. Cook the pasta in 3 quarts rapidly boiling salted water until al dente, about 8 minutes. Drain the pasta in a colander and rinse with cold water.

2. Meanwhile, heat the oil in a large nonstick frying pan. Cook the garlic over medium heat until soft but not brown, about 1 minute. Increase the heat to high and add the shiitakes. Cook for 3 minutes, or until soft. Stir in the flour and cook for 1 minute.

3. Gradually stir in the milk and bring the mixture to a boil, stirring well. It will thicken. Simmer for 2 minutes. Stir in the mustard, parsley, salt, pepper, nutmeg, and cayenne. The mixture should be very highly seasoned. Remove the pan from the heat and stir in the cheese.

4. Combine the sauce and macaroni in a mixing bowl and stir until mixed. Correct the seasoning. Spoon the mixture into a 6 × 10-inch baking dish coated with spray oil. Sprinkle the top with the bread crumbs. The recipe can be prepared up to 2 days ahead to this stage.

5. Bake the macaroni and cheese in a 350° F. oven for 30 minutes, or until thoroughly heated and golden brown.

Serves 6

291 CALORIES PER SERVING: 13 G PROTEIN; 5 G FAT; 47 G CARBOHYDRATE; 239 MG SODIUM; 5 MG CHOLESTEROL

DIDI'S THAI CURRIED NOODLES

*Here's another flavor-packed recipe from my assistant, Didi Emmons. Yellow or Mussamun ("Muslim-style") curry paste is a
spicy, golden Thai curry paste that contains no seafood products. (Red and green curry paste contain shrimp paste.)
Recognizable by its yellow label, Mussamun curry paste is available canned at Asian markets, gourmet
shops, and many supermarkets, where you can also find rice vermicelli. Alternatively, see Mail-Order
Sources. (You could use dry curry powder as a last resort.)* **Note**: *If you're unaccustomed
to spicy food, use 2 teaspoons curry paste. I like food that's so hot,
it brings tears to my eyes, so I use the full 2 tablespoons.*

6 ounces rice vermicelli (thin rice noodles)
5 dried Chinese black mushrooms
1½ cups hot water or Basic Vegetable Stock
   (page 247)
2 teaspoons to 2 tablespoons yellow Thai curry
   paste
3 tablespoons soy sauce
2 tablespoons fresh lime juice
1 teaspoon sugar
1 tablespoon canola oil
3 cloves garlic, minced

1 tablespoon lemongrass, finely chopped
   (1 stalk); if unavailable, substitute
   2 teaspoons grated lemon or lime zest
3 scallions, white part minced, green part thinly
   sliced
1 carrot, peeled and cut into matchstick slivers
½ red bell pepper, cut into matchstick slivers
2 cups mung bean sprouts
salt and freshly ground black pepper
¼ cup chopped fresh cilantro
1 tablespoon chopped dry-roasted peanuts

1. Soak the rice noodles in cold water to cover in a large bowl for 15 minutes, or until pliable. Soak the mushrooms in 1½ cups hot water or vegetable stock for 15 minutes, or until soft.

2. Drain the mushrooms, reserving the soaking liquid. Remove and discard the stems and thinly slice the caps. Dissolve the curry paste, the soy sauce, the lime juice, and the sugar in the mushroom liquid and set aside. Drain the noodles.

3. Just before serving, heat a wok or nonstick frying pan. Swirl in the oil. Stir-fry the garlic, lemongrass, and scallion whites for 15 seconds, or until fragrant. Add the carrot and bell pepper and stir-fry

over high heat for 2 minutes, or until fragrant but not brown. Add the noodles and half the bean sprouts and stir-fry for 1 minute.

4. Stir in the curry mixture and simmer until the noodles are just tender, 2 to 3 minutes, stirring often. Add salt, pepper, and correct seasoning, adding lime juice to taste. Stir in half the scallion greens and transfer the noodles to a platter. Sprinkle with the remaining bean sprouts and scallion greens, the cilantro, and the peanuts and serve at once.

Serves 4

253 CALORIES PER SERVING: 4 G PROTEIN; 5 G FAT; 51 G CARBOHYDRATE; 827 MG SODIUM; 0 MG CHOLESTEROL

SPAGHETTI WITH WHITE BEAN SAUCE

Here's an unexpected sauce for America's favorite pasta. (I sometimes think of it as my vegetarian "clam" sauce.) The logic of combining a grain product, like pasta, and beans goes beyond mere gustatory pleasure. Each contains essential amino acids, but not a complete set. Combining them gives you a complete source of protein.

FOR THE SAUCE
1 tablespoon olive oil
2 cloves garlic, minced
1 red onion, very finely chopped
½ red bell pepper, cut into ¼-inch dice
3 stalks celery, cut into ¼-inch dice
1 cup cooked white beans, such as navy beans or
  Great Northern beans (page 261)
1 cup Basic Vegetable Stock (page 247) or bean
  cooking liquid

¼ cup finely chopped flat-leaf parsley
½ teaspoon hot pepper flakes (optional)
salt and freshly ground black pepper
8 to 10 ounces spaghetti

1 to 2 ounces freshly grated Parmigiano-
  Reggiano or Romano cheese for serving
  (optional)

1. Prepare the sauce. Heat the olive oil in a nonstick frying pan. Add the garlic, onion, bell pepper, and celery and cook over medium heat until soft but not brown, about 4 minutes.

2. Stir in the white beans and cook for 1 minute. Add the vegetable stock, half the parsley, the pepper flakes (if using), and salt and pepper to taste. The sauce should be highly seasoned. Simmer until the beans are quite soft. Coarsely mash half the beans with a fork.

3. Cook the spaghetti in a large pot in 4 quarts rapidly boiling salted water until al dente, about 8 minutes. Drain well. Meanwhile, bring the sauce to a boil. Transfer the spaghetti and bean sauce to a large shallow bowl and mix well. Sprinkle the spaghetti with the remaining parsley and serve at once with freshly grated cheese on top (if using).

Serves 4 as an appetizer, 2 as a main course

672 CALORIES PER SERVING: 24 G PROTEIN; 10 G FAT; 122 G CARBOHYDRATE; 64 MG SODIUM; 0 MG CHOLESTEROL
Analysis based on main course serving

GRILLED ZUCCHINI LASAGNA WITH ROASTED RED PEPPER SAUCE

If I had to sum up this recipe in a single word, it would be vibrant. *The vibrant greens and reds of zucchini and roasted red peppers. The vibrant Mediterranean flavors of balsamic vinegar and saffron. To save time, you may wish to roast or grill the zucchini at the same time you do the peppers.*

FOR THE RED PEPPER SAUCE
4 large red bell peppers (about 1½ pounds)
1 tablespoon olive oil
1 onion, chopped
3 cloves garlic, chopped
¾ cup bread crumbs
1 tablespoon balsamic vinegar
¼ teaspoon saffron, soaked in 1 tablespoon hot water (optional)
approximately ⅔ cup Basic Vegetable Stock (page 247)

salt, freshly ground black pepper, and a pinch of cayenne pepper

TO FINISH THE LASAGNA
6 medium zucchinis (1½ pounds)
1 to 2 teaspoons extra-virgin olive oil
9 lasagna noodles
spray oil
20 basil leaves (optional)

1. Prepare the red pepper sauce. Roast, peel, core, and seed the red peppers as described on page 257. Heat the oil in a large nonstick skillet. Cook the onion and garlic over medium heat until soft but not brown, 3 to 4 minutes.

2. Combine the peppers, onion mixture, and bread crumbs in a food processor and purée to a smooth paste. Add the vinegar, saffron (if using), and enough vegetable stock to obtain a thick sauce. (The mixture should be the consistency of soft ice cream.) Correct the seasoning, adding salt, pepper, cayenne, and vinegar to taste: The sauce should be very highly seasoned. Preheat the grill to high.

3. Cut the zucchinis lengthwise into ¼-inch slices. Lightly brush each with olive oil and grill until limp (2 to 4 minutes per side). Alternatively, the zucchini can be broiled, oven-roasted, or sautéed in a nonstick frying pan.

4. Cook the lasagna noodles in 4 quarts rapidly boiling salted water for 8 minutes, or until al dente. Drain the noodles and rinse with cold water.

5. Preheat the oven to 350° F.

6. Lightly oil an attractive 8 × 11-inch baking dish with spray oil. Spread 3 lasagna noodles over the bottom. Arrange ⅓ of the zucchini strips over the noodles. Arrange ⅓ of the basil leaves (if using) on top of the zucchini and spread ⅓ of the pepper sauce on top. Make a second and third layer in this fashion. The lasagna can be prepared up to 24 hours ahead to this stage.

7. Bake the lasagna for 30 to 40 minutes or until thoroughly heated. Cut into rectangles for serving.

Serves 6

282 CALORIES PER SERVING: 9 G PROTEIN; 5 G FAT; 53 G CARBOHYDRATE; 99 MG SODIUM; 0 MG CHOLESTEROL

Grilled Zucchini Lasagna with Roasted Red Pepper Sauce

NEW WAVE KUGEL

Kugel is a Jewish noodle pudding. Traditional versions call for artery-clogging doses of eggs, butter, and sour cream.
This one uses low-fat dairy products to make a great holiday dish with minimal fat. To reduce
the fat further, you could replace the whole egg with 2 more egg whites.

8 ounces bow-tie noodles (5 cups uncooked)
1¼ cups no-fat sour cream
¼ cup skim milk
1 egg, lightly beaten
2 egg whites, lightly beaten
2½ cups low- or no-fat cottage cheese
1½ teaspoons vanilla extract
1½ teaspoons grated lemon zest

¼ to ½ cup sugar (or to taste)
spray oil

FOR THE TOPPING
2 tablespoons sugar
1 teaspoon cinnamon
I cup Grape-Nuts, Frosted Flakes, or other
   crunchy cereal

1. Preheat the oven to 350° F. Boil the noodles for 8 minutes, or until al dente. Drain well in a colander.

2. Meanwhile, combine the sour cream, milk, egg, egg whites, cottage cheese, vanilla, lemon zest, and sugar in a mixing bowl and stir to mix. Stir in the noodles and correct the seasoning, adding sugar or lemon zest to taste.

3. Spoon the noodle mixture into an 8 × 12-inch baking dish lightly sprayed with oil. Mix together the sugar and cinnamon for the topping and sprinkle over the kugel. Top with the cereal.

4. Bake the kugel for 50 to 60 minutes, or until the noodles are golden brown. Serve at once.

Serves 6 to 8

363 CALORIES PER SERVING: 22 G PROTEIN; 3 G FAT; 60 G CARBOHYDRATE; 600 MG SODIUM; 40 MG CHOLESTEROL
Analysis based on 6 large servings

CRISPY NOODLE CAKE

Here's my version of a Chinese noodle pancake. The secret is to cook the cake slowly in a little oil in a nonstick frying pan over low heat rather than to fry it in lots of oil over high heat, as is usually done. Fresh Chinese egg noodles can be found in the produce section of most supermarkets, not to mention at Asian markets, of course.

8 ounces Chinese egg noodles (preferably fresh)

FOR THE STIR-FRY
2 teaspoons canola oil for stir-frying, plus 2 to 3
    teaspoons oil for frying the pancake
4 scallions, white part minced, green part thinly
    sliced
3 cloves garlic, minced
1 tablespoon minced fresh ginger
½ red bell pepper, cut into matchstick slivers
½ green bell pepper (or more red), cut into
    matchstick slivers

2 cups very thinly sliced napa cabbage
3 tablespoons finely chopped fresh cilantro

FOR THE SAUCE
4 tablespoons rice vinegar
3 tablespoons soy sauce
½ teaspoon Asian sesame oil
1 tablespoon cornstarch

salt and freshly ground black pepper

1. Cook the noodles in at least 3 quarts boiling water for 5 minutes, or until al dente. Drain the noodles in a colander, refresh under cold water, and drain well.

2. Heat 2 teaspoons canola oil in a nonstick wok or frying pan. Add the scallion whites, garlic, and ginger and stir-fry over medium heat until fragrant but not brown, about 1 minute. Add the bell peppers and napa and cook over high heat for 2 minutes, or until the vegetables are crispy-tender. Stir in the noodles and cilantro.

3. For the sauce, combine the rice vinegar, soy sauce, and sesame oil with the cornstarch and whisk to a smooth paste. Stir this mixture into the noodle mixture and bring to a boil. The sauce will thicken. Correct the seasoning, adding salt and

pepper to taste. Transfer the mixture to a bowl to cool. Clean out the pan.

4. Just before serving, heat the remaining 2 teaspoons oil in a large (10-inch) nonstick frying pan over high heat. Add the noodle mixture and reduce the heat to medium-low. Pan-fry the pancake until crusty and a deep golden brown on the bottom, about 5 minutes, shaking the pan to keep the pancake from sticking. Press down gently with a spatula. Invert the pancake (you can do this by boldly flicking the pan with your wrist or by placing a plate over the pan, inverting the pancake onto it, and sliding it back into the pan). Cook the other side until crusty and golden brown, about 5 minutes. Cut into wedges. Serve at once.

Serves 4 as an appetizer, 2 to 3 as a main course

278 CALORIES PER SERVING: 9 G PROTEIN; 7.5 G FAT; 46 G CARBOHYDRATE; 794 MG SODIUM; 49 MG CHOLESTEROL

Analysis based on 4 servings

CHILLED NOODLES WITH SOUTHEAST ASIAN SEASONINGS

Part pasta and part salad, this vibrant dish makes a great summer refresher. There are several possibilities for noodles: Chinese wheat vermicelli, dan mian (thin fresh Chinese egg noodles), somen (thin Japanese wheat noodles), soba (Japanese buckwheat noodles), and even one of the rice or bean starch noodles so popular in Southeast Asia.

4 ounces thin Asian wheat or buckwheat noodles
salt
1 to 2 teaspoons sesame oil
1½ cups shredded napa (Chinese cabbage), cut crosswise
2 carrots, cut into matchstick slivers
1 cucumber, peeled, halved lengthwise, seeded, and cut into ¼-inch dice
1 to 2 teaspoons chopped fresh ginger
1 stalk fresh lemongrass, trimmed and minced (about 1 tablespoon)

1 to 3 jalapeño or serrano chilies, minced (for a milder dish, omit the seeds)
2 teaspoons light brown sugar
3 tablespoons fresh lime juice
2 to 4 teaspoons soy sauce
1 teaspoon Thai or Vietnamese hot sauce (optional)
salt and freshly ground black pepper
¼ cup chopped fresh cilantro
2 tablespoons chopped dry-roasted peanuts

1. Cook the noodles in boiling salted water until al dente, about 5 minutes. Drain in a colander, rinse with cold water, and drain well. Transfer the noodles to a mixing or salad bowl and toss with the sesame oil.

2. Stir in the cabbage, carrots, cucumber, ginger, lemongrass, chilies, sugar, lime juice, soy sauce, hot sauce (if using), salt, and pepper and half the cilantro. Correct the seasoning, adding lime juice, soy sauce, hot sauce, or salt to taste: The mixture should be highly seasoned. Sprinkle the noodles with the remaining cilantro and the peanuts and serve at once.

Serves 4 as an appetizer, 2 as a main course

377 CALORIES PER SERVING: 12 G PROTEIN; 8 G FAT; 68 G CARBOHYDRATE; 1519 MG SODIUM; 0 MG CHOLESTEROL
Analysis based on 2 servings

RIGATONI WITH TOMATOES AND BASIL

I first tasted this refreshing dish near Paestum, a spectacular ancient Greek temple site in southern Italy. It was made with pomodorini, tiny oval cherry tomatoes that seemed to explode with flavor. But the particular variety matters less than the ripeness of the tomato: Use the ripest, juiciest fruit you can find. (You know, the sort of tomato that goes splat if you drop it!) For the best results, use a good imported brand of pasta.
This dish is great for a summer buffet.

3 cups rigatoni (or other tube-shaped pasta)
salt
1 clove garlic, minced
1 large or 2 medium ripe tomatoes, peeled,
    seeded, and very finely chopped (about
    1½ cups)
¼ cup thinly slivered fresh basil leaves (plus a
    couple of whole sprigs for garnish)
¼ cup chopped fresh flat-leaf parsley

1 tablespoon drained capers (optional)
½ teaspoon dried oregano
½ teaspoon hot pepper flakes (or to taste)
2 tablespoons extra-virgin olive oil
1 to 2 tablespoons lemon juice (or to taste)
2 teaspoons balsamic vinegar
freshly ground black pepper

1. Cook the pasta in a large pot in 4 quarts rapidly boiling salted water until al dente, about 8 minutes. Drain pasta in a colander and keep hot.

2. Meanwhile, combine the garlic, tomatoes, slivered basil, parsley, capers (if using), oregano, pepper flakes, oil, lemon juice, vinegar, and pepper in a large serving bowl. Add the hot pasta and mix well. Let the ingredients cool to room temperature.

You can make the dish up to 6 hours ahead of time, but add the fresh herbs not more than 10 minutes before serving.

3. Just before serving, correct the seasoning, adding salt, pepper, or lemon juice to taste. Garnish with whole basil leaves.

Serves 6 as an appetizer, 4 as a light main course

328 CALORIES PER SERVING: 9 G PROTEIN; 8 G FAT; 60 G CARBOHYDRATE; 14.5 MG SODIUM; 0 MG CHOLESTEROL
Analysis based on 4 servings

SOBA (JAPANESE BUCKWHEAT NOODLE) STEW

Half stew and half soup, this buckwheat noodle dish is 100 percent delectable. It's versatile, too, as you can serve it cold or hot. (Served cold, it makes a great summer refresher.) The broth is flavored with kombu (dried kelp), which is available at natural foods stores and Japanese markets. If kelp is unavailable or undesirable, omit it and use Asian Vegetable Stock (page 250) or Basic Vegetable Stock (page 247) in place of the water.

FOR THE BROTH
9 cups water
1 6 × 2-inch piece of dried kelp (kombu)
1 head garlic, unpeeled, cut in half widthwise
3 carrots, peeled and cut into 1-inch pieces
2 medium onions, quartered (skins left on)
4 scallions (white part only, save greens for garnishing the stew), cut into 1-inch pieces
3 ¼-inch slices fresh ginger

TO FINISH THE STEW
4 ounces soba noodles (see Cook's Notes)
1 large carrot, cut into carrot flowers or thin slices (see Note below)
4 scallion greens, finely chopped
3 tablespoons tamari or soy sauce (or to taste)
3 tablespoons mirin (sweet rice wine—see Cook's Notes), or to taste
3 tablespoons rice vinegar (or to taste)
1½ teaspoons grated lemon zest
salt and freshly ground pepper

1. Combine the ingredients for the broth—water, kelp, garlic, carrots, onions, scallion whites, ginger—in a large saucepan. Gently simmer the mixture for 20 to 30 minutes, or until well flavored. Strain the broth into another pot, pressing the vegetables with the back of a spoon to extract the juices. Reserve the kelp.

2. Cut the kelp across the grain into 2-inch pieces, then along the grain into spaghetti-thin slivers. Depending on your fondness for sea vegetables, you may wish to add a lot of kelp to the stew or a little. I personally like 1 to 2 tablespoons per serving. If you plan to serve the stew cold, let the broth cool to room temperature, then refrigerate it.

3. Cook the soba noodles in 2 quarts boiling water until al dente, about 8 minutes. Add the carrot flowers after 4 minutes. Drain the noodles and car-

rots in a colander, rinse under cold water, and drain again.

4. Just before serving, stir the soba, carrot flowers, scallion greens, and slivered kelp into the broth. Stir in the soy sauce, mirin, vinegar, lemon zest, salt, and pepper. Correct the seasoning, adding soy sauce for saltiness, mirin for sweetness, or rice vinegar for tartness. The broth should be highly seasoned.

Serves 8 as a first course, 4 as a main course

Note: To make carrot flowers, slice the stem end off the carrot; then make V-shaped cuts, ⅛-inch deep and ¼ inch apart, running the length of the carrot. Cut the carrot widthwise into ⅛-inch slices. The indentations resulting from the V-shaped cuts will form the petals of a flower.

129 CALORIES PER SERVING: 5 G PROTEIN; 0 G FAT; 28 G CARBOHYDRATE; 1039 MG SODIUM; 0 MG CHOLESTEROL
Analysis based on 4 servings

VEGETABLE DISHES

CURRIED MASHED POTATOES

These aren't like the mashed potatoes my mom used to make! Not with the addition of curry-fried onions, which lend an Indian accent to an American classic. The mixture makes a great filling for turnovers and pasta dishes and is, of course, delectable by itself.

1 tablespoon olive oil
1 onion, finely chopped
2 cloves garlic, minced
1 to 1½ teaspoons curry powder (or to taste)
1½ pounds baking potatoes (3 large potatoes), peeled and cut into 1-inch dice

salt and freshly ground black pepper
½ cup no-fat sour cream
a pinch of cayenne pepper
¼ cup Basic Vegetable Stock (page 247) or skim milk (optional)

1. Heat the oil in large nonstick frying pan. Sauté the onion and garlic over medium heat for 6 to 8 minutes, or until golden brown, stirring often. Add the curry powder after 4 minutes.

2. Cook the potatoes in at least 2 quarts rapidly boiling salted water until very tender, about 10 to 15 minutes. (The potatoes can also be cooked in a microwave oven or pressure cooker.)

3. Thoroughly drain the potatoes in a colander. Return the spuds to the pot and mash with a potato masher or put through a ricer. Do not purée the potatoes in a food processor, or the mixture will become gummy.

4. Stir the onion mixture into the mashed potatoes with the sour cream, salt, pepper, and cayenne. If the potatoes seem dry, add a little vegetable stock or skim milk. Correct the seasonings and serve at once.

Serves 4 to 6

233 CALORIES PER SERVING: 5 G PROTEIN; 4 G FAT; 46 G CARBOHYDRATE; 63 MG SODIUM; 0 MG CHOLESTEROL

Analysis based on 4 servings

VEGETABLE BURGERS

Who says veggie burgers aren't mainstream? Chef Kerry Sear introduced these vegetable burgers
at the Garden Court restaurant at the Four Seasons Olympic Hotel in Seattle. They were so
popular, guests soon clamored for them at all three of the hotel's restaurants, not to
mention from room service. Fresh beets give these patties the crimson hue
of a rare beef hamburger. **Note***: For ease in preparation,*
the vegetables can be grated in a food processor.

1 tablespoon olive oil, plus 1 to 2 teaspoons for
  cooking the burgers
1 medium onion, peeled and coarsely grated
  (about 1 cup)
2 to 3 carrots, scrubbed and coarsely grated
  (1 cup)
1 to 2 turnips, peeled and coarsely grated (1 cup)
1 zucchini, scrubbed and coarsely grated (1 cup)
1 small or ½ large beet, peeled and coarsely
  grated (½ cup)
2 cloves garlic, minced
½ teaspoon ground cumin
½ cup instant rolled oats, soaked in ½ cup water
  for 5 minutes

1½ cups mashed potatoes
½ cup cooked rice
1 tablespoon minced fresh dill, tarragon,
  or basil
salt and freshly ground black pepper
spray oil or additional olive oil for sautéing

FOR SERVING
hamburger buns
sliced onion
sliced tomato
lettuce leaves
Miso Barbecue Sauce (page 217) or ketchup

1. Heat the oil in a large nonstick skillet. Add the grated onion, carrots, turnips, zucchini, beets, garlic, and cumin and cook over medium heat for 10 to 15 minutes, or until the vegetables are tender. Do not let brown. Remove the pan from the heat and let cool.

2. Place oats in a strainer and press with the back of a spoon to extract water. Stir the oats into the vegetable mixture with the potatoes, rice, minced herbs, salt, and pepper. Correct the seasoning, adding cumin, salt, or pepper to taste.

3. Wet your hands and form the mixture into 8 thick burgers. You'll need ½ to ⅔ cup mixture per burger. Place the burgers on a plate or baking sheet lightly sprayed with oil and chill for at least 2 hours.

4a. There are three ways to cook the burgers: by grilling, broiling, or sautéing. For the first you'll need a fine-meshed vegetable or fish grill. Thoroughly spray it with oil. Place the burgers on top. Grill over a medium flame for 3 to 4 minutes per side, or until thoroughly heated and lightly browned. Turn the burgers as gently as possible with a spatula. It's even easier if you use a hinged grill.

4b. To broil the burgers, preheat the broiler with the rack 3 inches from the flame. Place the burgers on a sheet of oiled foil. Brush or spray the burgers with a little more oil. Broil for 3 to 4 minutes per side, or until lightly browned, turning as gently as possible with a spatula.

4c. To sauté the burgers, heat 2 teaspoons oil in a

large nonstick frying pan. Cook the burgers over medium heat for 4 to 5 minutes per side, or until lightly browned, turning as gently as possible with a spatula.

5. Serve the burgers on buns with onion, tomato, lettuce, and your favorite condiments, such as barbecue sauce or ketchup.

Makes 8 burgers

112 CALORIES PER SERVING: 3 G PROTEIN; 3 G FAT; 20 G CARBOHYDRATE; 140 MG SODIUM; 0 MG CHOLESTEROL

BARBARA'S SWEET AND SOUR CABBAGE

Sometimes, the best recipes are those with the fewest ingredients and the simplest preparation. Consider my wife's sweet and sour cabbage. Most of the sweetness comes from the balsamic vinegar and Vidalia onions, so you don't need very much sugar.

1½ tablespoons olive oil
1 Vidalia onion or other sweet onion, finely chopped
2 to 3 tablespoons balsamic vinegar
1 medium green cabbage, cored and cut crosswise into ½-inch strips (6 to 8 cups strips)

1 to 2 tablespoons brown sugar or other sweetener
salt and plenty of freshly ground black pepper

1. Heat the olive oil in a large nonstick frying pan. Add the onions and cook over medium-low heat for 20 to 25 minutes, or until deep golden brown, stirring often. The secret here is to cook the onions slowly to caramelize the sugars.

2. Add 2 tablespoons balsamic vinegar and bring to a boil. Stir in the cabbage, 1 tablespoon brown sugar, a little salt, and lots of pepper. (If there's too much cabbage for the pan, start with half the cab-

bage. When it cooks down, add the remainder.) Cook the cabbage over medium-low heat, stirring occasionally, for 30 to 40 minutes, or until cooked through but not soft. It should have a little crunch.

3. Just before serving, correct the seasoning, adding vinegar, sugar, salt, or pepper to taste. The cabbage should be a little sweet, a little sour, and very peppery.

Serves 4

105 CALORIES PER SERVING: 2 G PROTEIN; 5 G FAT; 14 G CARBOHYDRATE; 22 MG SODIUM; 0 MG CHOLESTEROL

CUBAN SHEPHERD'S PIE

A childhood dish of my friend Elida Proenza, tambor de papa *is the Cuban version of Anglo-American shepherd's pie. Sofrito (a fragrant mixture of sautéed onion, garlic, and peppers) is the starting point for many Spanish-Caribbean dishes.*

3 to 4 large baking potatoes (3 pounds), peeled
   and cut into ½-inch dice
salt
1 clove garlic, minced
½ cup no-fat sour cream
2 egg whites, lightly beaten
freshly ground black pepper
2 to 4 tablespoons Basic Vegetable Stock (page
   247) or skim milk (optional)

FOR THE *SOFRITO*
2 tablespoons extra-virgin olive oil
1 onion, finely chopped
2 cloves garlic, minced
2 teaspoons minced fresh ginger

½ red bell pepper, finely chopped (½ cup)
1 teaspoon ground cumin

TO FINISH THE FILLING
2 stalks celery, cut into ¼-inch dice
3 carrots, cut into ¼-inch dice
1 large or 2 small tomatoes, peeled, seeded, and
   diced (1 cup)
1 cup cooked corn kernels
1 cup cooked peas
2 tablespoons tomato purée
¼ cup dry white wine

spray oil

1. Prepare the mashed potatoes: Cook the diced potatoes in 2 quarts salted water until very tender, about 10 minutes. Drain the potatoes in a colander. Return the potatoes to the dry pan and cook for a minute or so to evaporate any excess moisture. Mash the potatoes with a potato masher or pestle. Stir in the garlic, sour cream, egg whites, and salt and pepper to taste. If the mixture seems too dry, add a little vegetable stock or skim milk.

2. Preheat the oven to 400° F.

3. Meanwhile, prepare the *sofrito:* Heat the olive oil in a nonstick skillet. Add the onion, garlic, ginger, bell pepper, and cumin and cook over medium heat until just beginning to brown, 4 to 6 minutes, stirring occasionally.

4. To finish the filling, stir in the celery, carrots, tomatoes, corn, peas, tomato purée, and wine. Cook the mixture, stirring often, until the vegetables are

tender but not soft, about 10 minutes. The mixture should be quite dry. (If the vegetables should start to burn, add a little water or vegetable stock.) Correct the seasoning, adding salt and pepper to taste: The mixture should be highly seasoned.

5. Spray a 10-inch springform pan with oil. Spread half the potato mixture in the bottom. Spoon in the vegetable mixture. Spread the remaining potatoes on top. Smooth the top of the pie with a spatula. For a decorative touch, you can mark the top of the pie with a fork.

6. Bake the shepherd's pie for 20 minutes, or until just beginning to brown. Remove the pan from the oven and let cool for 3 minutes. Remove the sides of the pan. Cut the shepherd's pie into wedges for serving.

Serves 8

279 CALORIES PER SERVING: 8 G PROTEIN; 4 G FAT; 55 G CARBOHYDRATE; 106 MG SODIUM; 0 MG CHOLESTEROL

MUSHROOM SOUFFLÉ PIE

Soufflé pies make a great brunch or lunch dish. This one starts with a duxelles, *a French mushroom "forcemeat" made by cooking down a pound of mushrooms to a thick, aromatic paste. (This is a good way to use up mushrooms that have seen better days.) For extra flavor, you could use part or all exotic mushrooms, such as shiitakes or chanterelles. "Rust" Sauce (page 199) would make a tasty and colorful accompaniment.*

spray oil
¼ cup bread crumbs

1 pound fresh mushrooms
1 tablespoon lemon juice
1 tablespoon olive oil
3 shallots, minced (about 3 tablespoons)
2 cloves garlic, minced

⅓ cup minced flat-leaf parsley
1 tablespoon flour
1 cup no-fat sour cream
Salt and freshly ground black pepper
a pinch of cayenne pepper
5 egg whites
½ teaspoon cream of tartar

1. Spray a 9-inch nonstick or cast-iron skillet with spray oil. Sprinkle the inside with bread crumbs. Preheat the oven to 400° F.

2. Finely chop the mushrooms. If using a food processor, cut any large mushrooms in quarters or halves. Don't fill the processor bowl more than ⅓ of the way. Run the machine in bursts and don't overprocess, or you'll reduce the mushrooms to mush. Otherwise, chop the mushrooms by hand. Sprinkle the mushrooms with lemon juice to keep them from discoloring.

3. Heat the olive oil in a large nonstick frying pan. Cook the shallots and garlic over medium heat for 3 to 4 minutes, or until soft but not brown. Stir in the mushrooms (you may need to add them little by little) and increase the heat to high.

4. Cook the mushrooms, stirring frequently, for 10 minutes, or until all the liquid has evaporated. You should wind up with about 1 cup mushroom paste. Stir in the parsley and flour and cook for 1 minute. Stir in the no-fat sour cream and cook the mixture for 2 minutes, whisking steadily. Whisk in salt, pepper, and cayenne to taste. The mixture should be very thick and highly seasoned.

5. Beat the egg whites until shiny and firm, but not dry, adding the cream of tartar after 10 seconds. Stir ¼ of the whites into the mushroom mixture to lighten it. Fold the mushroom mixture back into the remaining whites, working as gently as possible. Spoon the mixture into the prepared frying pan.

6. Bake the soufflé for 15 minutes, or until puffed and firm but not dry. Invert the soufflé onto a round platter and cut it into wedges for serving. The soufflé can be served either hot or cold.

Serves 4 to 6 as an appetizer, 2 or 3 as an entrée

Note: It is normal for the soufflé to fall somewhat.

318 CALORIES PER SERVING: 20 G PROTEIN; 8 G FAT; 38 G CARBOHYDRATE; 498 MG SODIUM; 0 MG CHOLESTEROL
Analysis based on 2 servings

GRILLED CORN PUDDING

This tasty pudding makes a great dish for Thanksgiving. The recipe was inspired by a corn pudding I had at the whimsical Boston restaurant Biba. Grilling corn gives you a wonderful smoky flavor, but if you're in a hurry, you could use any type of cooked corn.

2 cups grilled corn kernels (3 fresh ears)
1 to 2 teaspoons extra-virgin olive oil
salt and freshly ground black pepper
1 cup skim milk
1 cup Basic Vegetable Stock (page 247)
1 clove garlic, minced
⅓ cup quick Cream of Wheat
¼ cup no-fat sour cream
2 tablespoons fresh dill or other fresh herb

2 tablespoons minced flat-leaf parsley
½ teaspoon of your favorite hot sauce
a pinch of cayenne pepper
1 whole egg
2 egg whites
½ cup freshly grated Parmesan cheese

spray oil

1. Preheat the oven to 350° F. Brush each ear of corn with olive oil and sprinkle with salt and pepper. Grill or broil the corn over medium-high heat until golden brown, 2 to 3 minutes per side. Let the corn cool. Lay the ears flat on a cutting board and cut the kernels off the cobs with lengthwise strokes of a chef's knife.

2. Bring the milk, vegetable stock, and garlic to a boil in a heavy saucepan. Whisk in the Cream of Wheat in a thin stream and simmer, continuing to stir, for 2 to 3 minutes, or until thick. Stir in the corn, sour cream, dill, parsley, hot sauce, and cayenne. Remove the pan from the heat and let

cool for 2 minutes. Whisk in the whole egg, egg whites, and cheese.

3. Spoon the mixture into an 8-inch gratin dish lightly greased with spray oil. Place the dish in a roasting pan with ½-inch boiling water.

4. Bake the pudding for 40 to 50 minutes, or until puffed and golden brown. Serve at once.

Serves 4 to 6

Note: You can also make individual puddings in ramekins, timbales, or popover molds. Reduce baking time to 25 to 30 minutes. Lightly spray the molds with oil.

219 CALORIES PER SERVING: 14 G PROTEIN; 7 G FAT; 27 G CARBOHYDRATE; 374 MG SODIUM; 107 MG CHOLESTEROL
Analysis based on 4 servings

WINTER VEGETABLE TAGINE

Tagines are Moroccan stews flavored with coriander, turmeric, cumin, saffron, and other spices. This one features a soulful assortment of winter vegetables and dried fruits. For a livelier flavor, start with whole spices: Roast them in a dry frying pan until very fragrant, then grind them in a spice mill. Tagines are traditionally served over couscous (page 129) with harissa (North African hot sauce) as an accompaniment.

2 tablespoons olive oil
1 large onion, finely chopped
3 cloves garlic, minced
1 tablespoon minced fresh ginger
2 teaspoons coriander
1 teaspoon turmeric
1 teaspoon ground cumin
1 cinnamon stick
1 bay leaf
½ pound potatoes, peeled and cut into ¾-inch dice (about 2 cups)
½ pound winter squash, peeled and cut into ¾-inch dice (about 2 cups)
½ pound parsnips, peeled and cut into ¾-inch dice (about 2 cups)

1 cup cooked chickpeas (page 261)
¾ cup dried apricots
¾ cup pitted prunes
¼ teaspoon saffron, infused in 1 tablespoon warm water
1 tablespoon tomato paste
1 teaspoon freshly grated lemon zest
6 cups Basic Vegetable Stock (page 247), or as needed
salt and freshly ground black pepper
a pinch of cayenne pepper
¼ cup chopped cilantro or flat-leaf parsley for garnish

1. Heat the olive oil in a large casserole pan. Add the onion and cook over medium heat for 2 minutes. Stir in the garlic and ginger and continue cooking for 2 minutes, or until the vegetables begin to brown.

2. Stir in the coriander, turmeric, cumin, cinnamon stick, and bay leaves and cook for 1 minute, or until the mixture is very fragrant. Stir in the potatoes, squash, parsnips, chickpeas, apricots, prunes, saffron, tomato paste, lemon zest, vegetable stock, salt, black pepper, and cayenne and bring to a boil.

Reduce the heat and simmer the tagine, uncovered, until the vegetables are tender but not soft; you need about 40 to 50 minutes' cooking time in all. If the stew begins to dry out, add more stock. It should be quite moist.

3. Just before serving, remove the cinnamon stick and bay leaf. Correct the seasoning, adding salt, pepper, cumin, or cayenne to taste: The stew should be highly seasoned. Sprinkle the tagine with the chopped cilantro and serve at once.

Makes 6 cups, serving 4 to 6

382 CALORIES PER SERVING: 7 G PROTEIN; 8 G FAT; 76 G CARBOHYDRATE; 220 MG SODIUM; 0 MG CHOLESTEROL
Analysis based on 4 servings of tagine. See page 129 for couscous recipe and serving analysis.

MEDITERRANEAN BAKED STUFFED ZUCCHINI

Baked stuffed vegetables are always in fashion. Serve them as an appetizer or a colorful side dish. Increase the portion size, and they become a sophisticated entrée. In this recipe, the zucchini is cut crosswise into cylinders, which are hollowed out with a melon baller to form barrel-shaped vessels for the stuffing.

3 zucchinis (9 to 10 inches long) or 4 zucchinis
  (7 to 8 inches long)

FOR THE STUFFING
2 cups mushrooms
1 teaspoon lemon juice
1 tablespoon olive oil
1 onion, minced
2 cloves garlic, minced

1 red bell pepper, cored, seeded, and minced
1 yellow bell pepper, cored, seeded, and minced
1 green bell pepper, cored, seeded, and minced
¼ teaspoon saffron, soaked in 1 tablespoon hot
  water
¼ teaspoon fennel seeds
½ cup Basic Vegetable Stock (page 247), or as
  needed
salt and freshly ground black pepper

1. Cut the ends off the zucchini. Cut each zucchini widthwise into 2-inch sections. Hollow each section with a melon baller, leaving ¼ inch at the bottom and on the sides intact to make a barrel-shaped container. You should have 12 "barrels."

2. Finely chop the mushrooms and sprinkle with lemon juice. (If using a food processor, don't fill the bowl more than ¼ full at a time, and run the machine in short bursts.)

3. Heat the olive oil in a nonstick frying pan. Cook the onion, garlic, and bell peppers over medium heat until soft but not brown, 3 to 4 min-

utes. Add the mushrooms, saffron, fennel, and vegetable stock and cook for 10 minutes, or until all the stock has been absorbed by the vegetables. Add salt and pepper to taste. The mixture should be highly seasoned.

4. Preheat the oven to 350° F. Fill each zucchini barrel with stuffing. Place the zucchinis in a baking dish with ¼ inch hot water. Bake the zucchinis for 15 to 20 minutes, or until the sides of the barrels feel soft. Serve at once.

*Makes 12 pieces, enough to serve 4 to 6 as an
appetizer or side dish*

101 CALORIES PER SERVING: 3 G PROTEIN; 4 G FAT; 16 G CARBOHYDRATE; 10 MG SODIUM; 0 MG CHOLESTEROL
Analysis based on 4 servings

Mediterranean Baked Stuffed Zucchini (top) and Couscous-Stuffed Baby Eggplants

COUSCOUS-STUFFED BABY EGGPLANTS

I like to use tiny Italian eggplants for stuffing, those small purple beauties that are only 4 to 6 inches long. Look for them in Italian markets, specialty greengrocers', and many supermarkets. The scoring and salting of the eggplant is called disgorging and it helps remove any bitter juices.

6 small Italian eggplants (4 to 6 inches long)
1 tablespoon kosher salt
1 tablespoon olive oil
4 shallots, minced (¼ cup)
2 cloves garlic, minced
1 yellow bell pepper, cored, seeded, and very finely diced
1 red bell pepper, cored, seeded, and very finely diced

2 tablespoons pine nuts
2 tablespoons currants
2 cups cooked Couscous (recipe follows)
1 tablespoon fresh lemon juice or to taste
¼ cup finely chopped flat-leaf parsley
¼ cup finely chopped fresh mint
salt and freshly ground black pepper

1. Preheat the oven to 375° F. Cut the eggplants in half lengthwise (through the stem end). Carefully score the cut side of each eggplant almost to but not through the skin. Sprinkle each eggplant with kosher salt. Let stand for 20 minutes. Rinse off any bitter juices that may gather on the surface and blot the eggplants dry.

2. Bake the eggplants cut side down on a nonstick baking sheet for 20 minutes, or until soft.

3. Scrape out most of the pulp with a spoon, leaving about ¼ inch flesh next to the skin. Finely chop half the pulp. Reserve the other half for stocks or stews.

4. Prepare the filling: Heat the olive oil in a nonstick frying pan. Cook the shallots, garlic, bell peppers, pine nuts, and currants over medium heat, or until the vegetables are soft but not brown, about 4 minutes. Stir in the couscous, lemon juice, parsley, mint, salt, pepper, and chopped eggplant. Correct the seasoning, adding salt or lemon juice to taste. Stuff this mixture back into the eggplant shells. The recipe can be prepared ahead to this stage.

5. In a baking dish sprayed with oil, bake the eggplants at 375° F. for 10 minutes, or until thoroughly heated. Serve at once.

Serves 6 as an appetizer, 3 or 4 as an entrée

292 CALORIES PER SERVING: 8 G PROTEIN; 8 G FAT; 48 G CARBOHYDRATE; 18 MG SODIUM; 0 MG CHOLESTEROL

Analysis based on 3 servings

TO PREPARE COUSCOUS

2 cups vegetable stock or water
1 cup quick-cook couscous
salt and freshly ground black pepper

1. Bring the stock to a boil. Stir in the couscous and salt and pepper. Bring the mixture back to a boil.
2. Cover the pan and remove from the heat. Let the couscous stand for 5 minutes. Correct the seasoning and fluff the couscous with a fork before serving.

Serves 4

150 CALORIES PER SERVING: 5 G PROTEIN; 0 G FAT; 31 G CARBOHYDRATE; 7 MG SODIUM; 0 MG CHOLESTEROL

SWEET POTATO AND PARSNIP CASSEROLE

Thanksgiving wouldn't be complete without a sweet potato casserole. This one owes its richness and moistness to vegetable stock, not butter. The parsnips add an unexpected touch of sweetness.

1½ tablespoons olive oil, plus 1 teaspoon for drizzling on top
3 large onions, thinly sliced (about 4 cups)

5 cloves garlic, minced
3 to 4 large sweet potatoes (about 2 pounds), peeled and cut into ¼-inch slices
1 pound parsnips, peeled and cut into ¼-inch slices
2 to 3 cups Basic Vegetable Stock (page 247)

1 cup no-fat sour cream
1 teaspoon fresh or dried thyme
salt and freshly ground black pepper
¼ cup fine, dry bread crumbs

1. Heat 1½ tablespoons olive oil in a large sauté pan (preferably nonstick). Add the onions and garlic and cook over medium heat, stirring often, until a deep golden brown, 8 to 10 minutes.
2. Stir the sweet potatoes and parsnips into the onions. Add the vegetable stock, sour cream, thyme, and a little salt and pepper. Simmer the mixture until the potatoes are tender and most of the liquid is absorbed, 15 to 20 minutes. Correct the seasoning, adding salt and pepper to taste. The recipe can be prepared ahead to this stage.
3. Preheat the oven to 400° F. Sprinkle the bread crumbs on top of the casserole and drizzle with the remaining olive oil. Bake the casserole for 20 to 30 minutes, or until the stock has been absorbed by the potatoes and the top is crusty and brown. (You can also brown the casserole under the broiler.)

Serves 8

220 CALORIES PER SERVING: 4.5 G PROTEIN; 3.75 G FAT; 43 G CARBOHYDRATE; 89 MG SODIUM; 0 MG CHOLESTEROL

CHINESE EGGPLANT WITH GINGER AND SCALLIONS

Eggplant used to be one of my favorite dishes at Chinese restaurants. Unfortunately, traditional recipes call for the eggplant to be deep-fried prior to stir-frying. No wonder medical studies report some Chinese dishes contain more fat than a Big Mac. My rendition calls for grilling the eggplant, which imparts a smoky flavor in addition to dramatically reducing the fat. This dish is best made with Chinese or Japanese eggplant, those small, long, slender, bright purple eggplants sold at Asian markets. But a regular eggplant will do in a pinch.

1½ pounds Chinese or Japanese eggplant
1 teaspoon Asian sesame oil

FOR THE SAUCE
3 tablespoons low-sodium soy sauce (or to taste)
2 tablespoons rice wine
2 tablespoons rice vinegar
1 tablespoon sugar
1 tablespoon cornstarch

1 tablespoon canola oil

3 cloves garlic, minced
2 teaspoons minced fresh ginger
3 scallions, white part minced, green part thinly sliced for garnish
1 to 3 serrano or jalapeño chilies, minced (for a milder dish, remove the seeds)

1. Preheat the grill to medium-high heat. Peel the eggplants and cut on the diagonal into ¼-inch slices. Brush the slices with sesame oil and grill over medium heat for 2 minutes per side or until golden brown. The recipe can be prepared up to 24 hours ahead to this stage.

2. For the sauce, combine the soy sauce, rice wine, vinegar, sugar, and cornstarch in a small bowl and stir to mix.

3. Heat a wok (preferably nonstick) over a high flame. Swirl in the canola oil. Add the garlic, ginger, scallion whites, and chilies and stir-fry for 10 seconds or until fragrant but not brown. Add the eggplant and stir-fry for 1 minute. Stir the sauce

and add it to the eggplant. Bring the mixture to a boil; the sauce should thicken. Transfer the eggplant to a platter or bowl and sprinkle with scallion greens. The eggplant can be served hot or cold as an appetizer or vegetable side dish.

Serves 4 to 6

Note: To transform this dish into a main course, you could add 8 ounces tofu. Press the tofu as described on page 257 and cut it into 1-inch cubes. Add it to the wok when you add the eggplant and stir-fry as described. You may need to add a little more soy sauce and vinegar for flavor.

117 CALORIES PER SERVING: 3 G PROTEIN; 5 G FAT; 17 G CARBOHYDRATE; 423 MG SODIUM; 0 MG CHOLESTEROL

Analysis based on 4 servings

HERBED POTATO KNISHES

These knishes certainly aren't like the ones grandmother used to make! Gone are yesterday's chicken fat and egg yolks. These knishes use caramelized onions and fresh herbs to achieve flavor with a minimum of fat.

1½ tablespoons olive oil
1 large onion, minced (about 2 cups)
2 cloves garlic, minced
2 egg whites, lightly beaten
3 to 4 tablespoons chopped fresh herbs,
   including basil, chives, tarragon, oregano,
   and/or thyme

1 tablespoon sweet Hungarian paprika
2½ pounds baking potatoes (3 to 4 potatoes),
   peeled and cut into ½-inch dice
salt and freshly ground black pepper
3 to 4 tablespoons flour, plus 1 cup for dredging
spray oil

1. Preheat the oven to 350° F.

2. Heat the olive oil in a large nonstick frying pan. Add the onion and cook over medium-low heat until nicely caramelized, about 10 to 15 minutes. Add the garlic after 5 minutes. Set the onion mixture aside to cool. Stir in the egg whites, herbs, and paprika.

3. Place the potatoes in a large pot with cold water to cover. Bring to a boil, reduce the heat, and simmer the potatoes for 8 to 10 minutes, or until very tender. (For extra flavor, you could cook the potatoes in vegetable stock.) Drain the potatoes in a colander and return them to the pan. Cook the potatoes over medium heat for 1 to 2 minutes to evaporate any excess liquid. Remove the pot from the heat and let cool slightly.

4. Mash the potatoes in the pot with a potato masher or pestle. (I like to leave a few small lumps for texture.) Stir in the onion mixture and salt and pepper to taste: The mixture should be highly seasoned. Stir in 3 to 4 tablespoons flour, or enough to obtain a mixture you can shape with your fingers.

5. Wet your hands and form the potato mixture into patties 1 inch thick and 3 inches across. Place the remaining flour in a bowl. Lightly dredge each knish in flour, shaking off the excess. Arrange the knishes on a a nonstick baking sheet lightly sprayed with oil. The knishes can be prepared ahead to this stage, covered with plastic, and refrigerated for up to 2 days.

6. Bake the knishes for 30 to 40 minutes, or until lightly browned and hot in the center (an inserted skewer will come out hot to the touch). If the knishes are slow in browning, you can run them under the broiler for a few minutes.

Serve the knishes by themselves or with Quince Compote (page 237) or no-fat sour cream (or—if you're feeling particularly indulgent—both).

Makes 8 knishes

177 CALORIES PER SERVING: 4 G PROTEIN; 3 G FAT; 35 G CARBOHYDRATE; 22 MG SODIUM; 0 MG CHOLESTEROL

THANKSGIVING STUFFED ACORN SQUASH

This colorful dish is Thanksgiving incarnate. You could use any number of breads, from Five-Grain Bread (page 78) to challah, corn bread, or whole wheat bread. The squash can be stuffed ahead of time and reheated at the last minute, which makes this an ideal dish for a holiday buffet. **Note:***For a fanciful presentation, "wolf" the squashes (cut them in half in a zigzag fashion), as pictured on page 132.*

4 small acorn squashes (preferably orange)
spray oil

FOR THE STUFFING
½ cup currants
1 cup warm Basic Vegetable Stock (page 247), or as needed
1½ tablespoons olive oil
2 onions, finely chopped
4 stalks celery, finely chopped
4 cloves garlic, minced

2 apples, cored and cut into ¼-inch dice (1 cup)
1½ cups cooked corn kernels from 1 ear (optional)
1¼ cups very coarse fresh bread crumbs or finely diced bread
5 tablespoons chopped fresh herbs, including flat-leaf parsley, basil, tarragon, thyme, and/or sage
1 teaspoon grated lemon zest
salt and freshly ground black pepper

1. Preheat the oven to 350° F.

2. Cut the squashes in half widthwise. Cut a ¼-inch slice off the top and bottom, so the halves sit straight without wobbling. Scoop out the seeds. Bake the squashes, cut side down, on a baking sheet oiled with spray oil until soft, about 40 minutes. Transfer the squashes to a cake rack to cool.

3. Prepare the stuffing: Plump the currants in the vegetable stock in a bowl for 10 minutes. Meanwhile, heat the olive oil in a large nonstick frying pan. Cook the onion, celery, and garlic over medium heat until soft but not brown, 3 to 4 minutes. Add the apple and corn (if using) and cook until the apple has lost its rawness, about 3 minutes.

4. Transfer the mixture to a large bowl and stir in the bread crumbs, herbs, lemon zest, currants with the stock, and salt and pepper to taste. The mixture should be highly seasoned and moist but not wet. Add stock or salt as needed. Spoon the stuffing into the baked squashes. The recipe can be prepared ahead to this stage.

5. Just before serving, bake the stuffed squashes in a 375° F. oven until thoroughly heated, 15 to 20 minutes.

Serves 8

271 CALORIES PER SERVING: 6 G PROTEIN; 6 G FAT; 53 G CARBOHYDRATE; 254 MG SODIUM; 0 MG CHOLESTEROL

GARLIC SOUFFLÉ

A full cup of garlic cloves may seem like a deadly dose of the malodorous root, but garlic loses its nose-jarring pungency when the cloves are poached in milk. It still has enough flavor to compensate for the reduced number of egg yolks.
Note: *Barbara's Chunky Tomato Sauce (page 212) would make a good accompaniment.*

spray oil
3 tablespoons toasted bread crumbs

1 cup peeled whole garlic cloves
1 cup skim milk
2 tablespoons flour
1 to 2 egg yolks

salt and freshly ground black pepper
a pinch each freshly grated nutmeg and cayenne
  pepper
6 egg whites
½ teaspoon cream of tartar

1. Thoroughly oil the bottom and sides of a 5-cup soufflé dish with the spray oil. Add the bread crumbs and rotate the dish to coat the bottom and sides with crumbs.

2. Preheat the oven to 375° F.

3. Combine the garlic and milk in a heavy 1-quart saucepan. Cook, covered, over medium-low heat for about 15 minutes, or until the garlic cloves are very soft.

4. Place the garlic, milk, and flour in a blender and purée to a smooth paste. Return the mixture to the saucepan and bring it back to a boil. Remove the pan from the heat and whisk in the egg yolks. The mixture should thicken. If it doesn't, return it to the heat for a minute or so, whisking steadily. Whisk in salt, pepper, nutmeg, and cayenne. The mixture should be very highly seasoned. Keep it warm.

5. Beat the egg whites until firm and glossy but not dry, adding the cream of tartar after 20 seconds.

6. Whisk ¼ of the egg whites into the yolk mixture. Fold this mixture back into the remaining whites as gently as possible. It is better to underfold than overfold.

7. Spoon the soufflé mixture into the prepared soufflé dish. Bake the soufflé until puffed and golden brown, 15 to 20 minutes. **Note:** People wait for soufflés, not the other way around. Serve at once!

Serves 4 as an appetizer, 2 or 3 as a main course

Note: Peeled whole cloves of garlic can be found at upscale food markets. If you use whole heads of garlic, break the heads into cloves with your fingers. Lightly pound each clove with the side of the knife to loosen the skin and slip it off.

260 CALORIES PER SERVING: 21 G PROTEIN; 4 G FAT; 35 G CARBOHYDRATE; 366 MG SODIUM; 108 MG CHOLESTEROL

Analysis based on 2 servings

Cold Grilled Vegetable and Smoked Cheese "Tart"

This colorful tart makes a great appetizer or entrée for a summertime lunch. The recipe comes from Mark Militello, owner of Miami's acclaimed restaurant Mark's Place. Smoked mozzarella can be found at Italian markets, natural foods stores, and gourmet shops. (If unavailable, use fresh.) The lacto-vegetarian could use a layer of cooked grains or beans (about 2 cups) instead of cheese. "Rust" Sauce (page 199) would make a good accompaniment.

3 cloves garlic, minced
2 to 3 tablespoons extra-virgin olive oil
4 medium zucchini
4 medium eggplants
3 medium red onions
8 ounces smoked mozzarella
5 vine-ripe tomatoes
salt and freshly ground black pepper

3 red bell peppers
3 yellow bell peppers (or more red)
3 tablespoons freshly grated Parmigiano-Reggiano cheese
3 to 4 tablespoons chopped fresh herbs, including chives, oregano, thyme, and/or flat-leaf parsley
1 bunch fresh basil, washed and stemmed

1. Preheat a barbecue grill to high. Stir the garlic into the olive oil and let marinate for 10 minutes. Cut the zucchini and eggplants lengthwise into ⅛-inch slices. (This is most easily done on a mandoline, but a chef's knife will work, too.) Cut the onions and mozzarella into ¼-inch slices, the tomatoes into ½-inch slices.

2. Lightly brush the sliced vegetables with olive oil and season with salt and pepper. Grill the vegetables until nicely browned on both sides: This will take 1 to 2 minutes per side for the zucchini, eggplant, and tomatoes; 2 to 3 minutes per side for the onions. Transfer the vegetables to a platter to cool.

3. Grill the peppers until charred on all sides: This will take about 8 to 10 minutes in all. Wrap the peppers in wet paper towels and let cool. Unwrap the peppers and scrape the charred skin off with a knife. Cut the peppers in half, core, and seed.

4. Lightly brush the inside of a 10-inch springform pan with olive oil and sprinkle it with the grated Parmesan cheese. Arrange half the eggplant slices inside the pan on the bottom, cutting as necessary so that the layer of slices fits the shape of the pan. Sprinkle with chopped herbs, salt, and pepper, and repeat this step after the addition of each layer. Add a layer of red peppers, then of mozzarella, grilled onions, half the basil leaves, and tomatoes. Add the remaining basil leaves, then the yellow peppers, eggplant, and zucchini.

5. Cover the top of the tart with plastic wrap and place a 9- or 10-inch springform pan bottom or cake pan on top; crown it with a cast-iron skillet, brick, or other heavy object. Refrigerate the tart for at least 6 hours, preferably overnight.

6. To unmold the tart, remove the weights and plastic wrap. Unfasten the side of the pan. Cut the tart into wedges and serve.

Serves 8 to 10

Note: Cookware shops sell fine-grid enamel or wire vegetable grills, which are great help for grilling the vegetables.

233 CALORIES PER SERVING: 21 G PROTEIN; 11 G FAT; 17 G CARBOHYDRATE; 435 MG SODIUM; 22 MG CHOLESTEROL

Analysis based on 8 servings

SAAG PANIR
INDIAN SPINACH CURRY WITH HOMEMADE CHEESE

Panir is a fresh Indian cheese that's mild and sweet, like mozzarella, and tooth-squeakingly crisp, like string cheese. In this recipe the cheese is simmered in a mild spinach curry. Indians traditionally cook spinach a long time—until soft and mushy—so I usually use frozen spinach when preparing this recipe.

FOR THE SAUCE
1 tablespoon olive oil
1 onion, finely chopped
1 tablespoon minced fresh ginger
3 cloves garlic, minced
1 teaspoon ground cumin
1 teaspoon ground coriander
1 cinnamon stick
salt, freshly ground black pepper, and a pinch of cayenne pepper

2 ripe tomatoes, peeled, seeded, and finely chopped
3 10-ounce packages frozen spinach, thawed
¼ cup Basic Vegetable Stock (page 247) or water
¾ cup no-fat sour cream
1 tablespoon fresh lemon juice (or to taste)
2 cups diced Panir (recipe follows)
¼ cup finely chopped cilantro or scallion greens for garnish

1. Heat the olive oil in a large heavy saucepan. Lightly brown the onions over medium heat (this will take 4 to 5 minutes), adding the ginger, garlic, cumin, coriander, cinnamon stick, salt, black pepper, and cayenne after 2 minutes.

2. Stir in the tomatoes and cook for 1 minute. Stir in the spinach and vegetable stock and gently simmer for 10 minutes, or until most of the liquid has evaporated. Stir in the sour cream and lemon juice and simmer for 3 minutes. Stir in the panir and cook until warmed but not melted. Correct the seasoning, adding salt and pepper to taste. Serve the Saag Panir over Basic Basmati Rice (page 260). Garnish with the cilantro or scallion greens.

Serves 4

258 CALORIES PER SERVING: 26 G PROTEIN; 10 G FAT; 20 G CARBOHYDRATE; 610 MG SODIUM; 20 MG CHOLESTEROL

Analysis based on serving of saag panir. See page 260 for Basic Basmati Rice recipe and serving analysis.

TO MAKE PANIR (INDIAN CHEESE)

Many people are intimidated by the prospect of making cheese from scratch, but it's really quite easy. Strict vegetarians will appreciate the use of lemon juice, not rennet, to separate the milk into curds and whey.

6 cups two percent milk
3 tablespoons fresh lemon juice

1. Bring the milk just to a boil in a large heavy saucepan. Remove the pan from the heat and stir in the lemon juice. The milk will curdle in about 10 seconds. Pour the mixture through a strainer lined with cheesecloth. Let drain for 10 minutes. Rinse the curds under cold water to remove the lemon taste and let drain.

2. Gather the corners of the cheesecloth together and tie the curds into a tight bundle. Place the bundle on a sloping cutting board in the sink. Place a heavy weight, like a cast-iron skillet, on top. Press the curds for 2 to 3 hours, or until firm. Unwrap the cheese and cut it into ½-inch cubes.

Makes 2 cups

MY CHILES RELLENOS

Chiles rellenos are one of the glories of Mexican gastronomy. But the first time I tasted the traditional version, cheese-stuffed poblano chilies dripping with oil from deep-frying, I could almost feel my arteries hardening! My low-fat rendition takes advantage of the poblano's unique flavor, but the filling features grilled corn kernels with only a minimal amount of cheese. To further reduce the fat, the chilies are baked, not deep-fried. See Cook's Notes for a full description of poblano chilies. If unavailable, you could use small green bell peppers or Anaheim chilies.

8 poblano chilies

FOR THE FILLING
1½ cups corn kernels, preferably grilled corn
   (page 252), but drained canned or frozen will
   work in a pinch
4 scallions, minced
2 cloves garlic, minced
¼ cup lightly toasted pine nuts
2 to 4 ounces goat cheese, crumbled, or sharp
   cheddar cheese, grated (optional)
1 tablespoon finely chopped fresh cilantro, dill,
   or flat-leaf parsley
salt and freshly ground black pepper

TO FINISH THE DISH
approximately 1 cup flour
3 egg whites, beaten with a pinch of salt
approximately 1 cup blue or yellow cornmeal
spray oil (optional)
1 to 2 teaspoons extra-virgin olive oil

Garlic Sauce or Chili Sauce (recipes follow)

1. Roast the chilies until charred on all sides over a high burner flame, on the barbecue grill, or under the broiler (see page 257). Wrap the roasted chilies in wet paper towels and let cool. Unwrap and scrape off the charred skin with a paring knife, keeping the chilies' tops and bottoms intact. Make a lengthwise incision in each chili—about 2 inches long, big enough to fit a spoonful of stuffing—taking care not to tear the chili. Use a melon baller or spoon to carefully scrape out the core and seeds.

2. For the filling, combine the corn, scallions, garlic, pine nuts, cheese (if using), cilantro, salt, and pepper in a mixing bowl. Correct the seasoning, adding salt or pepper to taste.

3. Spoon the filling into the chilies, taking care not to pierce the sides. Freeze the chilies for 15 minutes. Preheat the oven to 400° F.

4. To finish the dish, place the flour in a shallow bowl, the egg whites in a second bowl, and the cornmeal in a third bowl. Dip each chili first in flour, shaking off the excess, then in egg white, then finally in cornmeal. Place the chilies on a nonstick baking sheet or in a baking dish lightly sprayed with spray oil. Drizzle a little olive oil over each chili. Bake the chiles rellenos for 20 minutes, or until crusty and golden brown.

5. Serve the chiles with either the Garlic Sauce or the Chili Sauce, or with both. For a fancier presentation, you can cut the chiles crosswise into ½-inch slices and fan the slices out on plates or a platter.

Serves 8 as an appetizer, 4 as a main course

534 CALORIES PER SERVING: 20 G PROTEIN; 14 G FAT; 86 G CARBOHYDRATE; 334 MG SODIUM; 11 MG CHOLESTEROL
Analysis based on 4 servings

GARLIC SAUCE

Don't be alarmed by the seemingly enormous amount of garlic here. Poaching greatly reduces its pungency.

10 cloves garlic, peeled
approximately 1 cup Basic Vegetable Stock
 (page 247)

½ cup no-fat sour cream
¼ teaspoon ground cumin, or to taste
salt and freshly ground black pepper

1. Combine the garlic and vegetable stock in a heavy saucepan and gently simmer over medium heat until the garlic is very soft, about 10 minutes. Some of the stock will evaporate, some will be absorbed by the garlic. You want to wind up with about ½ cup stock. Add more as needed.

2. Stir in the sour cream, cumin, salt, and pepper. Purée the sauce in a blender. Correct the seasoning, adding cumin or salt to taste.

Makes 1 cup

7 CALORIES PER SERVING: 0.4 G PROTEIN; 0 G FAT; 1 G CARBOHYDRATE; 13 MG SODIUM; 0 MG CHOLESTEROL

CHILI SAUCE

Here's a rich, rust-colored sauce that's great for decorating plates. Try squirting it from squeeze bottles. To create a marbled effect, spread the plates with the above garlic sauce. Squirt parallel lines or concentric circles of chili sauce on top. Drag a knife point through the sauces to marble them. For the best results, use a mild, pure chili powder from New Mexico.

⅓ cup pure chili powder
¼ onion, coarsely chopped (about 3 tablespoons)
2 cloves garlic, peeled and coarsely chopped

1 cup Basic Vegetable Stock (page 247)
salt and freshly ground black pepper

1. Combine the chili powder, onion, garlic, vegetable stock, salt, and pepper in a blender and purée to a smooth paste. Transfer the mixture to a saucepan.

2. Bring the sauce to a boil, whisking steadily. Reduce the heat and gently simmer the sauce for 5 minutes, whisking occasionally. (The sauce scorches easily, so don't forget to whisk.) Add stock as necessary to thin the sauce to the consistency of heavy cream. Correct the seasoning, adding salt and pepper to taste.

Makes 1 cup

9 CALORIES PER SERVING: 0.4 G PROTEIN; 0.4 G FAT; 2 G CARBOHYDRATE; 26 MG SODIUM; 0 MG CHOLESTEROL

GRAIN DISHES

VEGETABLE PAELLA

Say the word paella, *and most people will think of shellfish. But a great many paellas exist in Spain, some made with no seafood at all. Peppers, corn, peas, and fava beans lend this paella plenty of flavor and color, while chickpeas complete the proteins found in the rice. Radiant like the sun and redolent with saffron and onion, vegetable paella makes a dramatic dish for entertaining. Valencia-style rice is a starchy short-grain rice available at Hispanic markets and many supermarkets. If unavailable, use Italian Arborio rice.* **Note**: *If you're in a hurry, you can replace the roasted peppers with sautéed peppers or bottled pimientoes.*

FOR THE *SOFRITO*
2 tablespoons extra-virgin olive oil
1 large onion, finely chopped (about 1½ cups)
5 cloves garlic, minced
1 red bell pepper, cored, seeded, and cut into
    ¼-inch dice (about 1 cup)
1 large ripe tomato, peeled, seeded, and cut into
    ¼-inch dice (about 1 cup)

TO FINISH THE PAELLA
2 cups Valencia-style or Arborio rice
6 to 7 cups Mediterranean Vegetable Stock (page
    249) or Basic Vegetable Stock (page 247)
salt
1 cup shucked green peas
1 cup shelled fava beans or lima beans
2 ears corn, shucked and cut crosswise into
    1-inch pieces

2 carrots, scraped or peeled and cut on the
    diagonal into ½-inch pieces
1 to 2 red bell peppers, roasted, skinned, cored,
    and seeded (see roasting instructions on
    page 257)
1 yellow bell pepper, roasted, skinned, cored,
    and seeded
1 cup dry white wine
¼ teaspoon saffron, soaked in 1 tablespoon hot
    water for 10 minutes
2 bay leaves
8 small cooked artichoke hearts
1 cup cooked chickpeas (page 261)
freshly ground black pepper and a hint of
    cayenne
3 tablespoons finely chopped flat-leaf parsley

1. Prepare the *sofrito*: Heat the olive oil in an attractive heavy 14-inch frying pan or paella pan. Sauté the onion, garlic, and raw red bell pepper over medium heat, stirring often, for 6 to 8 minutes, or until golden brown. Increase the heat to high and stir in the tomato. Cook for 1 minute, or until all the tomato liquid has evaporated. Remove the pan from the heat.

2. Meanwhile, wash the rice. (Place it in a bowl and add water to cover. Swirl it with your fingers and pour off the water. Continue adding water, swirling, and rinsing until the water runs clear.) Set aside.

3. Bring the vegetable stock to a boil in a large pot and add salt to taste. Boil the peas for 1 minute, or until tender. Transfer the peas with a slotted spoon to a colander, rinse with cold water, and drain. Boil the fava beans in the stock for 2 minutes or until tender. Transfer with a slotted spoon to the colander, rinse, and drain. Cook the corn in this fashion for 4 minutes or until tender; the carrots for 5 minutes. Set these boiled vegetables aside and reserve the stock. Cut the roasted peppers into 1-inch squares. The paella can be prepared several hours ahead to this stage.

4. Thirty minutes before serving, reheat the *sofrito*. Stir in the rice and cook it for 2 minutes, or until the grains are shiny. Stir in the white wine, saffron mixture, and bay leaves and bring to a boil. Stir in 5 cups vegetable stock and bring to a boil. Reduce the heat to medium and gently simmer the rice, uncovered, stirring occasionally, for 25 minutes, or until tender. If the rice starts to dry out, add the remaining stock. The rice should be very moist, like risotto.

5. Stir in most of the vegetables (including artichokes) and chickpeas and continue cooking for 3 minutes, or until the rice is soft but not mushy. Correct the seasoning, adding salt, black pepper, or cayenne to taste. Decorate the paella with the remaining vegetables and chickpeas, sprinkle with parsley, and serve at once.

Serves 8

524 CALORIES PER SERVING: 13 G PROTEIN; 5 G FAT; 103 G CARBOHYDRATE; 129 MG SODIUM; 0 MG CHOLESTEROL

BASIC POLENTA

Polenta, simply defined, is Italian cornmeal mush. But, oh, what mush! You can bake it, grill it, sauté it, or slather it with a dozen different sauces. Barbara's Chunky Tomato Sauce (page 212) or Red Bean Bolognese (page 213) would be great. My polenta differs from traditional recipes in two significant ways. To bolster the flavor without fat, I make it with vegetable stock instead of water. To prevent lumping, I make a cold-water slurry, rather than adding the cornmeal directly to boiling liquid.
__Note__: To make a thick polenta for grilling or broiling, use 6½ to 7 cups stock. To make a creamier polenta, for eating like mashed potatoes, use 8 cups stock.

2 cups coarse yellow cornmeal
6½ to 8 cups Basic Vegetable Stock (page 247)
1 clove garlic, minced (optional)
3 tablespoons chopped fresh herbs (optional)

salt and freshly ground black pepper

spray oil

1. In a mixing bowl, combine the cornmeal with 2 cups cold or cool stock and whisk to a smooth paste. Bring the remaining stock to a boil in a large heavy saucepan (preferably nonstick). Add the cornmeal mixture to the stock in a thin stream, whisking steadily. Boil the polenta for 3 minutes, whisking steadily.

2. Reduce the heat and stir in the garlic and herbs (if using) and a little salt and pepper. Gently simmer the polenta for 40 to 50 minutes, or until the mixture thickens enough to pull away from the sides of the pan. It should be the consistency of soft ice cream. It isn't necessary to whisk the polenta continuously, but you should give it a stir every 5 minutes. As it thickens, you may need to switch from a whisk to a wooden spoon. Correct the seasoning, adding salt and pepper to taste: The polenta should be highly seasoned.

3. The polenta can be eaten at this stage as you would mashed potatoes. Alternatively, pour it onto a nonstick jelly roll pan or 9-inch square cake pan lightly sprayed with oil. Let the polenta cool to room temperature, then refrigerate it until firm. Cut the cold polenta with a knife or cookie cutter into strips, squares, rectangles, or other fanciful shapes.

4. To reheat the polenta, bake it in a baking dish with a sauce on top, sauté it in a little olive oil in a nonstick frying pan, or brush it with oil and grill it. I particularly like grilling, as the polenta picks up a smoky flavor.

Makes six 3 x 5-inch rectangles, enough to serve 6 as an appetizer or side dish, 3 or 4 as a main course

Note: You can buy instant and quick polentas, but they're not nearly as good as the old-fashioned version.

149 CALORIES PER SERVING: 3 G PROTEIN; 2 G FAT; 31 G CARBOHYDRATE; 14 MG SODIUM; 0 MG CHOLESTEROL

Analysis based on 4 servings

POLENTA PAPRIKAS

Paprikas is the national dish of Hungary, a soulful stew of onions, peppers, and paprika enriched with sour cream, for which this Eastern European nation is so famous. I despaired of ever making a low-fat version until the American dairy industry responded to growing consumer health-consciousness by developing a fat-free sour cream. Land O'Lakes makes an excellent no-fat sour cream; this and other brands are available at most supermarkets.
A complete discussion of Polenta is found on page 143.

1½ tablespoons olive oil
1 large onion, very thinly sliced (2 cups)
2 cloves garlic, minced
2 red bell peppers, cored, seeded, and thinly sliced
1 green bell pepper, cored, seeded, and thinly sliced
1 large ripe tomato, peeled, seeded, and finely chopped

1 to 2 tablespoons sweet Hungarian paprika
1 cup no-fat sour cream
1 tablespoon tomato paste
¾ to 1 cup Basic Vegetable Stock (page 247)
salt and freshly ground black pepper

1 recipe Basic Polenta (page 143)
a pinch of cayenne pepper

1. Heat the olive oil in a large nonstick frying pan. Add the onion and cook over medium-low heat until it begins to soften, about 3 minutes. Add the garlic and sliced peppers and continue cooking until the vegetables are very soft but not brown, about 8 minutes. Stir in the tomato and cook for 2 minutes. Stir in the paprika and cook for 1 minute.

2. Stir the sour cream, tomato paste, and ¾ cup vegetable stock into the pepper mixture and bring to a boil, stirring gently. Reduce the heat and gently simmer the mixture for 2 minutes, or until thick and richly flavored. Add salt, pepper, cayenne, and additional paprika, if desired, to taste. If the sauce is too thick, thin with a little more vegetable stock.

3. Spoon the pepper mixture over the polenta and serve at once.

Serves 4

346 CALORIES PER SERVING: 9 G PROTEIN; 8 G FAT; 61 G CARBOHYDRATE; 160 MG SODIUM; 0 MG CHOLESTEROL

ANGÚ (BRAZILIAN CORNMEAL MUSH)

Angú (pronounced aing-GOO) is a sort of polenta, one of the many starchy side dishes one finds in Brazil. For the best results, use a fine stone-ground cornmeal. **Note**: *A bird pepper is a tiny, fiery chili found in African, Asian, and Indian markets. Any hot chili will do, though.*

1 tablespoon olive oil
1 onion, finely chopped
2 cloves garlic, minced
1 bird pepper or other hot chili, seeded and minced
1 poblano chili, cored, seeded, and very finely chopped, or ½ green bell pepper
½ red bell pepper, cored, seeded, and very finely chopped

2 cups Basic Vegetable Stock (page 247) or water
9 tablespoons (½ cup plus 1 tablespoon) fine cornmeal
salt and freshly ground black pepper
1 tablespoon cilantro

1. Heat the oil in a large nonstick saucepan. Cook the onion, garlic, chilies, and pepper over medium heat until soft but not brown, 3 to 4 minutes. Add the vegetable stock and bring to a boil.

2. Add the cornmeal in a thin stream through your fingers, whisking vigorously to prevent lumps. Bring the mixture to a boil, then reduce the heat and simmer for 4 to 5 minutes, stirring often. The mixture should be the consistency of soft ice cream.

If too thick, whisk in a little more stock. Stir in the cilantro and correct the seasoning, adding salt and pepper to taste.

Serves 4 to 6

Note: For a pretty presentation, spoon the angú into a tube pan or other fancifully shaped mold oiled with spray oil and let stand for 5 minutes. Invert the mold onto a platter.

124 CALORIES PER SERVING: 2 G PROTEIN; 4 G FAT; 20 G CARBOHYDRATE; 3 MG SODIUM; 0 MG CHOLESTEROL
Analysis based on 4 servings

TAMALES

Tamales are one of the most ancient and universal foods of the New World, enjoyed throughout the Caribbean, Central America, and the American Southwest. Dried corn husks are available at Hispanic markets, gourmet shops, and many supermarkets. You can also use fresh corn husks. This recipe replaces the lard found in traditional Southwestern tamales with puréed fresh corn—a trick that's as tasty as it is nutritious. Corn kernels cut fresh off the cob make the best tamales, but canned or frozen corn works almost as well.

24 fresh or dried corn husks
2 cups yellow or white corn kernels
1 cup masa harina (see note below) or cornmeal
1 to 2 teaspoons sugar or honey (optional, depending on the sweetness of the corn)
salt and freshly ground black pepper
2 to 4 tablespoons skim milk

one or both of the Pinto Bean and Cuban Potato fillings (recipes follow; if using both fillings, make just ½ of each)

FOR COOKING THE TAMALES
2 bay leaves
3 sprigs cilantro or flat-leaf parsley

1. If using fresh corn husks, rinse well. If using dried corn husks, soak in warm water for 1 hour, or until pliable.

2. Purée the corn kernels in a food processor. Blend in the masa harina or cornmeal, sugar (if using), salt and pepper, and enough milk to obtain a moist but firm paste. (It should be the consistency of soft ice cream.) Correct the seasoning, adding salt or sugar to taste. Transfer the corn mixture to a mixing bowl and stir in one of the fillings (see pages 148 and 149).

3. Roll one of the corn husks into a cone, wide end up: It should look like an ice-cream cone. Fold the cone in half, bringing the bottom point flush with the top. Hold the cone open in your left hand (or right hand if you're left-handed). Spoon 3 to 4 tablespoons filling into the cone.

4. Wrap another corn husk around the cone, wide end down. Fold the pointed end down flush with the bottom of the tamale to completely encase the filling. With a 14-inch piece of string, circle the length and width of the tamale, making a neat bundle.

5. Continue making tamales in this manner until all the filling and husks are used up. This will feel a little awkward at first, but by your third or fourth tamale, you'll be a pro.

6. Bring 3 quarts water to a boil in a large pot with the bay leaves and cilantro or parsley and salt and pepper to taste. Add the tamales. Reduce the heat and simmer the tamales, covered, for 1 hour, or until firm.

7. Drain the tamales in a colander and let stand for 3 minutes. Cut the strings. Instruct each guest to open his tamale and eat the filling with a fork. Do not eat the husk.

Makes 12 tamales, enough to serve 6 as an appetizer, 3 or 4 as an entrée

Note: Masa harina is a coarse flour made from cooked dried corn kernels. Look for it at Hispanic markets and in the flour or ethnic food section of most supermarkets. If it's unavailable, use cornmeal, preferably stone-ground. Fresh corn husks can be frozen during corn season for use throughout the year.

NUTRITIONAL INFORMATION LISTED BELOW EACH FILLING.

PINTO BEAN FILLING

Onions and chili powder give this filling a Southwestern flavor. Thanks to the combination of beans and corn, these tamales offer a complete source of protein.

1 tablespoon olive oil
¼ onion, very finely chopped (about ¼ cup)
3 cloves garlic, very finely chopped
1 poblano chili or ½ green bell pepper, cored, seeded, and finely chopped
1 jalapeño chili, seeded and finely chopped (for a spicier filling, leave the seeds in)

1½ cups cooked pinto beans or kidney beans, drained well
2 teaspoons chili powder (or to taste)
½ teaspoon ground cumin
salt and freshly ground black pepper
1 teaspoon fresh lime juice (or to taste)
2 tablespoons finely chopped cilantro

1. Heat the oil in a nonstick frying pan over medium heat. Add the onion, garlic, and chilies and cook for 2 minutes, or until soft but not brown.

2. Stir in the beans, chili powder, cumin, salt, black pepper, lime juice, and cilantro and cook for 2 minutes, or until richly flavored. Correct the seasoning, adding salt, pepper, or lime juice: The mixture should be highly seasoned.

Makes 2 cups, enough to fill 12 tamales

207 CALORIES PER SERVING: 8 G PROTEIN; 3 G FAT; 40 G CARBOHYDRATE; 17 MG SODIUM; 0 MG CHOLESTEROL
Analysis based on a serving of 2 tamales

CUBAN POTATO FILLING

Tamales are just as popular in Cuba as they are in Mexico and the Southwest. This filling features the unmistakable Cuban seasonings of cumin, cilantro, and garlic.

1 tablespoon olive oil
¼ onion, very finely chopped (about ¼ cup)
6 cloves garlic, very finely chopped
½ red bell pepper, cored, seeded, and finely chopped
1 small tomato, peeled, seeded, and diced (about ⅔ cup)

1 large or 2 small potatoes, peeled and cut into ½-inch dice
2 tablespoons finely chopped cilantro
½ teaspoon ground cumin
½ teaspoon dried oregano
salt and freshly ground black pepper

Heat the oil in a nonstick frying pan over medium heat. Add the onion, garlic, and bell pepper and cook for 2 minutes, or until soft but not brown. Stir in the tomato, potato, and cilantro and cook over high heat for 1 minute. Stir in the cumin, oregano, salt, and pepper.

Correct the seasoning, adding salt or cumin to taste: The mixture should be highly seasoned.

Makes 2 cups, enough to fill 12 tamales

180 CALORIES PER SERVING: 5 G PROTEIN; 3 G FAT; 36 G CARBOHYDRATE; 11 MG SODIUM; 0 MG CHOLESTEROL
Analysis based on a serving of 2 tamales

KASHA LOAF WITH MUSHROOMS AND DILL

Kasha (roasted buckwheat groats) isn't technically a grain—it's the seeds of a berry native to Russia. But it's certainly used as a grain, and more and more Americans are discovering its wonderful sweet, nutty, earthy flavor. Kasha can be found at natural foods stores, Jewish markets, and most supermarkets. In the last century, kasha was a mainstay of the Russian and Eastern European Jewish diet.

2 tablespoons extra-virgin olive oil
1 onion, finely chopped
2 cloves garlic, minced
½ green or red bell pepper, finely chopped
12 ounces mushrooms, finely chopped
1½ cups kasha
3 egg whites
1 whole egg (or 1 more white)
5 cups Basic Vegetable Stock (page 247) or water
2 carrots, cut into ½-inch dice

2 stalks celery, cut into ½-inch dice
2 parsnips, cut into ½-inch dice
salt, freshly ground black pepper, and a pinch of cayenne pepper
2 to 3 tablespoons fresh lemon juice (or to taste)
2 tablespoons chopped fresh dill (or 1 tablespoon dried)
1 tablespoon tamari or low-sodium soy sauce

spray oil

1. Heat the olive oil in a large saucepan (preferably nonstick). Add the onion, garlic, and bell pepper and cook over medium heat until soft but not brown, about 5 minutes. Add the mushrooms and increase the heat to high. Cook until the mushrooms are soft and most of the mushroom liquid has evaporated, about 5 minutes.

2. Combine the kasha and 1 egg white in a bowl and stir to mix. Add the kasha to the vegetable mixture. Cook the mixture over high heat for 2 minutes, or until the kasha grains are separate and dry.

3. Stir the vegetable stock, carrots, celery, parsnips, salt, black pepper, and cayenne into the kasha and bring to a boil. Reduce the heat, cover the pan, and gently simmer the kasha until it is tender and all the liquid has been absorbed, about 18 minutes. Stir the mixture occasionally to keep it from sticking on the bottom. Remove the pan from the heat and let the kasha cool.

4. Stir the whole egg and remaining 2 egg whites,

lemon juice, dill, and tamari into the kasha mixture. Correct the seasoning, adding salt, pepper, or lemon juice to taste: The mixture should be highly seasoned. Spray a 9 × 5-inch loaf pan generously with oil and spoon the mixture into the pan. Cover the pan with a lightly oiled piece of foil. Preheat the oven to 350° F.

5. Bake the kasha loaf for 40 to 50 minutes, or until set. (When done, an inserted skewer will come out clean and will feel very hot to the touch.) Remove the loaf from the oven and let cool for 5 minutes. Unmold the loaf onto a cutting board. Cut the kasha loaf into ½-inch slices for serving. An electric knife works best for slicing.

Serves 6 to 8

Note: There are several possibilities for accompaniments here, including "Rust" Sauce (page 199), Barbara's Chunky Tomato Sauce (page 212), Sugo di Pomodoro (page 211), and even dollops of nonfat sour cream.

291 CALORIES PER SERVING: 11 G PROTEIN; 7 G FAT; 51 G CARBOHYDRATE; 238 MG SODIUM; 36 MG CHOLESTEROL

Analysis based on 6 servings

CRUSTY MILLET CAKES WITH FETA CHEESE

For many Americans, millet is for the birds. (Quite literally so—millet is a primary ingredient in bird feed!) I believe there are better ways to use a grain whose fluffy texture and fine nutty flavor have endeared it to cooks throughout Africa and India. There are several possibilities for cheese, including feta, romano, and mizithra (a tangy Greek sheep or goat milk grating cheese). Whichever you use, choose a strong cheese to get the maximum amount of flavor for the fat.

1½ cups millet
salt
1 tablespoon extra-virgin olive oil (or as needed)
2 cloves garlic, minced
4 scallions, finely chopped

½ red bell pepper, diced as finely as possible
½ yellow bell pepper, diced as finely as possible
3 tablespoons finely chopped flat-leaf parsley
2 ounces feta cheese, crumbled (about ¼ cup)
freshly ground black pepper

1. Cook the millet in 8 cups rapidly boiling, lightly salted water for 20 to 30 minutes, or until tender. Drain the grain in a strainer and let cool. Do not rinse.

2. Heat 2 teaspoons olive oil in a nonstick skillet. Add the garlic, scallions, bell peppers, and parsley and cook over medium heat until soft but not brown, about 3 minutes. Combine these vegetables and the millet, cheese, salt, and pepper in a large bowl and mix well. Correct the seasoning, adding salt or pepper to taste.

3. Heat the remaining 1 teaspoon of oil in the skillet. Lightly wet your hands and form 3-inch patties of millet mixture. Cook the patties over medium-low heat for 5 minutes, or until crusty and well browned. Carefully turn the pancakes with a spatula (they're quite fragile) and brown the other side the same way. Add oil as necessary and work in several batches so as not to crowd the pan. Transfer the pancakes to a plate lined with paper towels to drain.

Makes 12 pancakes

Note: Finished millet cakes can be kept warm on a baking sheet in a low oven (300° F.) while you cook the rest, or you can work in 2 nonstick skillets. Barbara's Chunky Tomato Sauce (page 212) would make a nice accompaniment.

120 CALORIES PER SERVING: 4 G PROTEIN; 3 G FAT; 19 G CARBOHYDRATE; 54 MG SODIUM; 4 MG CHOLESTEROL
Analysis based on 1 pancake

QUINOA PILAF

Quinoa is one of my favorite grains. Its softly crunchy consistency and mild nutty flavor make a great change of pace from the usual rice. It's also highly nutritious, being loaded with calcium, phosphorus, and protein. Quinoa can be found at all natural food stores and at many supermarkets.

1 cup quinoa
1 tablespoon extra-virgin olive oil
1 small onion, finely chopped
1 clove garlic, minced (optional)
½ red, yellow, or green bell pepper, cored, seeded, and finely chopped

2 tablespoons pine nuts
2 cups Basic Vegetable Stock (page 247) or water
salt and freshly ground black pepper

1. Place the quinoa in a strainer and rinse with cold water. Drain well.

2. Heat the oil in a large nonstick skillet. Add the onion, garlic (if using), bell pepper, and pine nuts and cook over medium heat until the vegetables are soft but not brown, 3 to 4 minutes. Add the quinoa and cook for 1 minute.

3. Stir in the vegetable stock, salt, and pepper and bring to a boil. Reduce the heat to low (the liquid should gently simmer), cover the pan, and cook until the liquid is absorbed and the quinoa is tender, 15 to 20 minutes. Fluff the quinoa with a fork and correct the seasoning. Serve at once.

Serves 4 as a side dish, 2 as a main course

226 CALORIES PER SERVING: 7 G PROTEIN; 9 G FAT; 32 G CARBOHYDRATE; 10 MG SODIUM; 0 MG CHOLESTEROL
Analysis based on 2 servings

CREOLE-STYLE QUINOA

Here's a recipe inspired by my hometown, Miami. The sauce is characteristic of the cumin-scented enchilados (seafood stews) so beloved by Cubans. The optional addition of black beans gives you complementary proteins.

1 tablespoon extra-virgin olive oil
1 onion, finely chopped
3 cloves garlic, minced
½ red bell pepper, seeded and finely chopped
½ green bell pepper, seeded and finely chopped
1 large ripe tomato, finely chopped
1 teaspoon ground cumin (or to taste)
1 teaspoon dried oregano (or to taste)

1 cup dry white wine
½ cup tomato paste
2 bay leaves
salt and freshly ground black pepper
4 cups cooked quinoa (recipe follows)
1 cup cooked black beans (page 261), optional
¼ cup minced flat-leaf parsley or cilantro

1. Heat the olive oil in a large nonstick frying pan. Add the onion, garlic, and peppers and cook over medium heat for 4 to 5 minutes, or until just beginning to brown.

2. Stir in the tomato, cumin, and oregano and cook for 1 minute. Stir in the wine and bring to a boil. Stir in the tomato paste and bay leaves and gently simmer the sauce until thick and intensely flavored, about 5 minutes, adding salt and plenty of fresh black pepper to taste.

3. Stir in the quinoa, black beans (if using), and half the parsley. Cook over medium heat for 5 minutes, or until thoroughly heated, stirring often. Correct the seasoning, adding salt, cumin, or oregano to taste. Remove and discard the bay leaves. Sprinkle the Creole-Style Quinoa with the remaining parsley and serve at once.

Serves 4

507 CALORIES PER SERVING: 18 G PROTEIN; 9 G FAT; 83 G CARBOHYDRATE; 287 MG SODIUM; 0 MG CHOLESTEROL

TO PREPARE QUINOA

4 cups water
½ teaspoon salt (optional)
2 cups quinoa

1. Bring 4 cups water and the salt (if using) to a boil in a large heavy pot. Stir in the quinoa and bring to a boil.

2. Reduce the heat, cover the pan, and gently simmer the quinoa for 15 to 20 minutes, or until tender. Transfer the quinoa to a mixing bowl and let cool. Fluff the quinoa with a fork.

GRITS CAKES

Grits are revered in the South and reviled just about everywhere else. I've never understood why: They're tasty, nutritious, and versatile. And they're a heck of a lot easier to make than their Italian cousin, polenta. In this recipe, the grits are transformed into crusty pancakes. Barbara's Chunky Tomato Sauce (page 212) would make a great accompaniment.

4 cups Basic Vegetable Stock (page 247) or
    water
1 cup quick-cook grits
1 to 3 cloves garlic, minced

3 tablespoons finely chopped flat-leaf parsley or
    other fresh herbs
salt and freshly ground black pepper
1 tablespoon olive oil

1. Bring the vegetable stock to a boil in a large heavy saucepan (preferably nonstick). Whisk in the grits in a thin stream. Briskly simmer the grits for 3 to 4 minutes, or until thick. Stir in the garlic, parsley, and salt and pepper to taste. Remove the pan from the heat and let the mixture cool to room temperature.

2. Lightly wet your hands and form the grits mixture into 3-inch pancakes.

3. Heat 1 teaspoon oil in a nonstick frying pan. Add the grit cakes and pan-fry over medium-low heat until crusty and golden brown, 3 to 5 minutes per side. As the cakes cook, gently flatten them with the back of a spatula. Work in several batches so as not to crowd the pan. Add oil as necessary to

keep the pancakes from sticking. As the cakes are done, transfer them to paper towels to drain. Already-cooked cakes can be kept warm on a non-stick baking sheet in a 300° F. oven while you cook the rest. Serve at once.

*Makes 8 grits cakes, enough to serve 8 as an appetizer
or side dish, 3 or 4 as a main course*

Note: I like to serve these crusty cakes as a savory dish, but you could easily make grits cakes for breakfast. Prepare the recipe, substituting 2 cups skim milk and 2 cups water for the vegetable stock and 1 tablespoon cinnamon sugar for the garlic, herbs, and pepper. Serve the grits cakes with maple syrup or apple butter.

89 CALORIES PER SERVING: 2 G PROTEIN; 2 G FAT; 16 G CARBOHYDRATE; 0 MG SODIUM; 0 MG CHOLESTEROL

RISOTTO PRIMAVERA

Risotto is the Italian rice dish that thinks it's pasta. The steady stirring of the starchy rice produces a thick creamy sauce with a minimum of fat. For the best results, use Arborio rice from Italy. Valencia-style rice from Spain will work in a pinch. Feel free to vary the vegetables suggested below, depending on what's in season and looks freshest.

2 carrots
2 stalks celery
1 medium zucchini
1 yellow squash
1 cup *haricots verts* (French green beans) or the skinniest regular green beans you can find
5 to 6 cups Basic Vegetable Stock (page 247)
salt and freshly ground black pepper
½ cup peas
1 tablespoon extra-virgin olive oil

1 large leek, trimmed, washed, and very finely chopped (about 1 cup)
½ red or yellow bell pepper, cut into ¼-inch dice
1½ cups Arborio rice
½ cup dry white wine
¼ cup freshly grated Parmigiano-Reggiano cheese
2 tablespoons finely chopped basil or other fresh herbs, plus whole sprigs of basil for garnish

1. Cut the carrots, celery, zucchini, squash, and *haricots verts* into strips 1 inch long and ¼ inch wide. Bring the vegetable stock to a boil in a large saucepan with plenty of salt and pepper. Cook the carrots and celery for 2 minutes or until al dente; the zucchini, squash, green beans, and peas for 1 minute, or until al dente. Transfer all the vegetables with a slotted spoon to a colander. Place ice on top of the vegetables to cool them and drain well. Reserve stock.

2. Heat the oil in a large heavy saucepan (preferably nonstick). Cook the leek and diced pepper over medium heat for 3 to 4 minutes, or until soft but not brown, stirring often. Stir in the rice and cook for 1 minute, or until the grains are shiny.

3. Add the wine and bring to a boil, stirring con-

stantly. When most of the wine is absorbed, stir in ½ cup stock. Cook the rice at a brisk simmer, stirring frequently. When most of the liquid is absorbed, add another ½ cup stock. Continue adding the stock, ½ cup at a time, until 5 cups are used up. Stir in the vegetables the last 3 minutes. If the rice is still too firm after 20 minutes, add ½ to 1 cup more stock. When cooked, the risotto will have a creamy sauce, but the individual grains of rice should still be slightly firm.

4. Remove the pan from the heat and stir in the cheese, chopped basil, and salt and pepper to taste. Serve at once, garnishing each serving with a basil sprig.

Serves 4

426 CALORIES PER SERVING: 11 G PROTEIN; 6 G FAT; 77 G CARBOHYDRATE; 158 MG SODIUM; 5 MG CHOLESTEROL

ASPARAGUS AND BROWN RICE RISOTTO

Green asparagus and red onions give this risotto the pastel hues of springtime. To snap asparagus, grasp the stem end firmly in one hand. Bend the stalk with the other: The asparagus will break at its natural point of tenderness.

1 pound fresh asparagus
7 to 8 cups Basic Vegetable Stock (page 247)
1 tablespoon extra-virgin olive oil
1 red onion, very finely chopped
1 clove garlic, minced
1½ cups brown rice

½ cup dry white wine
¼ to ½ cup freshly grated Parmigiano-Reggiano cheese
2 tablespoons finely chopped flat-leaf parsley
salt and freshly ground black pepper

1. Break the fibrous stem ends off the asparagus stalks. Bring the vegetable stock to a boil in a large saucepan. Reduce the heat and simmer the asparagus stems for 8 to 10 minutes to flavor the stock, then remove them with a skimmer and discard. Keep the stock at a gentle simmer. Cut the asparagus stalks on the diagonal into 2-inch pieces and set aside.

2. Heat the oil in a large heavy saucepan (preferably nonstick). Cook the onion and garlic over medium heat for 3 to 4 minutes, or until soft but not brown, stirring often. Stir in the rice and cook for 1 minute, or until the grains are shiny.

3. Add the wine and bring to a boil, stirring constantly. When most of the wine is absorbed, stir in ½ cup stock. Cook the rice at a gentle boil, stirring frequently. When most of the liquid is absorbed, add another ½ cup stock. Continue adding the stock, ½ cup at a time, until 7 cups are used up. Stir in the asparagus after 30 minutes. If the rice is still too firm after 40 minutes, add ½ to 1 more cup stock, and continue cooking until liquid is absorbed and rice is tender. When cooked, the risotto will have a creamy sauce, but the individual grains of rice should still be slightly firm.

4. Remove the pan from the heat and stir in the cheese and parsley, and salt and pepper to taste. Serve at once.

Serves 4

378 CALORIES PER SERVING: 11 G PROTEIN; 8 G FAT; 62 G CARBOHYDRATE; 128 MG SODIUM; 5 MG CHOLESTEROL

RISOTTO PANCAKES

These crusty pancakes make a case for the superiority of leftovers. The Italian name for this dish is risotto al salto *(loosely translated, "jumping risotto," which is what the pancakes do when you flick the pan). You'll need a little extra olive oil for sautéing. If this takes you over your fat quota, omit the cheese in the basic risotto.*

**a batch of one of the two preceding risottos,
  cooked and cooled to room temperature
1 to 2 tablespoons olive oil**

1. Form 3½-inch patties with the risotto, wetting or lightly oiling your hands if necessary to keep the rice from sticking. You'll need about ½ cup risotto for each pancake.

2. Just before serving, heat 1 to 2 teaspoons of oil in 1 or 2 nonstick skillets. Add the pancakes to the pan(s) without crowding and cook over medium-low heat for 4 to 5 minutes per side, or until crusty and golden brown. As the pancakes cook, gently flatten them with the side of a spatula. Add oil as necessary, but by working in a nonstick pan over a low heat, you shouldn't need too much. As the pancakes are done, transfer them to paper towels to drain. Already-cooked pancakes can be kept warm on a nonstick baking sheet in a 300° F. oven while you cook the rest. Serve at once.

Makes about 12 pancakes, enough to serve 6 as an appetizer or side dish, 4 as a main course

414 CALORIES PER SERVING: 11 G PROTEIN; 9 G FAT; 67 G CARBOHYDRATE; 124 MG SODIUM; 5 MG CHOLESTEROL

Analysis based on 4 servings

BROWN RICE SUSHI

I love sushi. I love its jewel-like appearance, its contrast of textures and flavors, the way it fills you up without leaving you feeling stuffed. Here's an exceptionally healthful version of this Japanese mainstay: vegetable sushi made with nutritious brown rice. Nori (laver seaweed), wasabi (Japanese horseradish), and gari (pickled ginger) can be purchased at Asian markets, natural foods stores, gourmet shops, and many supermarkets, as can a sushi roller, which looks like a miniature bamboo mat. (For a complete discussion of these ingredients, see Cook's Notes and Mail-Order Sources.) **Note:** *This recipe is a little involved, but the results are well worth it.*

FOR THE RICE
3⅓ cups short-grain brown rice
4 cups water
5 to 6 tablespoons rice vinegar
5 tablespoons sugar or honey
4 teaspoons salt

TO FINISH THE SUSHI
10 to 12 dried black mushrooms
3 carrots, peeled and cut lengthwise into ¼-inch strips
1 cucumber, seeded and cut lengthwise into ¼-inch strips
1 red bell pepper, cored, seeded, and cut lengthwise into ¼-inch strips

1 yellow bell pepper, cored, seeded, and cut lengthwise into ¼-inch strips
4 cups spinach leaves, stemmed and washed
6 asparagus spears
salt

3 tablespoons wasabi powder (Japanese horseradish)
1½ tablespoons of hot water
6 sheets of nori seaweed, 7 by 8 inches in size
1 tablespoon black sesame seeds (optional)

FOR THE GARNISH
½ cup gari (Japanese pickled ginger)
½ cup tamari or soy sauce

1. Wash the rice. Place it in a large bowl with water to cover by 2 inches. Swirl the rice with your fingers to wash it. Pour off the water. Continue adding water and swirling the rice until the water comes clean. This may take 6 to 8 washings. Drain the rice well in a colander.

2. Combine the rice and 4 cups water in a large heavy pot with a tight-fitting lid. Bring the rice to a boil. Tightly cover the pot and boil the rice for 2 minutes. Reduce the heat to medium and briskly simmer for 5 minutes. Lower the heat to low and cook the rice for 20 minutes. Remove the pan from the heat and let sit, covered, for 15 minutes.

3. Meanwhile, combine the vinegar, sugar, and 4 teaspoons salt in a small saucepan and heat, stir-ring, until all the sugar is dissolved. Cool this mixture completely.

4. Transfer the rice into a large shallow non-metallic bowl. Sprinkle the rice with the vinegar mixture. Gently stir the rice with a wooden spoon, making a slicing motion, fanning the rice with a fan or paper plate with your other hand to cool it. Do this for 5 to 10 minutes, or until the rice is completely cool.

5. Meanwhile, prepare the vegetables. Soak the mushrooms in hot water to cover for 20 minutes. Discard the stems, blot the caps dry, and cut into ¼-inch slivers. Blanch the carrots, cucumber, bell peppers, spinach, and asparagus separately, in rapidly boiling salted water for 1 minute, or until

crispy-tender. (The spinach will take about 20 seconds.) As they're cooked, transfer the vegetables to a colander with a slotted spoon to drain. Refresh them under cold water and drain. Blot the vegetables dry on paper towels.

6. Mix the wasabi with 1½ tablespoons hot water. Let the mixture stand for 5 minutes.

7. Lay a sheet of nori on a sushi roller or clean dish towel, wide edge toward you. Take about 1 cup rice and spoon it in a row along the center of the nori, parallel to the wide edge. Using your fingertips or the back of a spoon (it helps to moisten whichever you use with a little water), spread the rice out to a thickness of ⅓ inch to cover the seaweed, leaving a 1-inch space at the bottom and top. Smear a little wasabi paste (about ¼ teaspoon) in a lengthwise stripe down the center of the rice. (Reserve any remaining wasabi for garnish.) Arrange an assortment of vegetable strips on top of the rice, alternating color and type.

8. Starting at the edge closest to you and using the sushi roller or dish towel to help you, roll the rectangle into a tight cylinder. Gently squeeze the cylinder with your hands to make a compact roll.

(This gets easier with practice.) Roll up the remaining seaweed, rice, and vegetables the same way. Using a thin, razor-sharp knife, cut each roll widthwise into 6 even slices. Arrange the slices on plates or a platter for serving, and sprinkle with the black sesame seeds (if you are using them).

9. Prepare the garnishes: Drain the pickled ginger and place a little mound on each guest's plate. Pour the soy sauce into tiny bowls, one per guest. Form the remaining wasabi with your fingertips into 6 little pyramids and place one on each plate. To eat the sushi, have each guest dissolve a little wasabi in the soy sauce. (Wasabi is hot stuff, so if you're not used to it, add it sparingly.) Dip the sushi in the soy mixture, then pop it into your mouth. Use the pickled ginger to clear your palate.

*Makes 6 rolls, 36 pieces, which will serve
12 as an appetizer, 6 as a main course*

Note: The rolls can be made up to an hour ahead but will taste best if you roll and cut them just before serving. I turn sushi making into a party, letting the guests help with making the rolls.

252 CALORIES PER SERVING: 7 G PROTEIN; 2 G FAT; 54 G CARBOHYDRATE; 1469 MG SODIUM; 0 MG CHOLESTEROL
Analysis based on 6 servings

WILD RICE TIMBALES

Sometimes, the tastiest recipes are the ones that result from leftovers. Consider these timbales, which are made from puréed cauliflower and wild rice. I like to bake the timbales in popover molds, but you can also use ramekins, muffin tins, or proper timbale molds. (A timbale is a small drum-shaped mold from France.)

1 tablespoon olive oil
1 small onion, finely chopped
3 cloves garlic, minced
2 cups diced cauliflower, plus 6 florets for
   garnish (⅓ to ½ head)
1 cup skim milk
½ teaspoon cumin
salt and freshly ground black pepper

2 egg whites
3 cups cooked Basic Wild Rice (page 259)
3 tablespoons chopped fresh herbs, including
   tarragon, chervil, basil, thyme, and/or chives
a pinch of cayenne pepper

spray oil

1. Preheat the oven to 350° F.

2. Heat the olive oil in a nonstick frying pan. Add the onion and garlic and cook over medium heat until soft but not brown, 3 to 4 minutes.

3. Add cauliflower, milk, cumin, salt, and pepper. Gently simmer the mixture until the cauliflower is very soft, about 10 minutes. Remove the 6 cauliflower florets for garnish, rinse under cold water, and set aside. Let the cauliflower mixture cool slightly, then purée in a food processor. Work in the egg whites. Transfer the mixture to a mixing bowl and stir in the rice and herbs. Correct the seasoning, adding salt, pepper, and cayenne to taste: The mixture should be highly seasoned.

4. Spoon the rice mixture into popover molds,

timbale molds, or ramekins lightly oiled with spray oil. Set the molds in a roasting pan with ½ inch hot water. Bake the timbales for 40 minutes, or until just set. An inserted skewer will come out clean when the timbales are cooked. Remove the timbales from the oven and let cool for 5 minutes.

5. Place a baking sheet over the timbales and invert the mold(s) onto it. The timbales should slide out easily. If they don't, give the mold a little shake. Use a spatula to transfer the timbales to plates. As an accompaniment you could serve Barbara's Chunky Tomato Sauce (page 212), or "Rust" Sauce (page 199).

Makes six 2 × 3-inch timbales, enough to serve 6 as an appetizer or side dish, 3 as an entrée

140 CALORIES PER SERVING: 7 G PROTEIN; 3 G FAT; 23 G CARBOHYDRATE; 48 MG SODIUM; 1 MG CHOLESTEROL

Analysis based on 6 servings

THREE FRIED RICES

Like french toast and hash, fried rice offers irrefutable proof of the virtue of leftovers. When most people think of fried rice, they have a Chinese incarnation in mind. Here's how this Asian favorite might be prepared in other parts of the world.

CARIBBEAN FRIED RICE

Fried rice turns up at a surprising number of Cuban restaurants. The reason is simple, explains Sonia Zaldivar, owner of Miami's celebrated Victor's Cafe: Cuba had a large influx of Chinese railroad workers at the end of the nineteenth century. The following recipe uses Victor's version as a starting point.

1½ to 2 tablespoons Spanish olive oil
2 cloves garlic, minced
2 teaspoons minced ginger
3 scallions, minced
½ Scotch bonnet or 1 jalapeño chili, seeded and minced (for a spicier dish, leave the seeds in)
½ green bell pepper, cut into ¼-inch dice
½ red bell pepper, cut into ¼-inch dice
1 carrot, cut into ¼-inch dice

1 celery stalk, cut into ¼-inch dice
¼ cup snow peas, strings removed
3 to 4 cups cooked white rice (preferably Uncle Ben's)
½ cup cooked black beans (optional)
½ cup cooked corn kernels (optional)
1 cup mung bean sprouts
1 tablespoon capers, drained
2 tablespoons soy sauce (or to taste)

1. Just before serving, heat a wok or large non-stick frying pan over a high flame. Swirl in the oil. Add the minced garlic, ginger, scallions, and chili. Stir-fry these ingredients for 15 seconds, or until fragrant but not brown.

2. Add the peppers, carrot, celery, and snow peas and stir-fry for 1 to 2 minutes, or until crispy-tender. Stir in the rice, beans and corn (if using), bean sprouts, and capers and stir-fry for 2 minutes, or until the ingredients are thoroughly heated. Stir in soy sauce to taste and serve.

Serves 6 as a side dish, 4 as a main course

285 CALORIES PER SERVING: 6 G PROTEIN; 6 G FAT; 52 G CARBOHYDRATE; 597 MG SODIUM; 0 MG CHOLESTEROL
Analysis based on 4 servings

THAI FRIED RICE

Fried rice gets a Thai twist at the restaurant Panawan in Mai Sariang in northern Thailand. Lemongrass is discussed in full in Cook's Notes. If unavailable, use 1 teaspoon freshly grated lemon zest.

FOR THE SAUCE
1½ to 2 tablespoons soy sauce
1½ tablespoons lime juice
2 teaspoons sugar or honey (or to taste)
1 to 2 teaspoons Thai hot sauce (or to taste)

1½ to 2 tablespoons canola oil
2 to 3 cloves garlic, minced
2 teaspoons ginger, minced
2 scallions, minced

1 stalk trimmed, minced fresh lemongrass (about 1 tablespoon)
1 carrot, sliced as thinly as possible
½ red bell pepper, cut into 1-inch pieces
1 cup napa or other Asian cabbage, thinly sliced
1 cup collard greens, cut into 1-inch pieces
3 to 4 cups cooked white rice (preferably Uncle Ben's)
1 cup mung bean sprouts
½ cup chopped fresh mint or cilantro

1. For the sauce, combine the soy sauce, lime juice, sugar, and hot sauce in a small bowl and stir to mix.

2. Just before serving, heat a wok or large nonstick frying pan over a high flame. Swirl in the oil. Add the garlic, ginger, scallions, and lemongrass. Stir-fry these ingredients for 15 seconds, or until fragrant but not brown. Add the carrot, bell pepper, napa, and collard greens and stir-fry for 1 to 2 minutes, or until crispy-tender.

3. Stir in the rice and bean sprouts and stir-fry for 2 minutes, or until the ingredients are thoroughly heated. Stir in the sauce and half the mint and cook for 30 seconds. Correct the seasoning, adding soy sauce or lime juice to taste. Sprinkle the remaining mint on top and serve at once.

Serves 6 as a side dish, 4 as a main course

285 CALORIES PER SERVING: 6 G PROTEIN; 6 G FAT; 52 G CARBOHYDRATE; 411 MG SODIUM; 0 MG CHOLESTEROL

Analysis based on 4 servings

MEDITERRANEAN FRIED RICE

Fried rice doesn't belong to the traditional Mediterranean repertory, but there's no reason you couldn't make it with such local ingredients as basil, pine nuts, and dried tomatoes. If using store-bought dried tomatoes, soak them in hot water for 15 minutes, or until soft.

FOR THE SAUCE
2 tablespoons lemon juice
2 teaspoons tomato paste
¼ teaspoon saffron soaked in 1 tablespoon warm Basic Vegetable Stock (page 247) or water for 15 minutes
salt and freshly ground black pepper

1½ to 2 tablespoons extra-virgin olive oil
2 to 3 cloves garlic, minced

1 leek, trimmed, washed, and finely chopped
¼ cup thinly sliced fennel or celery
3 to 4 cups cooked white rice
1 tomato, seeded and diced
¼ cup chickpeas
2 tablespoons lightly toasted pine nuts
8 black olives (preferably oil-cured)
3 dried tomatoes, cut into thin slices
1 bunch basil, stemmed

1. For the sauce, combine the lemon juice, tomato paste, saffron, salt, and pepper in a small bowl and whisk until smooth. Add plenty of salt and pepper: The mixture should be highly seasoned.

2. Just before serving, heat a wok or large non-stick frying pan over a high flame. Swirl in the oil. Add the garlic and leek and stir-fry for 15 seconds, or until fragrant but not brown. Add the fennel and stir-fry for 1 to 2 minutes, or until the fennel is tender.

3. Stir in the rice, tomato, chickpeas, pine nuts, olives, and dried tomatoes, and most of the basil. Stir-fry for 2 minutes, or until the ingredients are thoroughly heated. Stir in the sauce and cook for 30 seconds. Correct the seasoning, adding salt or lemon juice to taste. Decorate the rice with the remaining basil leaves and serve at once.

Serves 6 as a side dish, 4 as a main course

326 CALORIES PER SERVING: 8 G PROTEIN; 10 G FAT; 54 G CARBOHYDRATE; 125 MG SODIUM; 0 MG CHOLESTEROL

Analysis based on 4 servings

BEAN DISHES

SMOKY BAKED BEANS

Baked beans and brown bread were eaten by untold generations of New Englanders for Saturday-night supper. Fakin' Bacon, smoke-flavored tempeh (a cultured soybean product—see Cook's Notes), gives my vegetarian version the smoky flavor traditionally provided by bacon and salt pork. Fakin' Bacon can be found at most natural foods stores, or you can substitute another smoked soy food. But equally important is the rich caramel flavor that comes from lengthily baking the beans in a bean pot or heavy crock.

2 cups pea beans or navy beans (1 14-ounce bag)
12 cups water
4 slices smoked tempeh or tofu, cut into ¼-inch slivers
½ cup dark brown sugar, or to taste
⅔ cup ketchup

⅓ cup dark molasses
¼ cup cider vinegar
1 whole onion, finely chopped
2 cloves garlic, minced
2 teaspoons dry mustard
salt and freshly ground black pepper

1. Pick through the beans and rinse in a strainer. Soak the beans in 8 cups cold water in a mixing bowl for at least 4 hours, preferably overnight.

2. Drain the beans. Place the beans in a large pot with 12 cups of water. Boil the beans, covered, for 1 hour, or until the skins split and the beans are semisoft. Add water as necessary. Preheat the oven to 325° F.

3. Spoon the beans into a bean pot or crock with enough cooking liquid to cover by ½ inch. Stir in the tempeh, brown sugar, ketchup, molasses, vinegar, onion, garlic, mustard, salt, and pepper. Cover the crock and bake for 3 hours, or until beans are tender. Uncover the pot and continue cooking the beans for 30 to 60 minutes, or until the liquid has evaporated and the sauce is thick and syrupy. Correct the seasoning, adding salt or brown sugar to taste.

Serves 4

511 CALORIES PER SERVING: 21 G PROTEIN; 2.6 G FAT; 107 G CARBOHYDRATE; 404 MG SODIUM; 0 MG CHOLESTEROL

BLACK BEAN BURRITOS
WITH GRILLED TOMATO PICO DE GALLO

Burritos are the Tex-Mex equivalent of blintzes. My version features a spicy black-bean filling and
a smoky salsa made from fire-roasted tomatoes. For a dramatic presentation, the tortillas are rolled with the filling,
then sliced widthwise. What results are stunning black and white spiraled rolls.
And we've omitted the traditional deep-fat frying.

1 to 2 chipotle chilies (see Cook's Notes) or
 other hot peppers
1½ tablespoons olive oil
1 large onion, finely chopped (1½ cups chopped)
3 cloves garlic, minced
1 teaspoon ground cumin (or to taste)
1 teaspoon dried oregano (or to taste)
2 to 3 tablespoons white wine or bean cooking
 liquid

4 teaspoons red wine vinegar, or to taste
1 tablespoon tomato paste
salt and freshly ground black pepper
3½ cups cooked black beans (page 261)

FOR SERVING
4 10-inch flour tortillas
Charred Tomato Pico de Gallo (page 203)
2 tablespoons no-fat sour cream (or to taste)

1. If using dried chipotles, soak in warm water for 30 minutes, or until soft, and then drain. Stem and seed the chilies. (For hotter burritos, leave the seeds in.) If using canned chipotles, finely chop.

2. Heat the olive oil in a large nonstick frying pan. Add the onion, garlic, chipotle, cumin, and oregano and cook over medium heat for 4 to 5 minutes, or until golden brown. Stir in the wine, vinegar, tomato paste, salt, pepper, and beans. Cook for 5 to 10 minutes, or until the beans are very soft. Transfer half the beans to a bowl. Mash the remaining beans with a potato masher or pestle. Stir the whole beans into the mashed. Correct the seasoning, adding salt or vinegar to taste. Preheat the oven to 400° F.

3. Warm the tortillas on a baking sheet in the oven until soft and pliable, 1 to 2 minutes. (They can also be warmed in the microwave.)

4. Lay the warmed tortillas flat on a work surface. Spread each with a ⅓-inch layer of bean mixture (about 1 cup). Roll the tortillas up tight to make thick tubes. Using a very sharp knife, cut each roll widthwise into 1-inch pieces. Stand the pieces on end and arrange on plates or a large platter, leaving room in the center. Place small bowls or ramekins of the Charred Tomato Pico de Gallo in the center and top with dollops of no-fat sour cream.

Serves 6 to 8 as an appetizer, 4 as an entrée

Note: Chipotles aren't as hot as, say, Scotch bonnet chilies, but they will send most people lunging for a drink. If you're not accustomed to spicy food, you may wish to use ½ to 1. If you use canned beans, you'll need two 1-pound cans.

638 CALORIES PER SERVING: 29 G PROTEIN; 12.5 G FAT; 102.5 G CARBOHYDRATE; 82.5 MG SODIUM; 0 MG CHOLESTEROL

Analysis based on 4 servings

FAVA BEAN GRATIN

I first tasted this dish in the whitewashed hilltop town of Ostuni in Apulia in southern Italy at a restaurant called Spessite. It was so rich, I was sure it contained butter or bacon fat. Imagine my surprise to learn that it was a low-fat dish, made with fava beans, bean broth, and a whisper of extra-virgin olive oil. For the diced bread, use a country- or Italian-style white bread and cut it into ½-inch cubes.

4 cups cooked fava beans or small lima beans (recipe follows), along with ½ to 1 cup bean-cooking liquid or Basic Vegetable Stock (page 247)
2 to 3 tablespoons extra-virgin olive oil
1 large onion, finely chopped
2 cloves garlic, finely chopped
2 carrots, finely diced

2 stalks celery, finely diced
salt and freshly ground black pepper
½ cup chopped flat-leaf parsley
2 cups diced bread cubes (½-inch dice), toasted in the oven until crisp
spray oil
½ cup fresh bread crumbs

1. Drain the beans and let cool, reserving the cooking liquid (or use drained canned beans). Coarsely purée the beans in the food processor or mash in a mortar and pestle.

2. Heat 1½ tablespoons olive oil in a nonstick frying pan. Add the onion, garlic, carrots, celery, salt, and pepper and cook over medium heat until just beginning to brown, about 5 minutes. Stir in the parsley, the puréed beans, and enough bean cooking liquid or vegetable stock to obtain a light fluffy purée (you may need more than 1 cup, depending on how fresh the beans are). Stir in the diced bread. Correct the seasoning, adding salt and pepper to taste: The mixture should be highly seasoned. Preheat the oven to 400° F.

3. Spoon the fava bean mixture into an 8 × 12-inch baking or gratin dish lightly greased with spray oil. Combine the bread crumbs with the remaining oil in a small bowl and stir to mix. Spread the crumb mixture atop the gratin. Bake the gratin for 15 to 20 minutes, or until the top is crusty and brown. Alternatively, you can brown the crust under the broiler.

Serves 8 as an appetizer or side dish

193 CALORIES PER SERVING: 9 G PROTEIN; 4 G FAT; 31 G CARBOHYDRATE; 71 MG SODIUM; 0 MG CHOLESTEROL

To Cook Fava Beans

1¾ cups dried fava beans or small lima beans
1 bay leaf
1 small onion, peeled

1 clove
12 cups water
salt

1. Spread the beans on a baking sheet and pick through them, removing any pebbles. Rinse the beans in a colander. Soak the beans for at least 4 hours, preferably overnight, in 8 cups water in a large bowl.

2. Drain the beans. Pin the bay leaf to the onion with a clove. Place the beans and onion in a large heavy pot with 12 cups water. Bring the beans to a boil, reduce the heat, loosely cover the pot, and simmer for 1½ hours, or until the beans are soft. Add water as necessary to keep the beans submerged. Add salt to taste the last 5 minutes. **Note:** The cooking time can be shortened to about 30 to 40 minutes in a pressure cooker.

ELECTRIC CHILI

Electrifying is the best way to describe this vegetarian chili, which is ignited with chipotles (smoked jalapeño) chilies. Chipotles are available both canned and dried at Hispanic markets and gourmet shops. (If using canned chipotles, you don't need to soak them.) Chipotles don't come close to being the world's hottest chilies, but they do pack a wallop. If you're not used to spicy food, you may wish to use only one. You could further diminish the heat by using green bell peppers instead of poblanos. **Note**: *This recipe makes a perfectly tasty chili without the chipotles, but it won't be electric.*

1 to 3 chipotle chilies (see Cook's Notes)
2 tablespoons olive oil
1 large onion, finely chopped
1 carrot, very finely chopped
1 stalk celery, very finely chopped
4 cloves garlic, very finely chopped
2 poblano chilies or 1 large green bell pepper,
    cored, seeded, and finely chopped
1 cup corn kernels
1½ tablespoons mild chili powder
1 tablespoon ground cumin
1 tablespoon dried oregano
1 teaspoon ground bay leaf or 2 whole bay leaves

1½ cups beer
1 28-ounce can peeled tomatoes, puréed with
    their juices
1 tablespoon Pickapeppa sauce or vegetarian
    Worcestershire-style sauce
1 teaspoon Tabasco (optional)
2 teaspoons wine vinegar (or to taste)
5 cups cooked beans—a mixture of black, pinto,
    and kidney beans (page 261)
salt and freshly ground black pepper
2 tablespoons coarse yellow cornmeal
½ cup no-fat sour cream for garnish
½ cup chopped scallion greens for garnish

1. If using dried chipotles, stem, split, and seed the chilies and soak in ½ cup hot water for 15 minutes. Drain and finely chop the chipotles, reserving the soaking liquid. If using canned chipotles, finely chop.

2. Heat the olive oil in a large heavy pot. Add the chopped onion, carrot, celery, garlic, and poblano chilies and brown over medium heat. (This will take 5 to 6 minutes.)

3. Stir in the corn, chili powder, cumin, oregano, bay leaf, beer, tomato pulp, Pickapeppa sauce, Tabasco (if using), vinegar, beans, chipotles with their soaking liquid, salt, and pepper. Briskly simmer the chili, uncovered, for 20 minutes, or until most

of cooking liquid has been absorbed by the beans and the chili is well flavored.

4. Stir in the cornmeal in a thin stream to thicken the chili and cook for 1 minute. The chili can be prepared up to 3 days ahead to this stage and reheated. Indeed, its flavor will improve with age.

5. Just before serving, remove the bay leaves (if using). Correct the seasoning, adding salt, chili powder, or vinegar to taste. The chili should be highly seasoned. Ladle the chili into bowls and garnish each with a dollop of sour cream and a sprinkling of chopped scallions.

Serves 6

363 CALORIES PER SERVING: 17 G PROTEIN; 7 G FAT; 59 G CARBOHYDRATE; 398 MG SODIUM; 0 MG CHOLESTEROL

CHICKPEA VINDALOO

Have you ever noticed how food gets hotter the closer you get to the equator? Consider this vindaloo, a fiery curry from southern India. I like to serve it over Basic Basmati Rice (page 260) with dollops of yogurt and sprigs of cilantro.

1 tablespoon olive oil
1 medium onion, thinly sliced
2 teaspoons minced fresh ginger
2 cloves garlic, minced
1 teaspoon ground cumin
1 teaspoon ground turmeric
1 cinnamon stick
2 green cardamom pods
1 bay leaf
¼ to ½ teaspoon cayenne pepper, or as much as
   you can bear

2 cups thinly sliced mushrooms
2 ripe tomatoes, peeled, seeded, and chopped
   (about 1½ cups)
3 to 4 tablespoons wine vinegar or cider vinegar
2 cups cooked chickpeas (page 261)
2 potatoes, peeled and diced (about 2 cups)
2 to 3 cups Basic Vegetable Stock (page 247)
   or water
1 tablespoon tomato paste
½ cup nonfat yogurt
salt and freshly ground black pepper

1. Heat the oil in a large sauté pan. Cook the onion over medium heat for 2 minutes. Stir in the ginger, garlic, cumin, turmeric, cinnamon stick, cardamom pods, bay leaf, and cayenne and cook for 2 to 3 minutes longer, or until the onion is very soft.

2. Increase the heat to high and stir in the mushrooms and tomatoes. Cook for 2 to 3 minutes, or until most of the mushroom liquid has evaporated. Stir in the vinegar and bring to a boil.

3. Stir in the chickpeas, the potatoes, 2 cups vegetable stock, the tomato paste, the yogurt, the salt, and the pepper. Simmer the vindaloo for 10 minutes, or until the potatoes and chickpeas are tender. Add stock as necessary to keep the stew moist. Just before serving, correct the seasoning, adding vinegar, salt, or cayenne. Vindaloo should be very highly seasoned.

Serves 4

234 CALORIES PER SERVING: 9 G PROTEIN; 6 G FAT; 40 G CARBOHYDRATE; 409 MG SODIUM; 1 MG CHOLESTEROL

RED-COOKED BEANS

Red-cooking is a method associated with eastern China, where all sorts of foods are braised in a pungent mixture of soy sauce, rice wine, and star anise. (The last is a star-shaped spice with a smoky licoricy flavor—look for it in Asian markets.) This recipe can be prepared with any type of bean: I like to use pea beans or navy beans.

FOR THE GLAZE
1 cup Chinese rice wine or sherry
1 cup water
3 to 4 tablespoons soy sauce
¼ cup light brown sugar
2 star anises
1 cinnamon stick
3 pieces of dried tangerine peel (available in Asian markets) or 2 strips fresh tangerine or orange peel
2 cloves garlic, peeled
2 ¼-inch-thick slices fresh ginger
3 scallions, trimmed and finely chopped

2½ cups cooked beans (recipe follows)

1. For the glaze, combine the rice wine, water, soy sauce, brown sugar, star anises, cinnamon stick, peel, garlic, ginger, and scallions in a large heavy saucepan and bring to a boil. Boil the mixture until thick, glazy, and reduced to about ½ cup. This will take about 10 minutes. Stir the mixture occasionally as it cooks to keep it from boiling over.

2. Strain the mixture into a large nonstick frying pan and add the beans. Cook the beans over medium heat until thickly coated with glaze, 3 to 5 minutes. Correct the seasoning, adding soy sauce or sugar as needed: The beans should be sweet, salty, and aromatic.

Makes 2 ½ cups or 4 servings

Note: Red-cooked beans are delicious by themselves or over rice. They're also the filling for Peking Tacos (page 175).

261 CALORIES PER SERVING: 11 G PROTEIN; 1 G FAT; 45 G CARBOHYDRATE; 783 MG SODIUM; 0 MG CHOLESTEROL
Analysis based on 4 servings

To Cook Pea Beans or Navy Beans

1 cup dried pea beans or navy beans
1 bay leaf
1 small onion, peeled

1 clove
12 cups water
salt

1. Spread the beans on a baking sheet and pick through them, removing any pebbles. Rinse the beans in a colander. Soak them for at least 4 hours, preferably overnight, in 8 cups water in a large bowl.

2. Drain the beans. Pin the bay leaf to the onion with a clove. Place the beans and onion in a large heavy pot with 12 cups water. Bring the beans to a boil, reduce the heat, loosely cover the pot, and simmer 1 hour, or until the beans are soft. Add water as necessary to keep the beans submerged. Add salt to taste the last 5 minutes. **Note:** The cooking time can be shortened to about 20 minutes in a pressure cooker.

PEKING TACOS

Peking duck is one of the glories of Chinese gastronomy. Here's a vegetarian version, made with beans that are braised in an aromatic mixture of soy sauce, rice wine, and star anise. Bean sprouts, cucumber, and scallion brushes provide the crunch traditionally achieved by crisp shards of duck skin. Flour tortillas give this recipe a Mexican touch and save time to boot, but a purist could make mandarin pancakes from scratch, following a recipe in a Chinese cookbook, like Barbara Tropp's China Moon *(Workman Publishing, 1991).*

10 6-inch flour tortillas
2 cups mung bean sprouts
10 thick scallions
1 cucumber, peeled, seeded, and cut into 2-inch matchsticks

2½ cups Red-Cooked Beans (page 172)
½ cup hoisin sauce (see note on page 266)

1. Heat the tortillas until soft and pliable. To do so, bake them on baking sheets in a 400° F. oven for 1 to 2 minutes, or grill for 30 seconds per side, or cook in a nonstick frying pan for 30 seconds per side, or steam briefly in a steamer. Place the warm tortillas in a covered dish.

2. Place the bean sprouts in a strainer. Pour boiling water over them and drain well.

3. Make scallion brushes: Trim the roots and green parts off the thickest scallions you can find. You should be left with a white section 2½ inches long. Make a series of ½-inch-long lengthwise cuts in each end, rotating the scallion as you go to make cuts every ⅛ inch. Place the cut scallions in a bowl of ice water for 30 minutes. The cut ends will swell to look like brushes.

4. Arrange the bean sprouts, scallion brushes, cucumber, and beans in piles on a platter or in individual bowls. Place the hoisin sauce in a bowl.

5. To make the Peking Tacos, have each guest take a tortilla and brush it with hoisin sauce, using a scallion brush. Place a spoonful of red beans inside and top with some cucumber, some bean sprouts, and a scallion brush. Fold the tortilla into a cone or like an egg roll. Eat as you would a taco.

Makes 10, enough to serve 4 or 5

Note: There are two ways to serve this dish. You can use the do-it-yourself approach, letting each guest make his own taco. Or, for a dramatic presentation, you can make the tacos ahead of time, tying them with scallion greens, as pictured on page 174.

320 CALORIES PER SERVING: 10 G PROTEIN; 4 G FAT; 61 G CARBOHYDRATE; 298 MG SODIUM; 0 MG CHOLESTEROL

Analysis based on 4 servings

THREE BEAN GUMBO

Gumbo is one of the glories of Louisianian cooking. I've greatly reduced the amount of oil in the recipe, but thanks to the generous amount of spices and seasonings, I don't think you'll miss it. Gumbo, by the way, takes its name from an Afro-Caribbean word for okra. This finger-shaped vegetable serves as a thickener, as does another typical Louisianian ingredient, filé powder (ground sassafras leaves). Liquid Smoke adds a smoky flavor achieved in traditional recipes with tasso ham or andouille sausage. Alternatively, you could add a smoked tofu or tempeh product. Feel free to vary the type of beans.

3 tablespoons canola oil
¼ cup flour
3 onions, finely chopped (2½ to 3 cups)
4 stalks celery, finely chopped
2 green bell peppers, cored, seeded, and finely chopped
1 red bell pepper, cored, seeded, and finely chopped
5 cloves garlic, chopped
6 cups Basic Vegetable Stock (page 247)
1 cup cooked black beans
1 cup cooked red beans
1 cup cooked black-eyed peas
1 cup corn kernels
¼ cup chopped flat-leaf parsley
1 tablespoon Cajun seasoning

1 teaspoon sweet paprika
½ teaspoon dried thyme
½ teaspoon cumin
2 bay leaves
1 tablespoon Pickapeppa sauce or vegetarian Worcestershire sauce
1 teaspoon Tabasco or other hot sauce (or to taste)
¼ teaspoon Liquid Smoke (optional)
salt, freshly ground black pepper, and a pinch of cayenne pepper
10 ounces fresh okra, cut widthwise into ½-inch slices (about 3 cups)
1 tablespoon filé powder, which is sometimes sold as "filé gumbo" (optional)

1. Prepare the roux. Place the oil and flour in a large heavy saucepan (preferably nonstick and at least 3-quart capacity) over medium heat. Have all the chopped vegetables handy. Cook the roux, whisking constantly, for 2 to 3 minutes, or until it is dark golden brown. Whisk continuously to prevent the roux from burning.

2. Lower the heat and stir in the onions, celery, bell peppers, and garlic. Cook over low heat for 5 to 6 minutes, or until the vegetables are lightly browned, stirring often.

3. Stir in the vegetable stock little by little and bring to a boil. Stir in the black and red beans,

black-eyed peas, corn, parsley, Cajun seasoning, paprika, thyme, cumin, bay leaves, Pickapeppa sauce, Tabasco, Liquid Smoke (if using), salt, black pepper, and cayenne. Simmer the gumbo for 10 to 15 minutes, or until well flavored. Stir in the okra and cook for 3 minutes.

4. Just before serving, stir in the filé powder. Simmer the gumbo for 1 minute. Correct the seasoning, adding salt, hot sauce, and Cajun seasoning to taste: The mixture should be highly seasoned. Serve the gumbo over rice (see Basic Rice recipe, page 258) in soup dishes or large plates.

Serves 8

Note: For a pretty presentation, pack the rice into custard cups or coffee cups sprayed with oil. Invert the rice into a shallow bowl: You should wind up with a neat dome. Ladle the gumbo around the rice and serve at once.

208 CALORIES PER SERVING: 8 G PROTEIN; 6 G FAT; 34 G CARBOHYDRATE; 119 MG SODIUM; 0 MG CHOLESTEROL

Rice not included in serving analysis

CARIBBEAN BEAN BOUILLABAISSE

This richly flavored Caribbean bean stew is easy to make, but you need to know about some special ingredients. Pigeon peas (sometimes called gunga peas) are small oval Caribbean beans with a nutty, earthy flavor. Look for them dried or canned at Hispanic and Caribbean markets. If unavailable, substitute black-eyed peas, navy beans, or any other type of cooked bean. The Scotch bonnet is the world's hottest chili, so use sparingly. Coconut milk is used as a dairy product throughout the tropics. It's normally high in fat, but the Taste of Thai company makes a "lite" coconut milk that contains only 1.5 grams of fat per ounce. (If this is still too much fat, you can omit the coconut milk and increase the vegetable stock accordingly.) Serve this stew over rice or couscous.

3 cups cooked pigeon peas (page 261)
2 medium potatoes, peeled and cut into 1-inch
  pieces
salt
1 tablespoon olive oil
1 small onion, finely chopped
3 cloves garlic, minced
2 teaspoons ginger, finely chopped
½ Scotch bonnet chili or other hot chili, seeded
  and minced
1 small red bell pepper, cored, seeded, and finely
  chopped

1 teaspoon curry powder
1 teaspoon chili powder
½ teaspoon ground cumin
1 tomato, seeded and thinly sliced
3 tablespoons tomato paste
approximately 1 cup Basic Vegetable Stock
  (page 247)
½ cup "lite" coconut milk (or more vegetable
  stock)
¼ cup finely chopped cilantro or flat-leaf parsley
freshly ground black pepper and a pinch of
  cayenne pepper

1. If using canned pigeon peas, drain well. Place the potatoes in a large saucepan with 6 cups cold salted water. Bring the potatoes to a boil, reduce the heat to medium, and simmer for 8 to 10 minutes, or until tender. (If cooking the beans from scratch, you can cook the potatoes in the same water.) Drain the potatoes and set aside.

2. Heat the oil in a large skillet. Add the onion, garlic, ginger, chili, and bell pepper. Cook over medium heat for 4 to 5 minutes, or until just beginning to brown. Stir in the curry powder, chili powder, and cumin after 3 minutes. Add the tomato and cook for 1 minute. Stir in the tomato paste, vegetable stock, coconut milk, and half the cilantro. Bring the sauce to a boil.

3. Stir in the pigeon peas and potatoes and simmer the stew over medium heat until thickened and richly flavored, about 10 minutes. Correct the seasoning, adding salt, cumin, curry powder, black pepper, and cayenne to taste. The sauce should be highly seasoned. Sprinkle the stew with the remaining cilantro and serve at once.

Serves 4

270 CALORIES PER SERVING: 7 G PROTEIN; 6 G FAT; 49 G CARBOHYDRATE; 123 MG SODIUM; 0 MG CHOLESTEROL

LENTIL MUSHROOM BURGERS

Lentils and mushrooms give these vegetarian "burgers" a rich, earthy flavor that's almost reminiscent of beef.
The recipe comes from a terrific cook from Boston, my assistant Didi Emmons.

⅔ cup lentils, picked through and rinsed
1 medium potato, peeled and cut into ½-inch
   dice
1½ to 2 tablespoons extra-virgin olive oil
1 small onion, finely chopped
2 tablespoons finely chopped red bell pepper
2 carrots, finely chopped (about ½ cup)

1 clove garlic, minced
8 ounces fresh mushrooms, thinly sliced (about
   2 cups)
salt and freshly ground black pepper
1 egg white
3 tablespoons finely chopped fresh cilantro or dill
2 cups fresh bread crumbs (or as needed)

1. Cook the lentils in 5 cups boiling water until tender, 20 to 30 minutes. Add the potatoes the last 10 minutes and cook until soft. Drain the lentils and potatoes in a colander and let cool.

2. Meanwhile, heat 1 tablespoon olive oil in a nonstick frying pan. Add the onion, bell pepper, carrots, and garlic and cook over medium heat until soft, about 3 minutes. Stir in the mushrooms and cook until most of the mushroom liquid has evaporated, about 5 minutes. Season the mixture with salt and pepper to taste.

3. Combine the lentils, potatoes, mushroom mixture, and egg white in a food processor and coarsely purée. Grind in the cilantro and enough bread crumbs to obtain a very stiff paste. Correct

the seasoning, adding salt and pepper to taste. Wet your hands and form the mixture into eight 3-inch patties. Place the patties on a lightly oiled plate and chill for at least 2 hours.

4. Heat 1½ teaspoons oil in large nonstick frying pan. Cook the burgers over medium heat until crusty and golden brown, 3 to 5 minutes per side. Work in 2 batches if necessary to avoid crowding the pan. Add oil as necessary. To reduce the fat further, you could broil the burgers. (Brush with a little oil before broiling.)

5. Serve the burgers as is or on rolls with sliced tomatoes and lettuce.

Makes eight to ten 3-inch burgers,
enough to serve 4 to 8

278 CALORIES PER SERVING: 13 G PROTEIN; 7 G FAT; 43 G CARBOHYDRATE; 140 MG SODIUM; 0 MG CHOLESTEROL
Analysis based on 4 servings

CHICKPEA BURGERS

These burgers were inspired by dishes from two continents. Chickpea stew is a traditional Cuban farm dish. Falafel (chickpea fritters) is a popular Middle East snack. The unifying element is cumin, which both cultures use with gusto.
Note: *To make a very tasty chickpea stew, prepare the recipe through step 3.*

3 cups cooked chickpeas (page 261)
2 medium potatoes, peeled and cut into 1-inch
  pieces
salt
1 tablespoon olive oil
1 small onion, finely chopped
1 small red bell pepper, cored, seeded, and finely
  chopped
3 cloves garlic, minced
1 tomato, seeded and thinly sliced
3 tablespoons tomato paste

½ teaspoon ground cumin
2 tablespoons finely chopped flat-leaf parsley
freshly ground black pepper and a pinch of
  cayenne
2 to 4 tablespoons fine, dry bread crumbs

spray oil or olive oil for cooking the burgers
hamburger buns
sliced onion
sliced tomato
lettuce leaves

1. If using canned chickpeas, drain well. Place the potatoes in a large saucepan with 6 cups cold salted water. Bring the potatoes to a boil, reduce the heat to medium, and simmer for 8 to 10 minutes, or until tender. (If cooking the beans from scratch, you can cook the potatoes in the same water.) Drain the potatoes and set aside.

2. Heat the oil in a large skillet. Add the onion, bell pepper, and garlic and cook over medium heat for 3 to 4 minutes, or until just beginning to brown. Add the tomato and cook for 1 minute. Stir in the tomato paste, cumin, and parsley and simmer for 2 minutes.

3. Stir the chickpeas and potatoes into the tomato mixture. Gently simmer the stew over medium heat for 5 minutes, or until well flavored. Correct the seasoning, adding salt, pepper, cayenne, and cumin to taste. At this stage, the mixture can be served as a stew over rice or couscous. For burgers, let it cool to room temperature.

4. Coarsely purée the chickpea mixture in a food processor, adding bread crumbs if necessary to obtain a stiff paste. Wet your hands and form the mixture into eight 3-inch patties. Place the patties on a lightly oiled plate and chill for at least 2 hours.

5a. There are three ways to cook the burgers: grilling, broiling, and sautéing. For grilling, you'll need a fine-meshed vegetable or fish grill. Thoroughly spray it with oil. Place the burgers on top. Grill over high heat for 2 minutes per side, or until thoroughly heated and lightly browned. Turn the burgers as gently as possible with a spatula. It's easier if you use a hinged grill.

5b. To broil the burgers, preheat the broiler with the rack 3 inches from the heat source. Place the burgers on a sheet of lightly oiled foil. Brush or spray the burgers with a little more oil and broil for 3 to 4 minutes per side, or until lightly browned, turning as gently as possible with a spatula.

5c. To sauté the burgers, heat 2 teaspoons oil in a large nonstick frying pan. Cook the burgers over medium heat for 2 to 3 minutes per side, or until lightly browned, turning as gently as possible with a spatula.

6. Serve the burgers on buns with onion, tomato, lettuce, and your favorite condiments. The burgers will taste even better if you toast the buns on the grill.

Makes 8 burgers

130 CALORIES PER SERVING: 4 G PROTEIN; 3 G FAT; 22 G CARBOHYDRATE; 318 MG SODIUM; 0 MG CHOLESTEROL

ENCHILADAS WITH NO-FRY REFRIES AND SALSA VERDE

*Enchiladas could be thought of as Mexican manicotti—stuffed, rolled tortillas slathered with salsa and baked until bubbly.
My vegetarian version features "sensible" refried beans, which are made with vegetable stock instead of lard.
The combination of a grain (the corn in the tortillas) with the beans gives you a complete form of protein.*

12 corn tortillas
1 recipe No-Fry Refries (page 185)
spray oil

1 recipe Salsa Verde (page 184)
¼ cup no-fat sour cream

1. Preheat the oven to 350° F. Spread the tortillas on nonstick baking sheets and warm in the oven until soft and pliable, 3 to 4 minutes.

2. Spoon 3 to 4 tablespoons refried bean mixture in the center of each tortilla and roll it up into a compact tube. Arrange the tortillas in an attractive, ovenproof 8 × 12-inch baking dish lightly sprayed with oil. Spoon the Salsa Verde over the enchiladas and garnish the top with dollops of sour cream. **Note:** The recipe can be prepared up to 24 hours ahead to this stage and refrigerated.

3. Bake the enchiladas until thoroughly heated and bubbly, 10 to 15 minutes. Serve at once.

Serves 6 as a hearty appetizer, 4 to 6 as an entrée

456 CALORIES PER SERVING: 18 G PROTEIN; 8 G FAT; 81 G CARBOHYDRATE; 214 MG SODIUM; 0 MG CHOLESTEROL
Analysis based on 4 servings

SALSA VERDE (TOMATILLO SAUCE)

Tomatillo (pronounced tow-ma-TEE-yoh) is a large green berry that grows in a papery husk. It looks and tastes like a green cherry tomato, but it actually belongs to the Physalis family, whose members include ground cherries and Cape gooseberries. Native to Mexico, tomatillos are the primary ingredient in salsa verde, the piquant green sauce traditionally served with enchiladas. Tomatillos are available both fresh and canned at specialty greengrocers', Hispanic markets, and an increasing number of supermarkets.

1 pound fresh tomatillos, husked and coarsely chopped
1 small onion, coarsely chopped
2 cloves garlic, minced
1 to 3 serrano or jalapeño chilies, seeded and chopped (for a spicier sauce, leave the seeds in)

¼ cup chopped fresh cilantro
3 to 4 tablespoons Basic Vegetable Stock (page 247) or water (optional)
½ teaspoon sugar or honey (or to taste)
salt and freshly ground black pepper

1. Coarsely purée the tomatillos, onion, garlic, chilies, and cilantro in a blender or food processor. If the mixture is too thick to purée, add 3 to 4 tablespoons vegetable stock or water.

2. Blend sugar, salt, and pepper into the tomatillo mixture and transfer to a large nonstick frying pan. Cook over medium heat for 4 to 5 minutes, or until the sauce is well flavored and slightly thickened. Correct the seasoning, adding salt, pepper, and/or sugar to taste.

Makes about 2 cups

40 CALORIES PER SERVING: 1 G PROTEIN; 0 G FAT; 8 G CARBOHYDRATE; 16 MG SODIUM; 0 MG CHOLESTEROL

NO-FRY REFRIES

Refried beans are a cornerstone of Mexican cooking. Daunting doses of lard lend the traditional recipe richness.
My version uses vegetable broth to obtain a creamy consistency without fat.
The corn, which is optional, adds unexpected crunch and sweetness.

1 tablespoon olive oil
1 onion, finely chopped
3 cloves garlic, minced
½ green bell pepper, finely chopped
1 teaspoon ground cumin
1 teaspoon oregano
1 to 2 teaspoons chili powder (or to taste)

2½ cups cooked pinto beans (page 261)
¾ cup corn kernels (optional)
½ cup Basic Vegetable Stock (page 247) or bean cooking liquid
3 tablespoons finely chopped cilantro
salt and freshly ground black pepper

1. Heat the olive oil in a nonstick frying pan. Add the onion, garlic, and bell pepper and cook over medium heat until soft but not brown, 3 to 4 minutes. Stir in the cumin, oregano, and chili powder and cook for 1 minute.

2. Stir in the beans, corn, vegetable stock, cilantro, salt, and black pepper. Simmer the beans, loosely covered, for 5 to 10 minutes, or until tender and flavorful and most of the liquid has been absorbed.

3. Mash half or all of the beans with a pestle or the back of a spoon. (I like to mash half the beans, leaving the other half whole for texture.) Correct the seasonings, adding salt or chili powder to taste.

Makes about 2½ cups or 4 servings

Note: For a quick, simple dinner, wrap the refries in tortillas with chopped vegetables, salsa—like Jicama Salsa (page 200)—and no-fat sour cream.

203 CALORIES PER SERVING: 10 G PROTEIN; 4 G FAT; 33 G CARBOHYDRATE; 12 MG SODIUM; 0 MG CHOLESTEROL

Analysis based on 4 servings

VEGETARIAN MOLE POBLANO

This dish always prompts expressions of incredulity from people who have never tasted it. Chilies with chocolate? In pre-Columbian times, chocolate was used as a spice, not as candy, and its sweet-bitter flavor goes well with the pungency of chilies. This recipe may seem complicated because it contains a lot of ingredients, but in fact it's a series of simple steps.
Note: *The mole sauce is also delicious served over grilled or broiled tofu. Santa Fe Slaw (page 51) would make a great accompaniment.*

FOR THE MOLE SAUCE
5 to 6 dried Mexican chilies (if possible use a blend of ancho, pasilla, and mulato chilies)
2 tablespoons blanched or slivered almonds
2 tablespoons sesame seeds
1 onion, finely chopped
2 cloves garlic, minced
¼ cup chopped fresh cilantro
1 corn tortilla, cut into 1-inch dice
1 large ripe tomato, quartered
3 tablespoons raisins
¼ teaspoon aniseed
¼ teaspoon ground cloves
¼ teaspoon cinnamon
¼ teaspoon ground coriander seed

1 cup Basic Vegetable Stock (page 247)
2 to 3 teaspoons unsweetened cocoa powder (or to taste)
1 to 2 teaspoons sugar or honey
1 to 2 teaspoons red wine vinegar or lime juice
salt and freshly ground black pepper

TO FINISH THE MOLE
1 cup Basic Vegetable Stock (optional)
12 corn tortillas
1 batch of No-Fry Refries (page 185) or Black Bean Filling (recipe follows)

spray oil

1. Rinse the chilies, tear in half, and remove the stems, veins, and seeds. Soak the chilies in warm water to cover in a bowl for 1 hour or until pliable. Drain the chilies in a strainer.

2. Meanwhile, toast the almonds and sesame seeds on a baking sheet in a 350° F. oven until lightly browned, 6 to 8 minutes, or in a dry skillet over medium heat, 2 to 3 minutes.

3. Place the chilies, the almonds, half the sesame seeds, and the onion, garlic, cilantro, tortilla, tomato, raisins, aniseed, cloves, cinnamon, and coriander in a blender. Purée to a smooth paste. (A blender works better for puréeing than a food processor.) You'll need to scrape down the sides of the blender bowl several times.

4. Transfer the chili mixture to a large nonstick frying pan and cook over medium heat, stirring constantly, for 5 minutes or until thick and fragrant. Reduce the heat and stir in 1 cup stock and the cocoa, sugar, vinegar, and salt and pepper to taste. Simmer the sauce for 10 minutes, stirring occasionally. The sauce should be thick and very flavorful: add cocoa, vinegar, salt, or pepper as needed.

5. If using the additional 1 cup stock to finish the mole poblano, heat it in a frying pan. Dip each tortilla in the stock for 10 seconds, or until soft and pliable. Alternatively, the tortillas can be warmed on a nonstick baking sheet in the oven (400° F. for 1 to 2 minutes).

6. Place 3 tablespoons refries or black bean filling on each tortilla and roll it up into a tube. Arrange the tortillas in a large baking dish lightly oiled with spray oil. (**Note:** The recipe can be prepared several hours or even a day ahead. If prepar-

ing ahead, let the stuffed tortillas cool to room temperature, then cover with plastic wrap and refrigerate. Let them come to room temperature before adding the mole sauce and baking.)

7. Preheat the oven to 400° F. Just before serving, spoon the mole sauce on top and bake the mole poblano until thoroughly heated, about 10 minutes. Sprinkle the top with the remaining tablespoon of toasted sesame seeds and serve at once.

Serves 4 to 6

537 CALORIES PER SERVING: 22 G PROTEIN; 13 G FAT; 91 G CARBOHYDRATE; 187 MG SODIUM; 0 MG CHOLESTEROL

Analysis based on 4 servings

BLACK BEAN FILLING

If you don't have time to make No-Fry Refries (page 185), here's a simple filling that can be made with canned beans. A pinto or kidney bean filling would be made the same way.

1 tablespoon olive oil
1 onion, finely chopped
2 cloves garlic, minced
3 cups cooked black beans (page 261)
⅓ cup Basic Vegetable Stock (page 247) or bean cooking liquid

3 tablespoons finely chopped fresh cilantro (optional)
salt and freshly ground black pepper

1. Heat the olive oil in a large nonstick skillet. Add the onion and garlic and lightly brown over medium heat, 4 to 5 minutes. Stir in the beans and vegetable stock and simmer for 3 minutes, or until beans are soft.

2. Mash half the beans in the pan with a pestle or the back of a wooden spoon. (The puréed beans help bind the filling, while the whole beans add texture.) Stir in the cilantro (if using) and salt and pepper to taste.

Makes 3 cups

218 CALORIES PER SERVING: 12 G PROTEIN; 4 G FAT; 35 G CARBOHYDRATE; 3 MG SODIUM; 0 MG CHOLESTEROL

Analysis based on 4 servings

CATALAN BEAN STEW

The soulful cooking of Catalonia (the southeasternmost province of Spain) entered America's culinary consciousness with the publication of Colman Andrews's intriguing book Catalan Cuisine *(William Morrow, 1988). Fava beans are broad, fleshy beans popular from one end of southern Europe to the other. (Look for them at Italian markets and specialty produce shops.)*

2 dried red or brown chilies, such as pasilla or New Mexican reds, or 1 tablespoon Spanish or Hungarian sweet paprika
3 cups Basic Vegetable Stock (see page 247)
2 medium onions, peeled and quartered
4 ripe tomatoes
6 cloves garlic, peeled
2 slices of country-style white bread
3 parsnips or carrots, cut into ½-inch dice
1 potato, peeled and cut into ½-inch dice

½ cup finely chopped flat-leaf parsley
4 cups cooked fava beans or lima beans
1 cup cooked corn kernels, preferably Grilled Corn (page 252)
2 tablespoons sherry wine (or to taste)
1 tablespoon sherry vinegar or wine vinegar (or to taste)
salt and freshly ground black pepper
1 tablespoon finely chopped toasted almonds

1. Tear the chilies in half and remove the stems and seeds. (For a really spicy dish, you could leave the seeds in.) Soak the chilies in the stock for 1 hour or until soft. If using paprika, dissolve it in the stock. Preheat the oven to 350° F.

2. Place the onions and tomatoes on a baking sheet lined with foil and roast them for 20 minutes. Add the garlic and continue roasting for 20 minutes, or until the garlic is soft and the onions are golden brown. Darkly toast the bread in a toaster.

3. Transfer the chilies to a blender with a slotted spoon, reserving the stock. Add the onions, tomatoes, garlic, and toast and purée until smooth, adding stock as necessary to obtain a thick paste. **Note:** A blender works better than a food processor for this purpose.

4. Transfer the chili mixture to a large, nonstick frying pan and cook over medium heat, stirring of-

ten, for 3 minutes or until fragrant. Stir in the reserved stock, parsnips, and potatoes and half the parsley and cook, uncovered, stirring often, for 15 to 20 minutes, or until the vegetables are just tender. The recipe can be prepared ahead to this stage.

5. Stir in the fava beans, corn, sherry, and vinegar and simmer for 5 minutes, or until the beans and corn are thoroughly heated. Correct the seasoning, adding salt, sherry, or vinegar to taste. The mixture should be highly seasoned. If the stew is too thick, add a little more stock. If too thin, simmer the stew, uncovered, to evaporate the excess liquid.

6. Transfer the stew to a bowl or platter and sprinkle with the remaining parsley and the almonds. Rice (page 258) or polenta (page 143) would make a nice accompaniment.

Serves 4 to 6

452 CALORIES PER SERVING: 18 G PROTEIN; 3 G FAT; 91 G CARBOHYDRATE; 252 MG SODIUM; 0 MG CHOLESTEROL

Analysis based on 4 servings

SOY DISHES

TANGERINE AND HONEY–GLAZED TOFU

Florida meets the Far East in this recipe, which uses fresh tangerine juice and peel instead of the dried peel favored by the Chinese. The zest—the oil-rich outer rind—is most easily removed from the fruit in broad thin strips with a vegetable peeler. Oranges make a tasty glaze, should tangerines be out of season.

1½ pounds firm tofu (preferably reduced-fat
   tofu) or extra-firm silken tofu

FOR THE MARINADE-GLAZE
½ cup soy sauce
½ cup fresh tangerine juice
5 strips tangerine zest, ½ inch × 2 inches wide
⅓ cup honey
1 teaspoon Asian sesame oil

5 cloves garlic, minced
3 scallions, finely chopped
2 tablespoons minced fresh ginger
2 star anise (available at Asian markets)

spray oil
2 tablespoons finely chopped scallion greens
2 teaspoons black sesame seeds

1. If using regular firm tofu, cut it widthwise (through the narrowest side) into broad ½-inch-thick slices. Press these under a heavy skillet for 15 minutes as described on page 257. If using firm silken tofu, slice but do not press.

2. For the marinade-glaze, combine the soy sauce, juice, zest, honey, sesame oil, garlic, scallions, ginger, and star anise in a mixing bowl and whisk until smooth. Arrange the tofu in a glass or ceramic baking dish. Pour half the marinade on top. Marinate the tofu in the refrigerator for 1 to 2 hours, turning several times.

3. Prepare the glaze: Place the remaining marinade in a saucepan and boil until thick and syrupy,

about 3 minutes. Strain the glaze into a small bowl.

4. Just before serving, preheat the broiler. Drain the tofu slices and blot dry. Arrange the tofu in an attractive baking dish or heatproof platter lightly oiled with spray oil. Brush the tofu with the glaze and broil for 1 to 2 minutes, or until golden brown. Brush the tofu with glaze one final time before serving and sprinkle with the chopped scallion greens and black sesame seeds.

Serves 6 to 8 as an appetizer, 4 as a light entrée

Note: For an unusual hors d'oeuvre, cut the tofu into 1-inch squares. Pierce with toothpicks and serve.

383 CALORIES PER SERVING: 29 G PROTEIN; 17 G FAT; 36 G CARBOHYDRATE; 2084 MG SODIUM; 0 MG CHOLESTEROL*

Analysis based on 4 servings

__Note:__ Despite its reputation as a health food, tofu is actually high in fat. The issues surrounding tofu and a healthful diet are addressed in full on page xiii.

TOFU, PRUNE, AND PINEAPPLE KEBABS WITH APRICOT-GINGER GLAZE

Fresh pineapple lends the kebabs a tropical touch, while the prunes provide contrasting color and sweetness. The kebabs can be grilled, but you'll need a fine-meshed vegetable grill, preferably nonstick, greased with spray oil. (Grilling imparts a great smoky flavor.) The kebabs are also delicious broiled and are less likely to fall apart than when grilled. **Note:** *Do not use silken tofu for this recipe—it's too fragile.*

1 pound firm tofu, preferably reduced-fat
32 small pitted prunes (about 1½ pounds)
1 fresh pineapple

FOR THE APRICOT-GINGER GLAZE
½ cup apricot jam

½ cup soy sauce
3 cloves garlic, minced
1 tablespoon minced fresh ginger
1 teaspoon Asian sesame oil (or to taste)

1. Press the tofu under a heavy skillet for 30 minutes as described on page 257. Cut the tofu into 32 ¾-inch cubes. (Slice it in half through the narrowest edge. Cut each half in quarters lengthwise, then widthwise.)

2. Meanwhile, plump the prunes in warm water to cover for 30 minutes. Drain well. Peel and core the pineapple and cut it into 32 ¾-inch chunks.

3. For the glaze, combine the jam, soy sauce, garlic, ginger, and sesame oil in a heavy saucepan. Bring to a boil. Reduce the heat and simmer for 3 minutes, whisking steadily. Correct the seasoning, adding soy sauce or sesame oil to taste.

4. Marinate the tofu and prunes in the glaze for 2 hours, turning gently. Thread the ingredients onto eight 10-inch bamboo skewers, alternating tofu, prune, and pineapple. Reserve the marinade. Preheat the grill or broiler.

5. Grill the kebabs over a medium flame for 1 to 2 minutes per side or until cooked, basting with glaze. Or cook the kebabs under the broiler on a sheet of foil that has been spray-oiled. Brush the kebabs one last time with the glaze before serving.

Makes 8 kebabs, enough to serve 8 as an appetizer, 4 as an entrée

386 CALORIES PER KEBAB: 12.5 G PROTEIN; 6 G FAT; 79 G CARBOHYDRATE; 1043 MG SODIUM; 0 MG CHOLESTEROL*

*Note:** *Despite its reputation as a health food, tofu is actually high in fat. The issues surrounding tofu and a healthful diet are addressed in full on page xiii.*

Tofu, Prune, and Pineapple Kebabs with Apricot-Ginger Glaze

TOFU RANCHERO

Here's an eggless twist on a Mexican classic that makes a great dish for brunch. Freezing the tofu gives it a crumbly-chewy texture similar to scrambled eggs. Grilling imparts a smoky flavor to the salsa, but the vegetables can also be broiled or browned in a nonstick frying pan. **Note:** *This salsa is quite fiery. (As you've probably noticed by now, I have an asbestos palate!) For a milder salsa, seed and mince the chili or omit it entirely.*

1 pound tofu (preferably reduced-fat)

FOR THE SALSA
4 ripe tomatoes, cut in half and seeded
1 large onion, peeled and quartered (leave the furry root end intact)
2 teaspoons olive oil
3 cloves garlic, minced
1 to 3 jalapeño or serrano chilies, thinly sliced (omit the seeds if you have a tender tongue)

¼ cup chopped fresh cilantro, plus 4 sprigs for garnish
2 to 3 tablespoons fresh lime juice
salt and freshly ground black pepper to taste

TO FINISH THE RANCHEROS
4 flour tortillas
1 teaspoon olive oil
1 clove garlic, minced

1. Slice the tofu widthwise in quarters. Arrange the slices on a plate and freeze until hard.

2. Transfer the tofu to a colander over a bowl to thaw. Gently squeeze each slice to wring out any liquid. Coarsely crumble the tofu into a bowl.

3. Meanwhile, prepare the salsa: Grill or broil the tomato halves and onion quarters over medium heat until nicely browned, 3 to 5 minutes per side. Transfer these vegetables to a cutting board. Cut the tomatoes into ½-inch chunks, saving any juices. Coarsely chop the onion, discarding the root.

4. Heat the 2 teaspoons oil in a nonstick skillet. Add the garlic and chilies and cook over medium heat until soft but not brown, about 1 minute. Stir in the grilled tomatoes (with their juices), onion, chopped cilantro, lime juice, salt, and pepper. Gently simmer the salsa for 3 minutes to blend the flavors. Correct the seasoning, adding salt or lime juice to taste: The salsa should be highly seasoned.

5. Prepare the chips to finish the rancheros. Preheat the oven to 350° F. Season the tortillas with salt and pepper, and cut each one into 8 wedges. Bake the tortillas on a baking sheet until crisp and golden brown, 7 to 10 minutes. The recipe can be prepared ahead to this stage.

6. Just before serving, heat the remaining teaspoon of olive oil in a nonstick frying pan. Add the remaining 1 clove garlic and cook over medium heat until soft but not brown, about 1 minute. Stir in the tofu and cook until thoroughly heated, adding salt and pepper to taste. Reheat the salsa if necessary.

7. To assemble the tofu ranchero, spoon the salsa onto 4 plates or a platter. Mound the tofu in the center and garnish with sprigs of cilantro. Arrange the tortilla chips in and around the tofu, pointed ends toward the center.

Serves 4

338 CALORIES PER SERVING: 22 G PROTEIN; 16 G FAT; 33 G CARBOHYDRATE; 29 MG SODIUM; 0 MG CHOLESTEROL*

Note: *Despite its reputation as a health food, tofu is actually high in fat. The issues surrounding tofu and a healthful diet are addressed in full on page xiii.*

SWEET AND SOUR TOFU STIR-FRY

Here's a healthful remake of a Cantonese classic with a fraction of the fat normally used. The bright colors, vibrant flavors, and contrasting textures of the dish are guaranteed to make believers even of people who swear they can't stand tofu.

1 pound firm or extra-firm tofu (preferably reduced-fat tofu) or extra-firm silken tofu

FOR THE SAUCE
¼ cup fresh lemon juice
3 tablespoons tamari or light soy sauce
2 tablespoons honey
1 teaspoon sesame oil
1 teaspoon grated lemon zest

TO FINISH THE STIR-FRY
4 teaspoons canola oil
3 cloves garlic, minced
1 tablespoon minced fresh ginger

3 scallions, white part minced, green part thinly sliced
1 to 2 jalapeño or other hot chilies, seeded and minced (for a spicier stir-fry, leave the seeds in)
1 large carrot, cut into ¼-inch slices
1 red or yellow bell pepper, cored, seeded, and cut into 1-inch diamonds
1 green bell pepper, cored, seeded, and cut into 1-inch diamonds
1 small zucchini, cut into ¼-inch slices
1 small summer squash, cut into ¼-inch slices
2 teaspoons cornstarch

1. Cut the tofu in half widthwise. Place the tofu pieces on a gently sloping cutting board and place a cast-iron skillet or other heavy utensil on top. Press the tofu in this fashion for 20 minutes as described on page 257. (This extracts the excess liquid.) **Note:** If using firm silken tofu, omit this step. Meanwhile, prepare the remaining ingredients.

2. For the sauce, combine the lemon juice, tamari, honey, sesame oil, and lemon zest in a mixing bowl and whisk to mix. Cut the tofu into squares 1 × 1 × ½ inch. Place the tofu in a small bowl and pour half the sauce on top. Marinate the tofu in this mixture for 10 to 15 minutes, gently mixing once or twice.

3. Just before serving, heat a wok almost to smoking over a high flame. Swirl in the canola oil. Add the garlic, ginger, scallion whites, and chilies and stir-fry for 15 seconds, or until fragrant but not brown. Add the carrot and bell peppers and stir-fry for 1 minute. Add the zucchini and squash and stir-fry for 1 minute.

4. Add the tofu and stir-fry for 30 seconds or until thoroughly heated. Add the cornstarch to the remaining sauce and stir well to dissolve it. Stir the sauce into the tofu mixture and bring to a boil. Taste the stir-fry for seasoning, adding tamari, lemon juice, or honey to taste. Stir in the scallion greens and remove the wok from the heat. Serve at once.

Serves 4

302 CALORIES PER SERVING: 21 G PROTEIN; 16 G FAT; 25 G CARBOHYDRATE; 780 MG SODIUM; 0 MG CHOLESTEROL*

*****Note:** *Despite its reputation as a health food, tofu is actually high in fat. The issues surrounding tofu and a healthful diet are addressed in full on page xiii.*

TOFU STEW WITH SOUTHEAST ASIAN SEASONINGS

Call this dish soup or call it stew. I call it delicious. Lemongrass, lime juice, and fried garlic are popular seasonings in Burmese and Cambodian cooking. Lemongrass is discussed in full on page 266. Don't worry about what may seem like an excessive amount of oil for frying the garlic: Most of it is discarded. My favorite tofu for this dish is Mori-Nu Extra Firm Silken Tofu, which is sold in cardboard cartons at Asian markets, natural foods stores, and many gourmet shops. There's another advantage to using Mori-Nu: It will enable you to reduce the fat content by more than half. Thai basil has a stronger licorice flavor than regular basil and can be found in Asian markets.

3 tablespoons canola oil

6 cloves garlic, peeled and thinly sliced, plus 2 cloves, minced

2 tablespoons finely chopped lemongrass (1 to 2 stalks—see Cook's Notes)

1 to 3 jalapeños or other hot chilies, seeded and minced (optional—for a hotter stew, leave the seeds in)

4 shallots, thinly sliced

6 cups Asian Vegetable Stock (page 250) or Basic Vegetable Stock (page 247)

2 to 3 tablespoons low-sodium soy sauce (or to taste)

1 tablespoon Thai, Vietnamese, or Chinese chili paste (or to taste)

2 tomatoes, each cut into 8 wedges

1 pound tofu (preferably extra-firm silken tofu), cut into 1-inch cubes

2 teaspoons cornstarch

3 to 4 tablespoons fresh lime juice

½ cup chopped fresh cilantro

12 fresh basil leaves (preferably Thai basil)

salt (optional)

1. Heat the oil in a wok over medium heat to 350° F. Fry the sliced garlic until golden brown, about 30 seconds. Do not let the garlic brown too much or it will become bitter. Transfer the garlic with a slotted spoon to paper towels to drain. Discard all but 1½ tablespoons oil from the wok. **Note:** You can save this remaining garlic oil for other recipes. It has lots of flavor.

2. Add the minced garlic, lemongrass, chilies, and shallots to the wok. Stir-fry over medium heat until fragrant and soft but not brown, about 1 minute.

3. Add the vegetable stock, soy sauce, chili paste, tomatoes, and tofu. Gently simmer the stew for 5 minutes, or until the tomatoes are cooked. Keep the stirring to a minimum, so as not to break up the tofu.

4. Just before serving, dissolve the cornstarch in the lime juice and stir it into the stew. Bring just to a boil and remove the wok from the heat. Stir in the cilantro and basil leaves. Correct the seasoning, adding soy sauce, chili paste, lime juice, or salt to taste.

Serves 4

257 CALORIES PER SERVING: 20 G PROTEIN; 15 G FAT; 16 G CARBOHYDRATE; 363 MG SODIUM; 0 MG CHOLESTEROL*

****Note:** *Despite its reputation as a health food, tofu is actually high in fat. The issues surrounding tofu and a healthful diet are addressed in full on page xiii.*

BROCCOLI AND TOFU STIR-FRY WITH GARLICKY HOISIN SAUCE

Like all self-respecting stir-fries, this one offers a contrast of colors (green and white), textures (crisp and soft), and flavors (sweet and salty). The tofu is pressed to extract some of the liquid, which would make the stir-fry watery. (Do not use firm silken tofu for this dish: It tends to fall apart.) Hoisin sauce is a sweet-salty sauce made with sugar and soybeans. Look for it in the Asian-food section of most supermarkets and in Asian markets.

10 ounces firm tofu
4 dried black mushrooms
1 tablespoon rice wine or sherry
½ teaspoon freshly grated lemon zest
kosher salt
¼ teaspoon black pepper
½ bunch broccoli (3 cups 1-inch florets)

FOR THE SAUCE
1½ tablespoons hoisin sauce

2 teaspoons rice wine or sherry
2 teaspoons low-sodium soy sauce
½ teaspoon sugar or honey (optional)
1 teaspoon cornstarch

1 tablespoon canola oil
2 cloves garlic, minced
2 teaspoons minced fresh ginger
2 scallions, white part minced, green part finely chopped

1. Press the tofu for 30 minutes as described on page 257. Soak the mushrooms in warm water to cover for 30 minutes.

2. Blot the tofu dry and cut it into 1-inch squares, each ½ inch thick. Toss the tofu with the rice wine, lemon zest, and a little salt and pepper and let marinate for 10 minutes. Drain the soaked mushrooms (you can save the soaking liquid for soups). Stem the mushrooms and cut the caps in quarters.

3. Cut the broccoli into small (1-inch) florets, discarding the fibrous stalks. (These can be used to make the Brocco-Leekie Soup on page 39.) Blanch the broccoli in 2 quarts rapidly boiling salted water for 1 minute, or until almost tender, and drain in a colander. Chill the broccoli with ice (or refresh under cold water) and drain. Blot dry with a paper towel.

4. For the sauce, combine the hoisin sauce, rice

wine, soy sauce, sugar (if using), and cornstarch in a small bowl and mix well.

5. Just before serving, heat a wok (preferably non-stick) almost to smoking over a high flame. Swirl in the canola oil. Add the minced garlic, ginger, and scallions. Stir-fry these ingredients for 15 seconds, or until fragrant but not brown. Add the tofu, mushrooms, and broccoli and stir-fry for 1 to 2 minutes, or until thoroughly heated. Stir in the sauce and boil for 30 seconds. Correct the seasoning, adding soy sauce if necessary, and serve at once.

Serves 4 as an appetizer or side dish or 2 as a main course

Note: To "swirl in the oil," pour it in a thin stream in a circle around the inside edge of the wok 2 inches below the rim. This thoroughly coats the inside of the wok with oil.

182 CALORIES PER SERVING: 14 G PROTEIN; 10 G FAT; 13 G CARBOHYDRATE; 140 MG SODIUM; 0 MG CHOLESTEROL*

Analysis based on 4 servings

***Note:** Despite its reputation as a health food, tofu is actually high in fat. The issues surrounding tofu and a healthful diet are addressed in full on page xiii.*

Smoked Tofu (Tofu "Ham")

I created this dish for my wife, Barbara, who loves the rich smoky flavor of ham but no longer eats pork. Serve it on sandwiches or cut it into tiny squares for skewering on toothpicks as hors d'oeuvres. One of the best stovetop smokers is the Cameroon Stovetop Smoker Cooker. (See Mail-Order Sources for the smoker as well as the hardwood sawdust or chips used in the smoking process.) But a wok or heavy skillet can be turned into a smoker, following the simple instructions on page 35.

1 pound firm tofu (preferably reduced-fat)

FOR CURING THE TOFU
2 cups water
¼ cup sea salt
¼ cup brown sugar or honey
1 strip lemon zest

1 clove
1 allspice berry
5 peppercorns
1 bay leaf

1½ tablespoons hickory, oak, or other hardwood sawdust or chips

1. Lay the tofu flat and cut it lengthwise into 4 broad, flat slices.

2. For the curing brine, combine the water, salt, brown sugar, peel, clove, allspice, peppercorns, and bay leaf in a nonreactive mixing bowl and whisk until the sugar is dissolved. Marinate the tofu in the brine in the refrigerator for 2 to 3 hours, or until well flavored.

3. Remove the tofu from the brine and blot dry. Place the sawdust in the bottom of the smoker and the tofu on the rack. Smoke the tofu for 20 minutes, or until richly flavored with smoke. Let the tofu cool to room temperature, then refrigerate until serving.

Makes 4 slices

177 CALORIES PER SLICE: 18 G PROTEIN; 10 G FAT; 8 G CARBOHYDRATE; 550 MG SODIUM; 0 MG CHOLESTEROL*

***Note:** Despite its reputation as a health food, tofu is actually high in fat. The issues surrounding tofu and a healthful diet are addressed in full on page xiii.*

SAUCES AND CONDIMENTS

"RUST" SAUCE

Rouille (literally "rust" sauce) is a pungent red pepper sauce traditionally served in the south of France with bouillabaisse and other fish soups. The sauce acquires its earthy orange color from saffron and freshly roasted peppers. If you're in a hurry, you can replace the latter with bottled pimientos. I like to serve this sauce in stews, atop Bruschetta (page 8), or on toast points floated in soups.

2 large red bell peppers
¼ teaspoon saffron threads
about ¼ cup hot Basic Vegetable Stock
  (page 247) or water
3 slices country-style white bread, crusts
  removed

2 to 3 cloves garlic, coarsely chopped
1½ tablespoons extra-virgin olive oil
2 teaspoons fresh lemon juice (or to taste)
salt and freshly ground black pepper
¼ teaspoon cayenne pepper (or to taste)

1. Roast, peel, core, and seed the peppers as described on page 257. Cut the peppers into 1-inch squares. You should have about ½ cup.

2. Meanwhile, infuse the saffron in the hot vegetable stock for 10 minutes.

3. Combine the bell peppers, saffron in stock, bread, garlic, oil, lemon juice, salt, black pepper, and cayenne in a blender. Purée to a smooth, thick paste. If the sauce is too thick, add a little more vegetable stock. If too thin, add another slice of bread. Correct the seasoning, adding salt or lemon juice to taste.

Makes about 1 ⅓ cups

17 CALORIES PER TABLESPOON: 0.3 G PROTEIN; 1 G FAT; 2 G CARBOHYDRATE; 11 MG SODIUM; 0 MG CHOLESTEROL

JICAMA SALSA

Jicama is a crisp, tan-skinned, turnip-shaped root vegetable that tastes like a cross between an apple and a potato. Generally eaten raw, it adds a refreshing crunch to salsas and salads. This recipe comes from my friend, Southwestern cuisine mogul Mark Miller, who founded the Coyote Cafe and Red Sage. If mango isn't available, you can use fresh peach or cantaloupe. Sometimes I like to serve this salsa on a bed of lettuce as a salad.

1 pound fresh jicama, cut into ¼-inch dice
1 ripe mango (or cantaloupe), skinned, seeded, and cut into ¼-inch dice
1 red bell pepper, cored, seeded, and cut into ¼-inch dice
1 yellow bell pepper, cored, seeded, and cut into ¼-inch dice
2 scallions (green part only), finely chopped
2 serrano chilies (or to taste), seeded and minced

(for a hotter salsa, leave the seeds in)
2 teaspoons minced fresh ginger
½ cup chopped fresh mint or cilantro
¼ cup fresh lime juice (or to taste)
2 tablespoons rice vinegar
1 tablespoon extra-virgin olive oil
1 to 2 tablespoons brown sugar (or to taste)
salt and freshly ground black pepper

1. Combine the jicama, mango, bell peppers, scallions, chilies, ginger, mint, lime juice, vinegar, oil, sugar, salt, and pepper in a mixing bowl and toss to mix. Correct the seasoning, adding salt, sugar, lime juice, or vinegar as necessary: The salsa should be a little sweet and a little sour.

2. The salsa can be served right away, but the taste will improve if you let it sit for 30 minutes to allow the flavors to meld.

Makes 4 cups, enough to serve 6 to 8

Note: The vegetables can be diced and mixed ahead of time, but for the best results, don't add the seasonings more than 1 hour ahead.

94 CALORIES PER SERVING: 2 G PROTEIN; 3 G FAT; 18 G CARBOHYDRATE; 8 MG SODIUM; 0 MG CHOLESTEROL

Analysis based on 6 servings

PEACH SALSA

This salsa belongs to that growing family of American condiments that are part sauce and part salad.
I like to serve it with the Vegetable Burgers on page 120 or with the Smoked Tofu on page 197.
Mango or tangerine salsa would be made the same way.

2 large ripe peaches, peeled, pitted, and cut into ½-inch pieces (for a more rustic salad, leave the skins on)
½ red bell pepper, cored, seeded, and cut into ¼-inch dice
1 poblano chili or ½ green bell pepper, cored, seeded, and cut into ¼-inch dice
½ to 1 Scotch bonnet chili or other hot chili, seeded and minced (for a hotter salsa, leave the seeds in)
¼ red onion, finely diced (about ¼ cup)
¼ cup chopped fresh cilantro or mint
3 to 4 tablespoons fresh lime juice (or to taste)
salt and freshly ground black pepper
1 tablespoon extra-virgin olive oil (optional)
1 tablespoon brown sugar or honey (optional)

Combine the peaches, bell pepper, chilies, onion, cilantro, lime juice, salt, black pepper, olive oil (if using), and sugar (if using) for the salsa in a mixing bowl and gently toss to mix. Correct the seasoning, adding lime juice, salt, or sugar to taste. This salsa tastes best served within 1 hour of mixing.

Makes 2 cups, enough to serve 4 to 8

64 CALORIES PER SERVING: 1.6 G PROTEIN; 0 G FAT; 16 G CARBOHYDRATE; 0 MG SODIUM; 0 MG CHOLESTEROL
Analysis based on 4 servings

GINGERED CRANBERRY SAUCE

This cranberry sauce is quick to make, and once you know how easy it is, you'll be ashamed you ever bought the canned stuff. This sauce will delight people who love ginger and vanilla.

1 12-ounce bag fresh cranberries, washed and stemmed
½ cup sugar or honey (or to taste)
2 strips lemon zest (remove it with a vegetable peeler)

2 cinnamon sticks
½ vanilla bean, split
5 thin slices of fresh ginger
⅔ cup apple cider

1. Combine the cranberries, sugar, lemon zest, cinnamon sticks, vanilla bean, ginger, and cider in a large nonreactive saucepan. Gently simmer the cranberries, loosely covered, for 8 to 10 minutes, or until tender but not too soft. Uncover the pan the last 3 minutes to allow some of the liquid to evaporate.

2. Let the sauce cool to room temperature, then refrigerate. Remove the lemon zest, cinnamon, vanilla, and ginger before serving.

Makes about 2 cups,
which will serve 4 to 6

152 CALORIES PER SERVING: 0 G PROTEIN; 0 G FAT; 40 G CARBOHYDRATE; 0 MG SODIUM; 0 MG CHOLESTEROL
Analysis based on 4 servings

CHARRED TOMATO PICO DE GALLO

The name of this tangy salsa literally means "rooster's beak" in Spanish. The tomatoes can be grilled on a barbecue grill, roasted over an open gas flame, charred under the broiler, or even roasted in a hot skillet. (To char a tomato over an open gas flame, skewer it with a carving fork and slowly turn it over the flame.) If you're in a hurry, you can combine the ingredients without charring.

2 ripe tomatoes
1 to 4 jalapeño chilies
½ medium white onion, cut into ¼-inch dice
1 clove garlic, minced

¼ cup finely chopped fresh cilantro
2 tablespoons fresh lime juice, or to taste
salt and freshly ground black pepper

1. Char the tomatoes and jalapeños until the skins are black over a hot barbecue grill or an open gas flame, or under the broiler, or in a hot cast-iron skillet. Let cool. Scrape off the burnt skin with a paring knife. Seed the tomatoes and cut into ½-inch dice. Seed the chilies and finely chop. (For a hotter pico de gallo, leave the seeds in.)

2. Combine the tomatoes, chilies, onions, garlic, cilantro, lime juice, salt, and pepper in a non-reactive bowl and toss to mix. Correct the seasoning, adding salt or lime juice to taste.

Makes 1½ to 2 cups

4 CALORIES PER TABLESPOON: 0.2 G PROTEIN; 0 G FAT; 1 G CARBOHYDRATE; 1 MG SODIUM; 0 MG CHOLESTEROL

TOFU SALAD DRESSINGS

I love using tofu as a base for salad dressings. Puréed in a blender, it gives you a gorgeous creamy consistency that used to be achieved with heavy cream and egg yolks. It's also a good source of protein and calcium, which aren't usually found in salads. Any type of tofu will work in the following recipes, but I like the smooth texture you get from silken tofu, which is available in natural foods stores and many gourmet shops. (One good brand is Mori-Nu Silken Tofu, imported from Japan, which is sold in convenient waxed paper cartons.)

ASIAN SPICE DRESSING

Ginger, scallion, and mirin give this dressing an Asian accent. Mirin is a sweet rice wine from Japan (see Cook's Notes). Look for it in Asian markets and natural foods stores. White wine mixed with sugar makes an acceptable substitute.

8 ounces tofu (preferably silken)

2 tablespoons chopped scallion (white part), minced

1 to 2 cloves garlic

2 teaspoons minced ginger

1 to 2 serrano or jalapeño chilies, minced, or ½ teaspoon of your favorite hot sauce (optional)

2 tablespoons rice wine vinegar

2 tablespoons mirin

2 tablespoons reduced-sodium soy sauce or tamari

1 tablespoon sugar or maple syrup (2 tablespoons if using white wine instead of mirin)

1 teaspoon Asian sesame oil

¼ to ½ cup Basic Vegetable Stock (page 247) or water (or as needed)

salt and freshly ground black pepper

3 tablespoons minced cilantro

1. Combine the tofu, scallion, garlic, ginger, chilies, vinegar, mirin, soy sauce, sugar, sesame oil, vegetable stock, salt, and pepper in a blender and purée until smooth. Thin the dressing to the desired consistency with additional stock, if needed.

Correct the seasoning, adding vinegar, sugar, soy, or salt to taste.

2. Stir in the cilantro and serve.

Makes 2½ cups

12 CALORIES PER TABLESPOON: 1 G PROTEIN; 0.6 G FAT; 0.7 G CARBOHYDRATE; 52 MG SODIUM; 0 MG CHOLESTEROL

LEMON-GARLIC DRESSING

An invention of my assistant, Didi Emmons, this tangy dressing owes its vibrant flavor to freshly grated lemon zest.
Try it on a Niçoise-style salad.

½ pound tofu (preferably silken)
3 tablespoons fresh lemon juice
2 to 3 teaspoons grated lemon zest
⅔ cup Basic Vegetable Stock (page 247)
2 to 4 cloves garlic

½ teaspoon freshly ground black pepper
½ teaspoon salt
2 tablespoons extra-virgin olive oil
1 tablespoon miso (optional—see Cook's Notes)

Combine the tofu, lemon juice, zest, vegetable stock, garlic, pepper, salt, oil, and miso in a blender and purée until smooth. Thin the dressing to the desired consistency with additional stock, if needed.

Correct the seasoning, adding lemon juice, garlic, or salt to taste.

Makes 2 cups

18 CALORIES PER TABLESPOON: 1 G PROTEIN; 1 G FAT; 0.5 G CARBOHYDRATE; 34 MG SODIUM; 0 MG CHOLESTEROL

GREEN GODDESS DRESSING

According to food historian John Mariani, this verdant dressing (minus the tofu, of course) was created in the early 1920s at San Francisco's Palace Hotel to honor a play called The Green Goddess. *Most people are so used to the bottled version, they forget how glorious it can be when made from scratch with fresh herbs.* **Note:** *It's not essential to use all of the herbs called for below, but try to use as many as you can. It's preferable to use fresh herbs, even if they're not the ones mentioned, rather than dried.*

8 ounces tofu (preferably silken)
1½ tablespoons finely chopped fresh flat-leaf parsley
1½ tablespoons finely chopped fresh basil
1½ tablespoons finely chopped fresh tarragon
1½ tablespoons finely chopped fresh chives or scallion greens
2 teaspoons capers

1 to 2 cloves garlic, minced
2 to 3 tablespoons wine vinegar (preferably red)
2 tablespoons extra-virgin olive oil
¼ to ½ cup Basic Vegetable Stock (page 247) or water, or as needed
a few drops of fresh lemon juice
½ teaspoon sugar
salt and freshly ground black pepper

Combine the tofu, parsley, basil, tarragon, chives, capers, garlic, vinegar, oil, vegetable stock, lemon juice, sugar, salt, and pepper in a blender and purée until smooth. Thin the dressing to the desired consistency with additional water, if needed. Correct the seasoning, adding lemon juice, garlic, or salt to taste.

Makes 1½ cups

25 CALORIES PER TABLESPOON: 2 G PROTEIN; 2 G FAT; 0.8 G CARBOHYDRATE; 6 MG SODIUM; 0 MG CHOLESTEROL

GINGER MISO DRESSING

Miso is a tangy paste made from fermented soybeans and/or grains. (For a full discussion, see Cook's Notes.)
Like yogurt and raw-milk cheese, it contains live microorganisms, which makes it extremely healthful.
Note: *For a quick, tasty summer dish, try serving this "dressing" over cooked, chilled soba*
(Japanese buckwheat noodles) or other Asian noodles. It's also good with steamed Asian vegetables.

6 ounces tofu (preferably silken)
3 tablespoons miso
1 tablespoon mirin (see Cook's Notes)
2 teaspoons Asian sesame oil
2 teaspoons rice vinegar
2 teaspoons soy sauce

1 teaspoon sugar or honey
1 clove garlic, minced
2 teaspoons minced fresh ginger
2 to 4 tablespoons Basic Vegetable Stock (page 247), or as needed

Combine the tofu, miso, mirin, sesame oil, vinegar, soy sauce, sugar, garlic, ginger, and vegetable stock in a blender and purée until smooth, adding enough stock to obtain a pourable dressing. Correct the seasoning, adding soy sauce or rice vinegar to taste.

Makes 1 cup

29 CALORIES PER TABLESPOON: 2 G PROTEIN; 2 G FAT; 2 G CARBOHYDRATE; 162 MG SODIUM; 0 MG CHOLESTEROL

HONEY MUSTARD POPPY-SEED DRESSING

Sweet, hot, and crunchy, this dressing tastes great on salads and as a dip for crudités.
The recipe comes from the unerring taste buds of my assistant, Didi Emmons.

6 tablespoons no-fat sour cream
¼ cup nonfat yogurt
¼ cup honey
2 tablespoons Dijon-style mustard

2 tablespoons poppy seeds
2 tablespoons canola oil
1 clove garlic, minced
salt and freshly ground black pepper

Combine the sour cream, yogurt, honey, mustard, poppy seeds, oil, garlic, salt, and pepper in a mixing bowl and whisk until smooth. Correct the seasoning, adding honey, mustard, or salt to taste.

Makes 1 cup

44 CALORIES PER TABLESPOON: 1 G PROTEIN; 2 G FAT; 5 G CARBOHYDRATE; 38 MG SODIUM; 0 MG CHOLESTEROL

ONION JAM

This rich, tangy condiment looks like jam. But is sure doesn't taste like it! Onion jam is great spread on
Pita Chips (page 7) or Bruschetta (page 8). I also like to serve it with the Smoked Tofu
on page 197 or the Cold Grilled Vegetable and Smoked Cheese "Tart" on page 135.

1 pound red onions, peeled and sliced paper-thin
   (about 4 cups)
¼ cup balsamic vinegar
2 cups dry red wine
2 cups water

3 to 4 tablespoons honey
2 tablespoons sugar
a pinch of cayenne pepper
a pinch of ground cloves
salt and freshly ground black pepper

1. Place the onions, vinegar, wine, water, honey, sugar, cayenne, and cloves in a large nonreactive sauté pan. The onions should be completely covered. Bring the mixture to a boil, reduce the heat, and gently simmer the onions until the liquid is completely absorbed, about 45 minutes. Stir from time to time, more frequently at the end, to keep the onions from burning.

2. Correct the seasoning, adding salt, pepper, vinegar, or honey to taste: The mixture should be a little sweet, a little sour, and very highly seasoned.

Makes 1 cup

53 CALORIES PER TABLESPOON: 0.4 G PROTEIN; 0 G FAT; 9 G CARBOHYDRATE; 4 MG SODIUM; 0 MG CHOLESTEROL

SUGO DI POMODORO (APULIAN-STYLE TOMATO SAUCE)

There are probably as many tomato sauces in Italy as there are individual families. This one, Sugo di Pomodoro (literally "juice of tomatoes"), is a smooth, simple, silky sauce that goes great with gnocchi, spaghetti, and other pasta. The recipe comes from Carlo Sozzo, owner of a bucolic restaurant called La Locanda in a small Apulian village.

2 tablespoons extra-virgin olive oil
½ small onion, minced (about ¼ cup)
1 clove garlic, minced
1 28-ounce can imported peeled plum tomatoes

2 tablespoons minced basil (8 to 10 leaves)
1 tablespoon minced flat-leaf parsley
salt and freshly ground black pepper

1. Heat the olive oil in a large heavy saucepan. Add the onion and garlic and cook over medium-low heat until just beginning to brown, about 5 minutes. Remove the pan from the heat.

2. Purée the onion, garlic, and tomatoes with their juices in a food processor or blender until smooth. Strain the mixture through a strainer or sieve back into the saucepan. (Alternatively, the vegetables can be puréed through a vegetable mill.) Simmer the sauce, uncovered, over medium heat until thick and well flavored, about 8 minutes, stirring occasionally.

3. Stir in the basil, the parsley, and salt and pepper to taste. Simmer for 2 minutes and serve.

*Makes a little less than
2 cups, enough to serve 4 to 6*

104 CALORIES PER SERVING: 2 G PROTEIN; 8 G FAT; 8 G CARBOHYDRATE; 309 MG SODIUM; 0 MG CHOLESTEROL

Analysis based on 4 servings

BARBARA'S CHUNKY TOMATO SAUCE

My wife, Barbara, makes the world's best tomato sauce. She's certainly had lots of practice: We eat it three times a week!
If you can't get gorgeous, squishy, vine-ripened tomatoes, use a good imported canned variety.

4 ripe tomatoes (about 2½ pounds), peeled,
  seeded, and finely chopped, with juices
1 tablespoon olive oil
1 onion, finely chopped
3 shallots, finely chopped
4 cloves garlic, thinly sliced
2 tablespoons balsamic vinegar

5 tablespoons tomato paste
1 teaspoon dark brown sugar
3 tablespoons chopped fresh herbs (including
  basil, oregano, and/or flat-leaf parsley)
¼ to ½ teaspoon red pepper flakes
salt and freshly ground black pepper

1. Peel and seed the tomatoes, as described on page 256, working over a bowl and sieve to catch the juices.

2. Heat the olive oil in a large nonstick frying pan. Add the onion and cook over medium-low heat until a rich golden brown, 8 to 10 minutes. Reduce the heat slightly, add the shallots and garlic, and cook for 2 minutes, or until golden brown.

3. Add the balsamic vinegar and bring to a boil. Add the tomatoes with their juices and the tomato paste, brown sugar, herbs, pepper flakes, salt, and pepper. Gently simmer the sauce until thick and richly flavored, 10 to 15 minutes, stirring often with a wooden spoon. Correct the seasoning, adding salt, brown sugar, or vinegar to taste.

Makes 3 to 4 cups

Note: For extra zing, you can add 1 tablespoon each capers and diced pitted green olives to the sauce.

74 CALORIES PER ½-CUP SERVING: 2 G PROTEIN; 3 G FAT; 12 G CARBOHYDRATE; 119 MG SODIUM; 0 MG CHOLESTEROL

RED BEAN BOLOGNESE SAUCE

Bolognese, of course, is the rich, meaty red sauce from Bologna in the Italian province of Emilia-Romagna.
My vegetarian version features red beans and squash in place of the veal and ham found in traditional recipes.

1½ tablespoons olive oil
1 onion, finely chopped
3 cloves garlic, finely chopped
2 teaspoons minced fresh ginger
1 large carrot, finely chopped
1 stalk celery, finely chopped
3 ripe tomatoes, peeled, seeded, and diced
   (2 cups)
1½ cups finely diced winter squash (about
   ½ pound peeled butternut, acorn, or other
   squash)

1 cup cooked red beans or kidney beans
   (page 261)
½ cup dry white vermouth
1½ to 2 cups Basic Vegetable Stock (page 247)
3 tablespoons tomato paste
1 tablespoon balsamic or wine vinegar
1 Bouquet Garni of bay leaf, thyme, and parsley
   (page 263)
2 teaspoons dark brown sugar or honey
salt, freshly ground black pepper, and a pinch of
   cayenne pepper

1. Heat the oil in a large nonstick saucepan. Add the onion, garlic, ginger, carrot, and celery and cook over medium heat until lightly browned, 6 to 8 minutes. Stir in the tomatoes, squash, and beans and cook for 2 minutes.

2. Stir in the vermouth and bring to a boil. Stir in the stock, tomato paste, vinegar, bouquet garni, brown sugar, salt, black pepper, and cayenne. Simmer the sauce, stirring from time to time, for 30 minutes, or until the squash and beans are very soft and the sauce is thick and flavorful. Add stock as necessary to keep the sauce from thickening too much.

3. Remove the bouquet garni. Coarsely purée the sauce in a food processor or through a spice mill. (Alternatively, you can serve the sauce chunky.) Correct the seasoning, adding salt, pepper, and vinegar as necessary: The sauce should be highly seasoned. Serve Red Bean Bolognese Sauce over spaghetti, cappellini, or fettuccine.

Makes 4 cups

139 CALORIES PER ½-CUP SERVING: 4 G PROTEIN; 4 G FAT; 19 G CARBOHYDRATE; 64 MG SODIUM; 0 MG CHOLESTEROL

APPLE CHIPOTLE JELLY

Hot and smoky is this jelly, which goes great with grilled vegetables and veggie burgers, not to mention on sandwiches with low-fat cream cheese. Chipotles (smoked jalapeños) provide the firepower. The chipotle of choice is a long, wrinkled, tan-brown chili called chipotle grande. For a complete discussion of chipotles, see page 265.

1 to 2 tablespoons minced chipotle chilies (3 to 4 whole chilies)
2 cups apple juice
6½ cups sugar

1 cup cider vinegar
1 box (1¾ ounces) dry fruit pectin (such as Sure-Jell)

1. If using dried chipotles, soak them in ½ cup warm apple juice for 30 minutes, then remove the stems and mince the chilies. If using canned chipotles, mince them. For a milder jelly, you can remove the seeds.

2. Combine the sugar, remaining apple juice, vinegar, and chipotles in a large heavy saucepan and stir to mix. Simmer the mixture over medium heat, stirring gently, until the sugar is completely dissolved, about 5 minutes. Skim off any foam that rises to the surface.

3. Stir in the dry and liquid pectins and boil for 2 minutes. Skim well. Pour the mixture into sterile jelly jars (three 1-pint jars or six 1-cup jars) and cover tightly. Invert the jars for 10 minutes, then reinvert. Shake the jars from time to time as the jelly cools, to evenly distribute the pepper pieces. The jelly will keep for several months in a cool, dark place, unopened. Refrigerate it, once it is opened.

Makes 6 cups

52 CALORIES PER TABLESPOON: 0 G PROTEIN; 0 G FAT; 14 G CARBOHYDRATE; 1 MG SODIUM; 0 MG CHOLESTEROL

APPLE FIG CHUTNEY

Chutneys are a great way to spice up bland low-fat foods, like grains, beans, and tofu.
The spices can be tied in cheesecloth or wrapped in a piece of foil, which you then perforate with a fork.

2½ cups dried figs
1 cup raisins
2 cups hot apple cider
1 large apple or pear, cored and finely chopped
2 tablespoons fresh lemon juice
6 cloves
6 allspice berries
6 blades of mace (or ¼ teaspoon freshly grated
    nutmeg)

1 cinnamon stick
½ teaspoon grated lemon zest
1 cup brown sugar
1 cup cider vinegar
2 tablespoons finely chopped candied ginger
1 clove garlic, minced
1 tablespoon chili powder
salt, freshly ground black pepper, and a pinch of
    cayenne pepper

1. Plump the figs and raisins in the cider for 15 minutes. Toss the apple with the lemon juice to prevent browning. Tie the cloves, allspice berries, mace, cinnamon stick, and lemon zest in a square of cheesecloth or aluminum foil perforated with a fork.

2. Combine the figs, raisins, apple, bag of spices, brown sugar, vinegar, ginger, garlic, chili powder, salt, black pepper, and cayenne in a large nonreactive saucepan. Bring to a boil, reduce the heat, and simmer the chutney, covered, for 30 minutes. Un-

cover the pot and continue simmering for 30 minutes, or until thick and richly flavored. (If the chutney becomes too dry, add a little more cider.)

3. Correct the seasoning, adding brown sugar, vinegar, or cayenne to taste: The chutney should be highly seasoned. Transfer the chutney to sterile canning jars. Invert the jars for 10 minutes, then reinvert and let cool. The chutney will keep for several months, unopened, in a cool, dark place. Refrigerate it, once it is opened.

Makes 4 cups

37 CALORIES PER TABLESPOON: 0.2 G PROTEIN; 0.1 G FAT; 10 G CARBOHYDRATE; 3 MG SODIUM; 0 MG CHOLESTEROL

MISO BARBECUE SAUCE

Miso (fermented soybean paste—see Cook's Notes), lends this barbecue sauce a lively and complex flavor.
I like to serve it with the Chickpea Burgers on page 181 and the Smoked Tofu on page 197.

⅓ cup cider vinegar
⅓ cup ketchup
2 tablespoons tomato paste
2 tablespoons brown sugar
1 tablespoon molasses
2 teaspoons Pickapeppa sauce or vegetarian
   Worcestershire-style sauce

2 cloves garlic, minced
1 teaspoon minced fresh ginger
a few drops Liquid Smoke
2 tablespoons miso (preferably red miso)

1. Combine the vinegar, ketchup, tomato paste, brown sugar, molasses, Pickapeppa sauce, garlic, ginger, and Liquid Smoke in a saucepan and simmer for 3 minutes, whisking well. Let the sauce cool slightly.

2. Purée the sauce in a food processor or blender, adding the miso. Correct the seasoning, adding vinegar, brown sugar, miso, or Liquid Smoke to taste. Store in the refrigerator.

Makes 1 ½ cups

15 CALORIES PER TABLESPOON: 0.3 G PROTEIN; 0.1 G FAT; 4 G CARBOHYDRATE; 107 MG SODIUM; 0 MG CHOLESTEROL

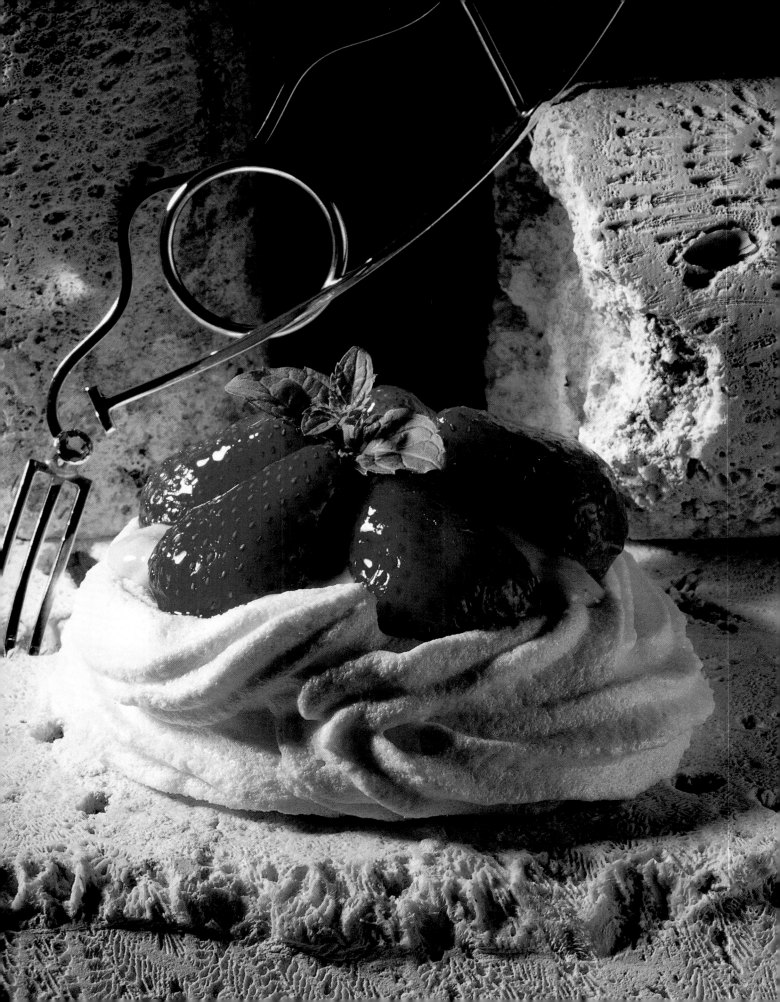

DESSERTS

STRAWBERRY MERINGUES WITH MAPLE CREAM

Who first contrived to combine sugar and stiffly beaten egg whites to make the airy dessert meringue? History fails to tell us, but some experts link the dish to the Swiss town of Meiringen. Regardless of its origins, meringue makes elegant low-fat desserts. This one features crisp meringue shells (which should be made a day before the rest of the recipe) filled with strawberries and maple cream.
Note: *Maple sugar is available at natural foods stores or via mail*
(see Mail-Order Sources). If it is unavailable, use confectioners' sugar or Sucanat.

spray oil
2 tablespoons flour

4 large egg whites
½ teaspoon cream of tartar
1 cup sugar
½ teaspoon vanilla extract

FOR THE MAPLE CREAM
5 tablespoons maple sugar
3 ounces low-fat cream cheese

½ cup no-fat sour cream
4 tablespoons silken tofu

FOR THE GLAZE (OPTIONAL)
3 tablespoons red currant jelly
1 tablespoon water

40 strawberries
10 sprigs of fresh mint

1. The day before, prepare the meringues. Spray 1 large or 2 small baking sheets with oil and lightly dust with flour. Trace ten 3½-inch circles, using a ramekin or cup as a guide. Preheat the oven to 200° F.

2. Beat the egg whites and cream of tartar to soft peaks in a mixer, starting on a slow speed and gradually increasing the speed to high. Add ¼ cup sugar and continue beating until the whites are firm and glossy. Gently fold in the remaining sugar (sift it if necessary) and the vanilla, working as gently as possible. Overfolding will deflate the whites.

3. Transfer the meringue to a piping bag fitted with a large star tip. Pipe out ten 3½-inch meringue circles. (It's easiest to start in the center and work outward.) Pipe a ring of meringue on top of each circle at the outside edge to form a shallow bowl-shaped container.

4. Bake the meringues for 8 hours, or until crisp and dry but not brown. I put them in the oven just before I go to bed and take them out the next morning. The idea is to dry them out without browning. Let the meringues cool completely, then gently lift them off the baking sheet with a flat spatula. **Note**: The meringues can be prepared ahead and stored in an airtight container.

5. Prepare the maple cream: Grind the maple sugar to a fine dust in a spice mill or blender. (This

step is optional, but it will give you a smoother cream.) Combine the maple sugar, cream cheese, sour cream, and tofu in a food processor and purée to a smooth paste, scraping down the edges of the bowl with a spatula.

6. Prepare the glaze (if using): Combine the jelly and water in a small saucepan and bring to a boil, whisking until smooth. Add water as necessary to obtain a brushable glaze. All of the parts of this dish can be prepared ahead of time and refrigerated, but should be assembled at the last minute.

7. Not more than 20 minutes before serving, spoon the cream into the meringue shells. Arrange the strawberries on top. Lightly brush the strawberries with glaze (if using). Crown each meringue with a mint sprig and serve at once.

Serves 10 normal people,
although I can eat 2 or 3 myself

149 CALORIES PER SERVING: 4 G PROTEIN; 2 G FAT; 30 G CARBOHYDRATE; 103 MG SODIUM; 3 MG CHOLESTEROL

ANGEL FOOD CAKE WITH EGGNOG SPICES

Eggnog is a quintessential holiday beverage. But more and more people are avoiding it on account of the high fat content of its principal ingredient: egg yolks. (There's also the slim but worrisome risk of salmonella associated with eating raw eggs.) This recipe features the eggnog spices (nutmeg, cinnamon, cloves, etc.) in a cake that is equally remarkable for its lightness, moistness, and virtual absence of fat.

1 cup sifted cake flour
1½ cups sifted sugar
1 teaspoon freshly grated nutmeg
½ teaspoon ground cinnamon
¼ teaspoon each ground allspice and mace
⅛ teaspoon each ground cloves and salt

12 large egg whites (about 1½ cups), at room
   temperature
1 teaspoon cream of tartar
1 teaspoon vanilla extract

confectioners' sugar for dusting

1. Preheat the oven to 350° F.

2. Combine the flour with ½ cup sugar and the nutmeg, cinnamon, allspice, mace, cloves, and salt in a large mixing bowl and sift together three times.

3. Beat the egg whites at slow speed for 1 minute. Add the cream of tartar and beat until the mixture is frothy. Increase the speed to high and beat the egg whites to soft peaks, adding the vanilla and the remaining 1 cup sugar in a thin stream. Do not overbeat.

4. Sift the flour mixture over the beaten whites in 3 parts, folding in gently after each sifting. Pour the batter into an ungreased 10-inch tube pan. Bake for 45 minutes, without opening the oven door. To test the cake for doneness, gently press the top with your finger. The top should feel firm to the touch and should spring back when you lift your finger. If necessary, bake the cake for 5 to 10 more minutes.

5. Remove the cake from the oven, invert the pan, and let cool. (If your pan doesn't have legs, invert it onto an upright bottle, with the neck of the bottle in the hole in the tube.) It's important to let the cake cool completely in an inverted position.

6. To unmold the cake, run a sharp knife around the inside of the pan and around the tube, working as gently as possible. Unmold the cake onto a platter. (You may need to give it a gentle shake.) Just before serving, dust the cake with confectioners' sugar. Cut into slices for serving.

Serves 8 to 10

216 CALORIES PER SERVING: 7 G PROTEIN; 0 G FAT; 48 G CARBOHYDRATE; 146 MG SODIUM; 0 MG CHOLESTEROL
Analysis based on 8 servings

COCOA PEAR DACQUOISE

A dacquoise is a cake made with nut-flavored meringue. (Dax is the town in France where it was invented.) This one features a pear-flavored meringue in place of the traditional buttercream filling. The recipe may seem a little involved, but actually it's a series of simple steps. And it can certainly be made ahead of time. The almonds increase the fat content slightly, but I've reduced the amount called for in most recipes and added cocoa powder for extra flavor.

FOR THE MERINGUES
spray oil
1 tablespoon flour
½ cup blanched almonds (2 ounces)
1 cup sugar
3 tablespoons unsweetened cocoa powder
2 tablespoons cornstarch
6 large egg whites, at room temperature
½ teaspoon cream of tartar

FOR THE FILLING
1 teaspoon unflavored gelatin
1 tablespoon cold water
3 ripe pears

2 tablespoons lemon juice
1¼ cups sugar
2 strips lemon zest
1 cinnamon stick
3 cloves
1 cup water
3 large egg whites
½ teaspoon cream of tartar
1 tablespoon Poire William (pear brandy)
   or kirsch

2 tablespoons unsweetened cocoa powder for
   garnish

1. Line 1 large or 2 small baking sheets with parchment paper and spray with oil. Sprinkle the paper with the flour and shake off the excess. Using a pot lid, trace out three 8-inch circles on the parchment paper. Cut a fourth circle out of cardboard and cover it with foil. Preheat the oven to 300° F.

2. Make the meringues. Lightly brown the almonds on a baking sheet in the oven. (This will take 8 to 12 minutes.) Let the nuts cool completely, then grind them with ¾ cup sugar, the 3 tablespoons cocoa powder, and the cornstarch to a fine powder in a food processor. (Run the machine in brief spurts. Don't overgrind, or the nuts will become oily.)

3. Beat the 6 egg whites at low speed for 20 seconds. Add the cream of tartar and gradually increase the speed of the mixer to high. Beat the whites until firm and glossy but not dry, adding the

remaining ¼ cup sugar in a thin stream as the whites stiffen. Gently fold in the almond-sugar mixture. Using a piping bag fitted with a ½-inch round tip, pipe the meringue in 3 circles on the parchment paper.

4. Bake the meringues for 50 to 60 minutes, or until firm. Rotate the baking sheets midway to ensure even cooking. Remove the meringues from the oven and let cool for 2 minutes. Using a long spatula, gently loosen the meringues from the parchment paper. Place the pot lid on top and trim the edges with a sharp knife to form perfect circles. Transfer the meringues to a cake rack to cool completely.

5. Meanwhile, prepare the filling. Sprinkle the gelatin over 1 tablespoon cold water in a metal measuring cup. Let stand about 5 minutes, until spongy. Place the measuring cup in a pan of sim-

mering water until the gelatin melts—about 2 minutes. Peel and core the pears and cut into ½-inch dice. Sprinkle with lemon juice to prevent discoloring. Combine 1 cup sugar with the lemon zest, cinnamon stick, cloves, and 1 cup water in a heavy saucepan. Bring the mixture to a boil, reduce the heat, and add the pears. Gently simmer the pears for 2 to 3 minutes, or until tender. Remove the pears, lemon zest, and spices with a slotted spoon. Drain the pears on a paper towel and let cool. Discard the lemon zest and spices. Boil the poaching liquid until thick and syrupy. Continue cooking until it reaches the soft-ball stage (240° F. on a candy thermometer).

6. Meanwhile, beat the 3 egg whites at low speed for 20 seconds. Add the cream of tartar and gradually increase the speed of the mixer to high. Beat the whites until firm and glossy but not dry, adding the remaining ¼ cup sugar in a thin stream as the whites stiffen. Pour the hot soft-ball sugar into the whites in a thin stream and continue beating until cool. Beat in the melted gelatin. Fold in the diced pear and pear brandy.

7. To assemble the dacquoise, affix one of the meringue rounds to the cardboard, using a dab of pear meringue to hold it. Spread half the pear mixture on top. Place the second round on top and spread it with the remaining pear mixture. Place the third round, smooth side up, on top. Lightly sprinkle the top with cocoa powder from a sifter.

8. Refrigerate the dacquoise for at least 6 hours, preferably overnight, before serving. Cut into wedges for serving.

Serves 8 to 10

331 CALORIES PER SERVING: 7 G PROTEIN; 4 G FAT; 71 G CARBOHYDRATE; 95 MG SODIUM; 0 MG CHOLESTEROL

BIG CHOCOLATE CAKE WITH SOUR CREAM ICING

When I first served this cake at a holiday dinner, my guests were flabbergasted to learn how little fat it contained. The secret is to use prune purée to give the cake the dense, moist, fudgy texture generally acquired with butter and egg yolks. I like to make my own Prune Purée following the recipe on page 253. But you can also use a commercial prune pastry filling, like the one made by Baker Brand and available in the baking section of most supermarkets.
Note: *The cocoa-powder checkerboard is optional, but it sure looks terrific.*

FOR THE CAKE
1½ cups all-purpose flour
1 cup unsweetened cocoa powder, preferably
   Droste
2 teaspoons baking powder
1 teaspoon baking soda
½ teaspoon cinnamon
⅛ teaspoon ground cloves
salt
¾ cup Prune Purée (page 253)
1¼ cups water
4 egg whites
2 teaspoons vanilla

1⅔ cups sugar
spray oil

FOR THE SOUR CREAM ICING
6 ounces semisweet chocolate (use the best you
   can buy)
1 cup no-fat sour cream, at room temperature
2 tablespoons orange liqueur

TO FINISH THE CAKE
½ cup apricot or cherry preserves
⅓ cup unsweetened cocoa powder (optional)

1. Preheat the oven to 350° F.

2. Sift the flour, cocoa powder, baking powder, baking soda, cinnamon, cloves, and salt into a mixing bowl. Combine the prune purée, water, egg whites, vanilla, and sugar in another mixing bowl and whisk until smooth. Stir the flour mixture into the prune mixture, whisking just to mix. Divide this mixture between two 9-inch cake pans oiled with spray oil and lined with 9-inch circles of parchment paper or foil.

3. Bake the cakes for 20 to 25 minutes, or until the top is firm but not dry. An inserted skewer should come out clean. Let the cakes cool for 5 minutes, then invert onto cake racks. Peel off the parchment paper.

4. Prepare the icing: Melt the chocolate in a mixing bowl over a pan of gently simmering water.

Don't let even the tiniest drop of water come in contact with the chocolate, or it will harden. Whisk the sour cream and orange liqueur into the chocolate. Chill the icing in the refrigerator for 15 minutes, or until it begins to firm up. Beat the icing with a whisk or beater until light and fluffy, 1 to 2 minutes. **Note:** Most of the fat in this recipe resides in the icing. If you're on a really low-fat diet, you could make the cake without the icing.

5. Assemble the cake: Place one of the cakes on a 9-inch springform pan bottom or cardboard circle. Spread the apricot preserves on top. Place the second cake on top, smooth side up. Spread the icing over the top and side of the cake, using a spatula. Wet the spatula and smooth the top.

6. To make the cocoa checkerboard, cut 12 strips of paper, 1 inch wide and 10 inches long. Gently

lay 6 of the paper strips on top of the cake, 1 inch apart, each one perfectly parallel to the next. Sift half the cocoa on top of the cake, using a sifter or strainer. Gently remove the paper strips and discard. Lay the other 6 strips on top of the cake, again parallel and 1 inch apart, at a 60° angle to the first. Sprinkle with the remaining cocoa. Remove and discard the paper strips. Cut the cake into wedges for serving.

Serves 8 to 10

471 CALORIES PER SERVING: 9 G PROTEIN; 8 G FAT; 99 G CARBOHYDRATE; 275 MG SODIUM; 0 MG CHOLESTEROL
Analysis based on 8 servings

ALMOND ORANGE CHEESECAKE

Here's a silk-smooth cheesecake in the finest New York tradition. The richness comes from the flavorings: freshly grated orange zest, almond extract, and toasted slivered almonds. To toast the almonds, bake them on a baking sheet in a 400° F. oven for 5 minutes or until golden brown. Immediately transfer the almonds to a plate to cool. The almonds can also be toasted in a dry skillet on the stove.
Note: *I usually make this cheesecake without a crust, but you can certainly add one, like Graham Cracker Grape-Nut Crust (page 230). If you're feeling fancy, you can decorate the cheesecake with sliced strawberries, orange segments, and/or kiwi slices.*

1 pound low-fat cream cheese, at room temperature
1½ cups nonfat Yogurt Cheese (page 263)
1¼ cups sugar
1 cup no-fat sour cream
2 eggs, lightly beaten
4 egg whites, lightly beaten

1 tablespoon finely grated orange zest
1 teaspoon almond extract
1 teaspoon vanilla

spray oil

¼ cup lightly toasted slivered almonds

1. Preheat the oven to 350° F.

2. Cream the cream cheese in a mixer or food processor. Beat in the yogurt cheese and sugar and whisk until smooth. Add the sour cream and beat until smooth. Add the eggs and whites, a little at a time, and beat until smooth, scraping down the sides of the bowl frequently. Beat in the orange zest, almond extract, and vanilla, adding sugar, zest, or almond extract to taste.

3. Pour the cheesecake batter into a 9-inch springform pan (make sure the bottom fits tightly) sprayed with oil. Jacket the bottom and sides of the pan with a piece of foil. Set the springform pan in a roasting pan containing 1 inch hot water. (The foil prevents the water from seeping into the springform pan.) Carefully place the roasting pan in the oven and bake the cheesecake for 50 to 60 minutes,

or until just set. (To test for doneness, gently tap the side of the pan. The mixture should jiggle ever so slightly.)

4. Remove the roasting pan from the oven and let the cheesecake cool in the water bath for 10 minutes. Transfer the cheesecake to a cake rack to cool to room temperature, then refrigerate for at least 6 hours, preferably overnight.

5. Just before serving, run a sharp slender knife around the inside of the springform pan and remove the side. Press half the almonds into the sides of the cheesecake. Use the remainder to decorate the top. Cut the cheesecake into wedges for serving, using a sharp, slender knife dipped in hot water and wiped off between cuts.

Serves 8 to 10

353 CALORIES PER SERVING: 16 G PROTEIN; 12 G FAT; 43 G CARBOHYDRATE; 463 MG SODIUM; 79 MG CHOLESTEROL
Analysis based on 8 servings

LEMON-GINGER RICOTTA CHEESECAKE

Americans don't have a monopoly on cheesecake. Ricotta cheesecakes, for example, are popular in southern Italy.
This one owes its zesty flavor to the addition of lemon, candied citron, fresh ginger, and candied ginger.
You'd never guess it's made with low-fat dairy products.

1 batch of Graham Cracker Grape-Nut Crust
   (recipe follows)

FOR THE FILLING
3 cups low- or no-fat ricotta cheese
¾ cup Yogurt Cheese (page 263)
½ cup no-fat sour cream
2 eggs
4 egg whites

1 cup sugar
1 tablespoon finely grated lemon zest
¼ cup lemon juice
1½ teaspoons grated fresh ginger
1 teaspoon vanilla
3 tablespoons candied ginger
3 tablespoons candied citron

spray oil

1. Preheat the oven to 350° F. Spray the bottom and sides of a 9½-inch springform pan with spray oil and press the prepared Graham Cracker Grape-Nut Crust into the pan.

2. Prepare the filling: Combine the ricotta, Yogurt Cheese, sour cream, eggs, egg whites, sugar, zest, lemon juice, grated ginger, vanilla, candied ginger, and citron in a mixer or mixing bowl and beat or whisk until smooth. Pour the filling into the prepared pan. Bake the cheesecake for about 1 hour, or until the filling is almost set: It should jiggle just slightly when the pan is shaken.

3. Transfer the cheesecake to a cake rack and let cool to room temperature. Refrigerate the cheesecake for at least 6 hours before serving. Cut into wedges and serve.

Serves 10 to 12

338 CALORIES PER SERVING: 15 G PROTEIN; 11 G FAT; 45 G CARBOHYDRATE; 276 MG SODIUM; 68 MG CHOLESTEROL
Analysis based on 10 servings

GRAHAM CRACKER GRAPE-NUT CRUST

*Grape-Nuts give this crust plenty of crunch, while the cider and canola oil stand
in for the traditional artery-clogging doses of butter.*

**1 cup graham cracker crumbs (8 to 10 whole
crackers ground in a food processor)**
⅔ cup Grape-Nuts or other crunchy cereal
2 tablespoons canola oil

3 tablespoons apple cider or water

spray oil

1. Combine the graham cracker crumbs, Grape-Nuts, oil, and cider in a food processor and process until crumbly.

2. Press this mixture into the bottom of a 9½-inch nonstick springform pan oiled with spray oil.

Makes one 9½-inch crust

97 CALORIES PER SERVING: 2 G PROTEIN; 4 G FAT; 15 G CARBOHYDRATE; 106 MG SODIUM; 0 MG CHOLESTEROL

Analysis based on 8 servings

DIDI'S INDIAN PUDDING CAKE

Indian pudding is probably America's most ancient dessert. But there's nothing old-fashioned about this heart-healthful cake, created by my assistant, Didi Emmons. Canola oil, no-fat sour cream, and egg whites replace the butter and whole eggs in traditional Indian pudding, but with all the spices and seasonings, you don't miss them. For a real splurge, you could serve the cake with Molasses "Whipped Cream" (page 232).

⅓ cup canola oil
⅓ cup no-fat sour cream
¼ cup molasses
1 tablespoon dark rum
1 teaspoon vanilla
¾ cup brown sugar
1 cup coarse yellow cornmeal
½ cup unbleached all-purpose white flour
1 teaspoon baking powder
2 teaspoons minced fresh ginger
2 teaspoons cinnamon

1 teaspoon ground cardamom
¼ teaspoon ground cloves
¼ teaspoon freshly grated nutmeg
salt
5 egg whites
¼ teaspoon cream of tartar

confectioner's sugar for dusting (optional)

spray oil

1. Preheat the oven to 350° F. Grease a 9-inch round cake pan (preferably nonstick) with spray oil.

2. Combine the oil, sour cream, molasses, rum, and vanilla in a mixing bowl and whisk to mix. Whisk in all but 2 tablespoons of the brown sugar. In another mixing bowl combine the cornmeal, flour, baking powder, ginger, cinnamon, cardamom, cloves, nutmeg, and salt and whisk to mix.

3. Beat the egg whites with the cream of tartar to stiff peaks, adding the remaining 2 tablespoons brown sugar as the whites stiffen. Gently fold ½ of the whites into the molasses mixture, then gently fold in half the cornmeal mixture. Gently fold in the remaining whites, followed by the remaining cornmeal mixture.

4. Spoon the batter into the prepared cake pan and bake for 35 to 40 minutes, or until the cake is firm to the touch. When the cake is done, an inserted toothpick will come out clean. Remove the cake from the oven and let cool to room temperature, then invert onto a platter or plate. Dust with confectioners' sugar, if desired.

Note: It's normal for the cake to fall slightly. (I like to spoon Molasses "Whipped Cream" [page 232] into the depression in the center.) Cut the Indian Pudding Cake into wedge-shaped slices and serve.

Serves 10 to 12

Note: If you're not using a nonstick cake pan, it's a good idea to line the pan with parchment paper before spraying with oil.

233 CALORIES PER SERVING: 4 G PROTEIN; 8 G FAT; 37 G CARBOHYDRATE; 90 MG SODIUM; 0 MG CHOLESTEROL
Analysis based on 10 servings

LOW-FAT "WHIPPED CREAM"

Here's a super-tasty topping that can be used like whipped cream but contains only a fraction of the fat and calories. The silken tofu gives it a light creamy texture. This is a great topping for people who want to reduce their fat intake but still sink their spoons into something rich and gooey. **Note***: This cream makes a great frosting for cakes.*

**3 ounces no-fat cream cheese, at room
    temperature**
½ cup no-fat sour cream
1 teaspoon vanilla

**4 to 6 tablespoons confectioners' sugar or maple
    sugar**
¼ cup silken tofu

Combine the cream cheese, sour cream, vanilla, confectioners' sugar, and tofu in a food processor and purée until smooth, scraping down the sides of the bowl several times. This will take 2 to 3 min- utes. Correct the seasoning, adding confectioners' sugar or vanilla to taste.

Makes 1 cup

22 CALORIES PER TABLESPOON: 2 G PROTEIN; 0.3 G FAT; 3 G CARBOHYDRATE; 43 MG SODIUM; 0 MG CHOLESTEROL

MOLASSES "WHIPPED CREAM"

Prepare the recipe for Low-Fat "Whipped Cream," reducing the confectioners' sugar by 1 tablespoon and adding 1 to 2 tablespoons molasses.

24 CALORIES PER TABLESPOON: 2 G PROTEIN; 0.3 G FAT; 3 G CARBOHYDRATE; 43 MG SODIUM; 0 MG CHOLESTEROL

LEMON "WHIPPED CREAM"

Prepare the recipe for Low-Fat "Whipped Cream," increasing the confectioners' sugar by 1 tablespoon, reducing the sour cream by 1 table- spoon, and adding 1 tablespoon lemon juice and 1 teaspoon grated lemon zest.

24 CALORIES PER TABLESPOON: 2 G PROTEIN; 0.3 G FAT; 3 G CARBOHYDRATE; 43 MG SODIUM; 0 MG CHOLESTEROL

UNCOOKED APPLE PIE

I first tasted this extraordinary apple pie at Delights of the Garden, an Atlanta-based vegetarian restaurant that serves only raw foods. Extraordinary is the word for it—not only on account of its crisp crust and flavorful filling, but for the fact that not a single ingredient has been cooked. Here's how I imagine they make it.

FOR THE CRUST
½ cup dried banana chips (available at natural foods stores)
½ cup dried mango, apricots, or pitted dates
½ cup dried pineapple
¼ cup raisins
¼ cup orange juice

spray oil

FOR THE FILLING
4 firm apples (like Granny Smiths)
2 teaspoons lemon juice

1 cup dried apples
1 teaspoon cinnamon
a little freshly grated nutmeg
2 tablespoons honey

FOR THE TOPPING
3 tablespoons dried banana chips
3 tablespoons dried pineapple
3 tablespoons dried mango or apricots

1. Lightly spray a 10-inch pie pan (preferably nonstick) with spray oil.

2. Prepare the crust: Combine the banana chips, dried mango and pineapple, raisins, and orange juice in a food processor and purée to a thick paste. Press this paste into the bottom and sides of the pie pan. Chill the crust while you prepare the filling.

3. Prepare the filling: Core the apples. Cut 2 of the apples into ¼-inch dice and toss with the lemon juice in a mixing bowl. Set aside. Finely chop the dried apples in the food processor. Add the remaining 2 apples, cinnamon, nutmeg, and honey to the processor and grind the mixture to a coarse purée. You'll need to scrape the sides of the bowl with a rubber spatula several times. Correct the seasoning, adding cinnamon, nutmeg, or honey to taste. Stir the purée into the diced apples and spoon this mixture into the crust.

4. Finely chop the dried banana chips, pineapple, and mango in a food processor. Sprinkle the topping over the apple filling. Let the pie chill for at least 30 minutes before serving. Refrigerated, it will keep for several days. Cut the pie into wedges and serve at once.

Serves 8

204 CALORIES PER SERVING: 1 G PROTEIN; 4 G FAT; 46 G CARBOHYDRATE; 18 MG SODIUM; 0 MG CHOLESTEROL

LEMON SOUFFLÉ

Fresh lemon juice and lemon zest (the fruit's oil-rich outer rind) give this soufflé such a vibrant flavor, you don't miss the large number of egg yolks called for in traditional recipes. Another advantage of this soufflé is that it can be made in 30 minutes. As an accompaniment, I would serve the Shocking Red Raspberry Sauce on page 203 of my first book, Steve Raichlen's High Flavor, Low-Fat Cooking.

TO PREPARE THE SOUFFLÉ DISHES
spray oil
2 to 3 tablespoons sugar for sprinkling

TO MAKE THE SOUFFLÉ
2 tablespoons cornstarch
1 cup skim milk
1 tablespoon grated lemon zest
⅓ cup sugar, plus 2 tablespoons sugar for beating the whites
5 to 6 tablespoons fresh lemon juice
1 egg yolk (optional)
5 egg whites
½ teaspoon cream of tartar

1. Thoroughly grease a 5-cup soufflé dish or six 3-inch ramekins, bottom and sides, with spray oil. Sprinkle the inside with sugar and shake out the excess. Preheat the oven to 400° F.

2. Place 1 tablespoon cornstarch and ¼ cup milk in a heavy saucepan and stir to a smooth paste. Whisk in the remaining milk, the lemon zest, and the ⅓ cup sugar. Bring the mixture to a boil, whisking steadily: It should thicken.

3. Combine the lemon juice with the remaining 1 tablespoon cornstarch in a heavy saucepan and whisk to a smooth paste. Bring the mixture to a boil: It should thicken. Whisk the lemon mixture into the milk mixture and simmer for 1 minute, or until thick. Remove the pan from the heat and whisk in the egg yolk (if using). Check the mixture for seasoning, adding sugar or lemon juice to taste.

4. Meanwhile, beat the egg whites and cream of tartar to soft peaks. Gradually add the 2 tablespoons sugar and continue beating until the whites are firm and glossy but not dry. Whisk ¼ of the whites into the hot lemon mixture to lighten it. Fold this mixture into the remaining whites, working as gently as possible.

5. Spoon the soufflé mixture into the soufflé dish or ramekins and smooth the top with a wet spatula. If the whites are properly beaten and folded into the hot lemon mixture, the soufflé(s) can be made up to 2 hours ahead of time and kept at room temperature until baking.

6. Bake the soufflé(s) until dramatically puffed and mostly set. (When shaken, it should jiggle a little, not a lot.) Little soufflés will take 8 to 12 minutes, one large soufflé 15 to 20 minutes. Do not open the oven door the first 7 minutes of baking.

Serves 4 to 6

170 CALORIES PER SERVING: 7 G PROTEIN; 0 G FAT; 37 G CARBOHYDRATE; 130 MG SODIUM; 1 MG CHOLESTEROL

Analysis based on 4 servings

ALMOND BEAN CURD WITH EXOTIC FRUITS

Almond Bean Curd is a playful dessert that reflects the Chinese fondness for foods that aren't what they appear to be. The illusion in this case is a dish that looks like bean curd (tofu), tastes like almonds, and wiggles like Jell-O. The bean curd is served in a light syrup with fruit salad to make a dessert that's as refreshing as it's offbeat. Agar-agar is a seaweed extract that behaves like gelatin but contains no animal products. Look for it at health and natural foods stores and Asian markets.

FOR THE ALMOND BEAN CURD
3½ cups water
6 tablespoons agar-agar flakes or powder
¾ cup sweetened condensed milk
2 tablespoons sugar or honey
2 teaspoons almond extract

FOR THE SALAD AND SYRUP
2 strips lemon zest
2 cinnamon sticks

2 cloves
3 cups water
1 cup sugar
3 to 4 cups mixed diced fruit (preferably fresh),
    such as lychees, seedless grapes, ripe pears,
    apples, bananas, peaches, mandarin orange
    segments, and/or mangos

6 sprigs fresh mint for garnish

1. Prepare the almond bean curd: Bring the water to a boil. Whisk in the agar-agar and briskly simmer the mixture for a minute or so, or until the agar-agar flakes dissolve. Remove the pan from the heat and stir in the sweetened condensed milk and sugar and almond extract to taste. Let the mixture cool to room temperature, then pour it into a 9-inch cake pan. Chill the mixture in the refrigerator until set.

2. Prepare the syrup. Tie the lemon zest, cinnamon sticks, and cloves in cheesecloth. Add to the water and sugar in a large saucepan and bring to a boil. Reduce the heat and gently simmer the syrup for 10 minutes, or until well flavored. Add the fruit and simmer for 1 to 2 minutes, or until just tender but not soft. Let the syrup and fruit cool to room temperature, then refrigerate it until cold.

3. Using a sharp knife, cut the almond bean curd into 2-inch diamonds. Run a knife around the inside of the pan. Invert the pan and firmly tap it on a cutting board. The bean curd should fall out, but if it doesn't, pry out one diamond with a spoon. Stir the bean curd pieces into the fruit mixture. Ladle the mixture into glass bowls or wine goblets. Garnish each with a mint sprig and serve at once. A spoon is the proper utensil for eating this dessert.

Serves 6

316 CALORIES PER SERVING: 5 G PROTEIN; 4 G FAT; 69 G CARBOHYDRATE; 52 MG SODIUM; 13 MG CHOLESTEROL

QUINCE COMPOTE

Quince is a cousin of the apple—a firm, round, light green–skinned fruit with a perfumed white flesh that turns pink when cooked. It is popular in the Mediterranean and the Near East, but an oddball in this country (although I see it in more and more supermarkets). Astringent in its raw state, it becomes mild and sweet when cooked. Rose water lends this compote an exotic touch (look for it in Indian and Near East markets). If unavailable, use your favorite liqueur.

4 to 5 quinces (about 2 pounds)
2 cups water
½ to 1 cup sugar (or to taste)
3 cardamom pods
2 cloves

1 cinnamon stick
3 strips lemon zest, plus the juice of a whole lemon
1 teaspoon rose water

1. Cut the quinces in half lengthwise and core with a melon baller or spoon. Coarsely chop the quinces. Combine them with the water, sugar, cardamom pods, cloves, cinnamon stick, lemon zest and juice, and rose water in a heavy saucepan and bring to a boil.

2. Reduce the heat, cover the pan, and gently simmer the quinces for 30 minutes, or until tender. If the mixture dries out too much, add a little more water. If it's too soupy at the end, uncover the pan the last 10 minutes. You're looking for the consistency of chunky apple sauce. Let the compote cool to room temperature, then refrigerate.

3. Correct the flavoring, adding sugar, lemon juice, or a few drops of rose water to taste: The compote should be richly flavored.

Makes about 4 cups, enough to serve 6 to 8

149 CALORIES PER SERVING: 1 G PROTEIN; 0 G FAT; 39 G CARBOHYDRATE; 6 MG SODIUM; 0 MG CHOLESTEROL
Analysis based on 6 servings

BISCOTTI

Ten years ago, few Americans had ever heard of biscotti. Today, we can't seem to live without them. These crisp Italian cookies—so perfect for dipping in coffee or tea—turn up in cafés and gourmet shops around the country, but they're easy to make at home.

GINGER CARDAMOM BISCOTTI

Cornstarch and confectioners' sugar have a softening effect on the dough, which enables you to use less fat and fewer eggs than are found in traditional recipes. These and the following biscotti were developed by my assistant, Didi Emmons.

2 eggs
2 egg whites
½ cup confectioners' sugar
9 tablespoons (½ cup plus 1 tablespoon) brown sugar
2 tablespoons canola oil
1 teaspoon vanilla extract
2½ to 2¾ cups unbleached all-purpose flour (or as needed)

¼ cup cornstarch
¼ cup cornmeal (preferabiy stone-ground)
¼ teaspoon salt (optional)
1 teaspoon baking powder
½ teaspoon baking soda
1 teaspoon ground cardamom
¼ cup finely chopped candied ginger

1. Preheat the oven to 350° F. Combine the eggs, whites, sugars, oil, and vanilla in a mixing bowl and whisk until smooth. Sift in the flour, cornstarch, cornmeal, salt (if using), baking powder, baking soda, and cardamom. Add the ginger and stir just to mix. You should wind up with a soft, pliable dough.

2. Cut the dough in half. Place each half on a baking sheet and gently pat into a rectangle 14 to 15 inches long, 5 to 6 inches wide, and ¾ inch high. Score the top of each rectangle with a knife, making shallow cuts on the diagonal every ½ inch.

3. Bake the biscotti for 25 minutes, or until the tops are firm to the touch. Remove the pan from the oven and let cool for 3 minutes.

4. Using a serrated knife, cut each cake into ½-inch slices, following the lines you scored on top. Place the slices, cut side down, on the baking sheet and bake for 10 minutes. Turn the biscotti and bake for 10 minutes more, or until crusty.

5. Transfer the biscotti to a cake rack to cool to room temperature. Store in an airtight container. The traditional way to eat biscotti is to dip them in coffee or wine, but I also like to munch them straight.

Makes about 30

90 CALORIES PER BISCOTTO: 2 G PROTEIN; 1 G FAT; 17 G CARBOHYDRATE; 35 MG SODIUM; 14 MG CHOLESTEROL

CHOCOLATE CHIP BISCOTTI

These biscotti were created for my wife, Barbara, an incurable chocoholic! My favorite cocoa powder is Droste from Holland.

2 eggs
2 egg whites
½ cup confectioners' sugar
10 tablespoons (½ cup plus 2 tablespoons)
 granulated sugar
2 tablespoons canola oil
1 teaspoon vanilla extract
2½ to 2¾ cups unbleached all-purpose flour

½ cup unsweetened cocoa powder (preferably
 Dutch)
¼ cup cornstarch
¼ cup cornmeal (preferably stone-ground)
¼ teaspoon salt (optional)
1 teaspoon baking powder
½ teaspoon baking soda
⅓ cup chocolate chips

1. Preheat the oven to 350° F. Combine the eggs, whites, sugars, oil, and vanilla in a mixing bowl and whisk until smooth. Sift in the flour, cocoa, cornstarch, cornmeal, salt (if using), baking powder, and baking soda. Add the chocolate chips and stir just to mix. You should wind up with a soft, pliable dough.

2. Cut the dough in half. Place each half on a baking sheet and gently pat into a rectangle 14 to 15 inches long, 5 to 6 inches wide, and ¾ inch high. Score the top of each rectangle with a knife, making shallow cuts on the diagonal every ½ inch.

3. Bake the biscotti for 25 minutes, or until the tops are firm to the touch. Remove the pan from the oven and let cool for 3 minutes.

4. Using a serrated knife, cut each cake into ½-inch slices following the lines you scored on top. Place the slices, cut side down, on the baking sheet and bake for 10 minutes. Turn the biscotti and bake for 10 minutes more, or until crusty.

5. Transfer the biscotti to a cake rack to cool to room temperature. Store in an airtight container. The traditional way to eat biscotti is to dip them in coffee or wine, but I also like to munch them straight.

Makes about 30 biscotti

98 CALORIES PER BISCOTTO; 2 G PROTEIN; 2 G FAT; 19 G CARBOHYDRATE; 35 MG SODIUM; 14 MG CHOLESTEROL

OATMEAL RAISIN COOKIES

An increasing number of health-conscious cooks are using fruit purées in place of butter or oil in baked goods. I actually prefer the following cookies, which are made with applesauce, to the traditional version made with butter.

¾ cup applesauce
1¼ cups packed light brown sugar
2 egg whites
⅓ cup skim milk
1½ teaspoons vanilla
½ cup all-purpose flour
1 teaspoon baking soda
½ teaspoon salt (optional)
1 teaspoon cinnamon

½ teaspoon ground cardamom
¼ teaspoon freshly grated nutmeg
⅛ teaspoon ground cloves
1½ teaspoons grated orange zest
3 cups quick-cooking oats
1 cup raisins

spray oil (optional)

1. Preheat the oven to 375° F. Combine the applesauce, sugar, egg whites, milk, and vanilla in a mixing bowl and whisk until smooth. Add the flour, baking soda, salt (if using), cinnamon, cardamom, nutmeg, cloves, and orange zest and stir just to mix. Stir in the oats and raisins.

2. Grease 3 cookie sheets with spray oil. (This is unnecessary with nonstick pans.) Spoon the batter onto the cookie sheets, 2 heaping tablespoons at a time, leaving 3 inches between cookies. Gently flatten each cookie with a wet spatula.

3. Bake the cookies for 12 to 14 minutes, or until firm and lightly browned on the bottom. (Watch them closely: They burn faster than butter-based cookies.) Let the cookies cool on the cookie sheet for 1 minute, then transfer to a wire rack to cool completely. Store any cookies you don't eat right on the spot in an airtight container.

Makes about twenty 3-inch cookies

140 CALORIES PER COOKIE: 3 G PROTEIN; 1 G FAT; 31 G CARBOHYDRATE; 54 MG SODIUM; 0 MG CHOLESTEROL

SIN-FREE BROWNIES

These brownies are the perfect revenge for people who have put up with unsatisfying diets. Prune purée provides the moistness and richness usually associated with butter or shortening. A recipe for Prune Purée is found on page 253. Alternatively, you can use commercial prune filling (available in the baking supply section of most supermarkets—one good brand is Baker brand). To further reduce the fat, golden raisins are used instead of oil-laden nuts. This recipe produces fudgy brownies. If you prefer cake-style brownies, try the Big Chocolate Cake with Sour Cream Icing (page 225).

½ cup golden raisins
4 ounces unsweetened chocolate, coarsely
 chopped
½ cup Prune Purée (page 253)
3 egg whites
1 cup sugar, plus 2 tablespoons for sprinkling
¼ teaspoon salt (optional)
2 teaspoons vanilla

1 tablespoon instant coffee
½ teaspoon cinnamon
¼ teaspoon cloves
½ cup flour

spray oil

3 tablespoons confectioners' sugar (optional)

1. Preheat the oven to 350° F.
2. Plump the raisins in hot water to cover in a bowl for 15 minutes. Drain well in a colander. Melt the chocolate in a bowl over a pan of barely simmering water or in the microwave. Do not let even the smallest droplet of water come in contact with the chocolate, or it will harden and become difficult to work with.
3. Combine the prune purée, egg whites, 1 cup sugar, salt (if using), vanilla, instant coffee, cinnamon, and cloves in a large mixing bowl and whisk or beat until smooth. Beat in the melted chocolate. Add the flour and raisins and beat just to mix.
4. Spoon the batter into an 8-inch square baking

pan (preferably nonstick) oiled with spray oil. (If a nonstick pan is unavailable, you may wish to line the pan with a square of parchment paper before spraying.) Sprinkle the top of the brownies with the remaining 2 tablespoons sugar. (This makes the top crusty.)
5. Bake the brownies for 25 minutes, or until the top is springy to the touch. Transfer the brownies to a cake rack to cool, then cut into squares with a butter knife. For a pretty presentation, sprinkle the brownies with confectioners' sugar right before serving.

Makes 12 to 14 brownies

169 CALORIES PER BROWNIE: 3 G PROTEIN; 5 G FAT; 33 G CARBOHYDRATE; 16 MG SODIUM; 0 MG CHOLESTEROL
Analysis based on 12 servings

CRANBERRY HONEY SORBET

This creamy sorbet makes a great, light finale to the groaning board we call Thanksgiving dinner.
It's also a good way to use up flat champagne.

1 12-ounce bag fresh cranberries
1 cup honey
the grated zest of 1 orange (about 1 teaspoon)
1 cup fresh orange juice
the grated zest and juice of 1 lemon (1 teaspoon zest, 3 tablespoons juice—or additional juice as desired)

1 tablespoon minced fresh ginger
1 cup flat champagne or other dry white wine
1½ cups water
sprigs of fresh mint for garnish

1. Combine the cranberries, honey, orange and lemon zests and juices, ginger, champagne, and water in a saucepan and bring to a boil. Reduce the heat and gently simmer the cranberries until very soft, about 8 minutes. Purée the mixture in a food processor. Let cool to room temperature, then chill in the refrigerator.

2. Freeze the sorbet in an ice-cream machine, following the manufacturer's instructions. Serve the sorbet in martini glasses or wineglasses, garnishing each with a sprig of mint.

Makes about 4 cups, which will serve 8

187 CALORIES PER SERVING: 1 G PROTEIN; 0 G FAT; 44 G CARBOHYDRATE; 4 MG SODIUM; 0 MG CHOLESTEROL

Granitas

Granitas are the simplest and most refreshing of all frozen desserts. The traditional method calls for the mixture to be frozen in a bowl, being scraped with a fork as it freezes to separate it into loose ice crystals. The advantage of this method is that it requires no special equipment. But I also like the smooth, creamy consistency achieved by using an ice-cream machine.

Cappuccino Granita

2 cups hot espresso
⅔ cup sugar (or to taste)

½ cup evaporated skim milk
½ teaspoon ground cinnamon

1. Combine the coffee and sugar in a mixing bowl and whisk until the sugar is completely dissolved. Stir in the evaporated milk and cinnamon. Taste the mixture for sweetness, adding sugar as desired. Let the mixture cool to room temperature, then refrigerate it until cold.

2. Freeze the mixture in an ice-cream machine, following the manufacturer's instructions. For best results, serve at once.

Serves 6

Note: If you don't have an ice-cream machine, place the granita in a shallow bowl in the freezer. Scrape the mixture with a fork three or four times as it freezes to break it into icy crystals. Scrape it again just before serving to loosen the crystals.

100 CALORIES PER SERVING: 2 G PROTEIN; 0 G FAT; 24 G CARBOHYDRATE; 26 MG SODIUM; 1 MG CHOLESTEROL

LEMON MINT GRANITA

2 cups water
¾ cup sugar (or to taste)
⅓ cup freshly squeezed lemon juice (or to taste)

1 tablespoon grated lemon zest
2 tablespoons finely chopped fresh mint
 (optional)

1. Combine the water and sugar in a nonreactive saucepan. Bring the mixture to a boil, stirring occasionally, until the sugar is dissolved. Let the mixture cool to room temperature, then stir in the lemon juice, lemon zest, and mint (if using). Taste the mixture for sweetness, adding sugar or lemon juice as desired. Let the mixture cool to room temperature, then refrigerate it until cold.

2. Freeze the mixture in an ice-cream machine, following the manufacturer's instructions. For the best results, serve at once.

Serves 6

Note: If you don't have an ice-cream machine, place the granita in a shallow bowl in the freezer. Scrape the mixture with a fork three or four times as it freezes to break it into icy crystals. Scrape it again just before serving to loosen the crystals.

97 CALORIES PER SERVING: 0 G PROTEIN; 0 G FAT; 27 G CARBOHYDRATE; 3 MG SODIUM; 0 MG CHOLESTEROL

PEACH GRANITA

4 very ripe peaches (2 cups purée)
1½ cups water

¾ cup sugar (or to taste)
2 tablespoons fresh lemon juice (or to taste)

1. Plunge the peaches in boiling water for 1 minute. Rinse under cold water and pull off the skins. Cut each peach in half and pull out the pit. Purée the peaches in a blender or food processor: You should have 2 cups purée. **Note:** For a more rustic granita, purée the peaches with the skins on.

2. Combine the water and sugar in a nonreactive saucepan. Bring the mixture to a boil, stirring occasionally to dissolve the sugar. Let the mixture cool to room temperature, then stir in the peach purée and lemon juice. Taste the mixture for sweetness,

adding sugar as desired. Let the mixture cool to room temperature, then refrigerate it until cold.

3. Freeze the mixture in an ice-cream machine, following the manufacturer's instructions. For the best results, serve at once.

Serves 6

Note: If you don't have an ice-cream machine, place the granita in a shallow bowl in the freezer. Scrape the mixture with a fork three or four times as it freezes to break it into icy crystals. Scrape it again just before serving to loosen the crystals.

116 CALORIES PER SERVING: 0 G PROTEIN; 0 G FAT; 31 G CARBOHYDRATE; 2 MG SODIUM; 0 MG CHOLESTEROL

BASIC RECIPES

BASIC VEGETABLE STOCK

Stock is the cornerstone of fine cooking from Paris to Phnom Penh. Stock is particularly useful to the low-fat cook, as it can be used as a substitute for butter, cream, and oil in myriad dishes. Almost any vegetable or vegetable trimming is a candidate for stock: corn cobs and husks, summer and winter squash, red and yellow peppers, green beans, zucchini, mushrooms, potatoes, collard greens, and kale stalks. Stock is a great place to put tomato seeds and skins. Use green peppers, eggplants, turnips, and cabbage in limited quantities, as their flavor tends to be overpowering. Avoid beets, which will turn a stock red, and asparagus, which will turn it green.

1 large onion, skin on, quartered
2 leeks, trimmed, washed, and cut into 1-inch pieces
2 carrots, cut into 1-inch pieces
2 stalks celery, cut into 1-inch pieces
2 tomatoes, cut into 1-inch pieces
6 cloves garlic, skin on, cut in half
2 quarts chopped vegetables or vegetable trimmings (see headnote above for some suggested vegetables)

2 tablespoons tomato paste
1 large Bouquet Garni (page 263)
½ cup mixed chopped fresh herbs, including basil, oregano, chives, and/or parsley stems (optional)
4 quarts water
freshly ground black pepper
sea salt or soy sauce (optional)

1. Combine the onion, leeks, carrots, celery, tomatoes, garlic, chopped vegetables, tomato paste, bouquet garni, herbs (if using), and water in a stockpot and bring to a boil. Reduce the heat and simmer the stock, uncovered, adding water as necessary to keep the vegetables covered, for 1 to 1½ hours, or until well flavored. (A certain amount of evaporation will take place—this helps concentrate the flavor.) Skim the stock as necessary and season with pepper and salt or soy sauce to taste at the end. Alternatively, the stock can be cooked in a pressure cooker for 15 minutes.

2. Strain the stock, pressing with the back of a spoon to extract as much liquid as possible from the vegetables. Cool the stock to room temperature, then refrigerate or freeze. (Refrigerated stock will keep 3 to 4 days; frozen it will keep for 6 months.) For a thicker, richer stock, force the liquid and vegetables through a vegetable mill or purée in a blender, then strain.

Makes 2½ to 3½ quarts (depending on the vegetables used, the size of the pot, and the length of the cooking time)

Note: I like to freeze 1-cup portions of vegetable stock, so I always have the right amount on hand.

ROASTED VEGETABLE STOCK

For a richer, more full-flavored vegetable stock, roast the vegetables in a lightly oiled roasting pan in a 400° F. oven for 45 minutes, or until nicely browned. Transfer the vegetables to a stockpot. Deglaze the roasting pan with ½ cup dry white wine and add the deglazing mixture to the stockpot as well. Prepare as in the preceding recipe.

MEDITERRANEAN VEGETABLE STOCK

Saffron, fennel, and red bell peppers give this stock a Mediterranean accent. Use it for dishes of Spanish, Italian, Provençal, and even North African origin.

2 bay leaves
4 thyme sprigs or 1 teaspoon dried thyme
20 black peppercorns
1 medium onion, peeled and coarsely chopped
1 leek, trimmed, washed, and coarsely chopped
6 cloves garlic, peeled and cut in half
2 stalks celery, coarsely chopped
2 carrots, coarsely chopped
1 red bell pepper, cored, seeded, and coarsely chopped
½ small or ¼ large fennel, coarsely chopped, or 1 teaspoon fennel seeds

2 tomatoes, coarsely chopped
½ cup fresh basil leaves and stems
½ cup flat-leaf parsley leaves and stems
2 strips orange zest
1 cup dry white vermouth
½ cup fresh orange juice
¼ teaspoon saffron, soaked in 1 tablespoon hot water
about 8 cups water
sea salt (optional)

1. Tie the bay leaves, thyme, and peppercorns in a piece of cheesecloth or wrap them in a piece of foil and pierce all over with a fork.

2. Combine the onion, leek, garlic, celery, carrots, bell pepper, fennel, tomatoes, basil, parsley, zest, vermouth, juice, saffron, and water in a large saucepan or stockpot and bring to a boil. Reduce the heat and simmer the mixture uncovered for 1 hour, or until the vegetables are very tender, adding water as necessary to keep the vegetables covered. Alternatively, the stock can be cooked in a pressure cooker for about 15 minutes.

3. Strain the stock, pressing with the back of a spoon to extract as much liquid as possible from the vegetables. Let the stock cool to room temperature, then refrigerate or freeze it. (Refrigerated stock will keep 3 to 4 days; frozen it keeps for 6 months.) For a thicker, richer stock, remove the bouquet garni and orange peel and force the liquid and vegetables through a vegetable mill or purée in a blender, then strain.

Makes 5 to 6 cups

Note: To make a wonderful Mediterranean vegetable soup, discard the bouquet garni and purée the stock and vegetables in a blender. Season with salt and pepper and serve. This will make 8 cups soup.

ASIAN VEGETABLE STOCK

Ginger, star anise, and black mushrooms lend this stock an Asian flavor. These ingredients can be found at Asian markets and in the ethnic foods section of most supermarkets. Use this stock for Asian-style soups and stir-fries.

2 star anises
1 teaspoon Sichuan peppercorns
1 onion, coarsely chopped
1 carrot, coarsely chopped
1 bunch scallions, coarsely chopped
8 cloves garlic, cut in half
1-inch piece fresh ginger, cut into ¼-inch slices
1 bunch cilantro with stems, coarsely chopped
  (about 1 cup)

3 cups coarsely chopped bok choy, napa, and
  other Chinese vegetables
2 dried Chinese or Japanese black mushrooms
  (shiitakes)
2 tablespoons soy sauce (or to taste)
10 cups water (or as needed)

1. Tie the star anise and Sichuan peppercorns in a piece of cheesecloth or wrap them in a piece of foil and pierce all over with a fork.

2. Combine the onion, carrot, scallions, garlic, ginger, cilantro, Chinese vegetables, shiitakes, soy sauce, and water in a large saucepan or stockpot and bring to a boil. Reduce the heat and simmer the stock, uncovered, adding water as necessary to keep the vegetables submerged, for 1 hour, or until the vegetables are very tender. Alternatively, the stock can be cooked in a pressure cooker for about 15 minutes.

3. Remove the spice bundle and black mushrooms. Discard the former and reserve the latter for stuffings. For a clear stock, strain the liquid into another container, pressing with the back of a spoon to extract the juices, then refrigerate it or freeze it. (Refrigerated stock will keep 3 to 4 days; frozen it will keep for 6 months.) For a thicker, richer stock, force the liquid and vegetables through a vegetable mill or purée in a blender, then strain.

Makes 6 cups

Note: To make a wonderful Asian vegetable soup, discard the bouquet garni and purée the broth and vegetables in a blender. Season with soy sauce and pepper and serve. This will make about 8 cups soup.

MUSHROOM STOCK

Dried mushrooms make a rich, soulful, extravagant vegetable stock. Use mushroom stock in soups, stews, and other dishes where an earthy flavor is desired.

1½ tablespoons olive oil
1 large onion, finely chopped
2 leeks, trimmed, washed, and finely chopped
3 stalks celery, finely chopped
8 cloves garlic, finely chopped
¾ cup dried shiitakes, boletus, or other exotic
    mushrooms (about 1½ ounces)

1 Bouquet Garni (page 263)
10 to 12 cups water
freshly ground black pepper
sea salt or soy sauce

1. Heat the oil in a large saucepan. Add the onions, leeks, celery, and garlic and lightly brown over medium heat. Add the mushrooms, bouquet garni, water, and pepper.

2. Simmer the stock, uncovered, for 1½ hours, or until richly flavored, adding water as necessary to keep the vegetables covered. Season to taste with salt or soy sauce and pepper. Alternatively, the stock can be cooked in a pressure cooker for 15 minutes.

3. Strain the stock, pressing with the back of a spoon to extract as much liquid as possible from the mushrooms. Cool the stock to room temperature, then refrigerate or freeze it. (Refrigerated stock will keep 3 to 4 days; frozen it will keep for 6 months.)

Makes about 5 cups

GRILLED CORN

Grilled corn turns up in many of the recipes in this book. The reason is simple: Grilling imparts a rich, smoky flavor that evokes backyard barbecues and smokehouses. Save the corn husks for the Tamales on page 147.
(Keep them in the freezer.)

4 ears fresh sweet corn, shucked
2 to 3 teaspoons extra-virgin olive oil
salt and freshly ground black pepper

1. Preheat the barbecue grill. Brush each ear of corn with olive oil and sprinkle with salt and pepper.

2. Grill the corn over medium-high heat until golden brown, 2 to 3 minutes per side, 8 to 10 minutes in all. Add salt and pepper as necessary. If serving as a vegetable, serve at once.

Note: To obtain grilled corn kernels, let the corn cool. Lay it flat on a cutting board and cut the kernels off the cobs in lengthwise swaths with a sharp knife.

Serves 2 to 4 as a vegetable; makes 3 cups kernels

113 CALORIES PER SERVING: 2.5 G PROTEIN; 4.5 G FAT; 20 G CARBOHYDRATE; 13 MG SODIUM; 0 MG CHOLESTEROL
Analysis based on 1 ear of corn per serving

PRUNE PURÉE

In the last few years, health-conscious cooks have begun using prune purée in place of butter or shortening to give moistness and richness to baked goods.

8 ounces pitted prunes (about 1¼ cups)
1 cup boiling water
2 tablespoons sugar

1. Plump the prunes in the water in a bowl for 15 minutes.

2. Combine the prunes, ⅓ cup of the soaking liquid (or as needed), and the sugar in a food processor and purée to a smooth paste.

Makes 1 ¼ cups

95 CALORIES PER ¼ CUP: 1 G PROTEIN; 0 G FAT; 25 G CARBOHYDRATE; 2 MG SODIUM; 0 MG CHOLESTEROL

DRIED TOMATOES

Centuries ago, tomato lovers in southern Italy devised an ingenious method for preserving the vibrant flavor of a vine-ripened summer tomato throughout the year. The tomatoes were split open, salted, and dried on wooden racks in the hot sun. The drying process intensified and enhanced the flavor, giving it the tangy, almost meaty quality one finds in prosciutto. Dried tomatoes are a cinch to make at home (and are much more economical). The results are much superior to the leathery dried tomatoes one finds in plastic packs at the supermarket.

16 ripe plum tomatoes or 8 large round tomatoes
spray oil
1 teaspoon kosher salt (or to taste)
freshly ground black pepper

3 to 4 cloves garlic, minced
1 bunch fresh basil
2 to 3 teaspoons extra-virgin olive oil

1. Preheat the oven to 200° F. Wash and dry the tomatoes. If using plum tomatoes, cut them in half lengthwise. If using regular tomatoes, cut in half widthwise. Arrange the tomatoes on a baking sheet oiled with spray oil. Generously sprinkle the tomatoes with kosher salt, pepper, and minced garlic. Stem the basil and place one leaf on each tomato. Lightly drizzle the tomatoes with olive oil.

2. Bake the tomatoes at 200° F. for 12 to 14 hours, or until shrunken, wrinkled, and almost dry. Don't let the tomatoes dry out completely (they'll become tough) and don't let them brown.

3. Let the tomatoes cool to room temperature, then transfer to a sterile jar. Some people like to add olive oil to cover. (You can use a few drops of the intensely flavored oil on salads or steamed vegetables.) Dried tomatoes should be stored in the refrigerator. (Without oil tomatoes will keep for 4 to 5 days; in olive oil they will keep for 6 months.) But ours never seem to last more than a day!

Makes about 1 cup

Note: I usually put the tomatoes in the oven just before I go to bed and take them out the next morning. But the first time you try the recipe, do so while you're awake, as baking times vary widely from oven to oven.

21 CALORIES PER TOMATO: 1 G PROTEIN; 1 G FAT; 3 G CARBOHYDRATE; 124 MG SODIUM; 0 MG CHOLESTEROL

HOW TO PEEL A TOMATO

Many recipes in this book call for peeled and seeded tomatoes. Why bother doing either? Tomato skins (especially when cooked) can form red filaments that get caught in your teeth. Tomato seeds come in a watery pulp that can dilute the flavor of the dish. So here are 2 methods for peeling and seeding a tomato. By the way, never refrigerate tomatoes. If they're not ripe, they may ripen at room temperature. They'll never ripen if refrigerated. If they are ripe, refrigeration will make them mealy.

ripe tomatoes

METHOD ONE

1. Using the tip of a paring knife, cut out the stem end and cut a shallow X in the rounded end. Plunge the tomato in rapidly boiling water for 15 to 60 seconds. (The riper the tomato, the shorter the cooking time required.)

2. Let the tomato cool on a plate until you can comfortably handle it, then pull off the skin with your fingers. It should slip off in broad strips.

METHOD TWO

This method has the added advantage of producing a decorative tomato rose. Starting from the bottom (the end opposite the stem), pare off the skin in a single continuous strip, ½ to ¾ inch wide, the way Meg Ryan peeled an apple in *Sleepless in Seattle*. Roll up the strip as you would a roll of paper. Set the roll on end: It will look like a rose.

TO SEED A TOMATO

Cut the tomato in half widthwise and squeeze each half in the palm of your hand, cut side down, to wring out the seeds and liquid. Work over a bowl and strainer. Push the pulp through the strainer with the back of a spoon. Reserve the tomato liquid that collects at the bottom of the bowl for sauces, soups, or even drinking.

1 peeled, seeded tomato produces about ¾ cup chopped tomato

HOW TO ROAST AND PEEL A PEPPER

Peppers are among the few foods you're actually allowed to burn. Indeed, charring the skin imparts a distinctive smoky flavor and brings out a pepper's sweetness. Here's how to do it.

4 hard, firm, shiny bell peppers

1. Place the peppers directly on a gas or electric burner preheated to the hottest setting. Roast the peppers until completely charred and black on all sides, turning with tongs. This will take about 6 to 8 minutes. Be sure to roast the ends of the peppers as well. Peppers can also be roasted under the broiler or over a high flame on the grill.

2. Wrap the roasted peppers in wet paper towels for 5 minutes or place them in a sealed paper bag. (This helps steam off the skin.) To peel the peppers, scrape off the charred skin with a paring knife, stiff brush, or your fingers.

3. To core and seed the peppers, cut them in half lengthwise. Cut out the stem end. Trim or scrape away any white pith and seeds inside. Roasted peppers are delectable marinated in balsamic vinegar and olive oil. Slice them into salads or purée them in soups and sauces.

Makes about 1 cup

HOW TO PRESS TOFU

Tofu comes packed in water. Many recipes call for the tofu to be pressed before cooking to remove the excess moisture. Pressing also helps firm up the tofu, which keeps it from falling apart during stir-frying or grilling.
***Note**: Firm silken tofu (see Cook's Notes) does not need to be pressed.*

1 pound firm or extra-firm tofu

1. Lay the block of tofu flat on a cutting board. Holding your knife parallel to the cutting board, cut the tofu in half. (You'll cut through the short side to obtain 2 broad thin rectangles.)

2. Prop up one end of the cutting board (do so on a pot or bowl), so the board slopes downward at a 30° to 45° angle. Place the pieces of tofu in the center. Place a heavy weight, such as a cast-iron skillet or a brick wrapped in aluminum foil, on top. Press the tofu for 30 to 60 minutes in this fashion. Blot the tofu dry on paper towels, then slice and cook as desired.

Serves 2 to 4

329 CALORIES PER SERVING: 36 G PROTEIN; 20 G FAT; 10 G CARBOHYDRATE; 32 MG SODIUM; 0 MG CHOLESTEROL

Analysis based on 2 servings

BASIC RICE

Our Cuban friend, Elida Proenza, makes the best white rice I've ever tasted: It's sweet and moist, yet every individual
grain stays separate. The secret? Elida washes the rice before cooking it. Her rice of choice?
Like many Cubans, she prefers Uncle Ben's!

1½ cups rice
2¼ cups water

½ teaspoon salt (or to taste)
1 tablespoon extra-virgin olive oil (optional)

1. Wash the rice. Place it in a large bowl with water to cover by 2 inches. Swirl the rice with your fingers to wash it. Pour off the cloudy water. Continue adding water and swirling the rice until the water comes clean. This will take 6 to 8 washings. Pour off the water.

2. Bring the 2¼ cups water, salt, and oil (if using) to a boil in a large heavy saucepan with a tight-fitting lid. Add the rice and bring to a boil.

Reduce the heat to a gentle simmer. Cover the pan and cook the rice over low heat for 18 to 20 minutes, or until tender. (If the rice is still wet at this time, uncover the pan and cook for a few more minutes.)

3. Remove the pan from the heat and let stand for 2 minutes. Fluff the rice with a fork.

Serves 4

253 CALORIES PER SERVING: 5 G PROTEIN; 0 G FAT; 56 G CARBOHYDRATE; 274 MG SODIUM; 0 MG CHOLESTEROL

BASIC WILD RICE

Wild rice is neither, technically speaking, rice (it's an aquatic grass seed), nor wild. (It's cultivated on paddies in northern Minnesota and elsewhere.) Withal, it's a uniquely American grain, with a distinctive nutty flavor and a firmly chewy consistency you can really sink your teeth into. There are several ways to cook wild rice. In my first book, Steven Raichlen's High-Flavor, Low-Fat Cooking, you'll find the "pasta" method. (The rice is soaked overnight, then boiled in lots of water like pasta.) This recipe is quicker, requiring no advance soaking.

1 cup wild rice
8 cups water or Basic Vegetable Stock (page 247)
salt and freshly ground black pepper

OPTIONAL FLAVORINGS
1 bay leaf
1 very small onion
1 clove
3 cloves garlic, peeled

1. Wash the rice in a strainer or colander. Place the rice, water, salt, and pepper in a large heavy pot and bring to a rapid boil. If using the optional flavorings, pin the bay leaf to the onion with a clove; add the onion and garlic to the rice.

2. Cover the pot, reduce the heat to medium, and simmer the rice for 30 minutes.

3. Remove the pan from the heat and let the rice sit for 30 minutes, or until softened to the desired consistency. Drain off any excess water in a colander. Discard the spices and vegetables and season the rice with salt and pepper to taste.

Makes 3½ to 4 cups, enough to serve 4 to 6

143 CALORIES PER SERVING: 6 G PROTEIN; 0 G FAT; 30 G CARBOHYDRATE; 14 MG SODIUM; 0 MG CHOLESTEROL

BASIC BROWN RICE

This recipe is simplicity itself, but it never fails to produce brown rice that is tender yet pleasingly chewy. The recipe is dedicated with affection to my friend Katherine Kenny, who makes it almost daily.

1 cup brown rice

1. Wash the rice. Place it in a large bowl with tap water to cover by 2 inches. Swirl the rice with your fingers to wash it. Pour off the cloudy water. Continue adding water and swirling the rice until the water comes clean. This may take several washings.

2 cups spring water

2. Combine the rice and spring water in a large heavy saucepan and bring to a boil.
3. Reduce the heat to a gentle simmer, loosely cover the pot, and cook the rice for 35 minutes, or until tender.

Makes 3 cups, enough to serve 4

171 CALORIES PER SERVING: 4 G PROTEIN; 1 G FAT; 36 G CARBOHYDRATE; 7 MG SODIUM; 0 MG CHOLESTEROL

BASIC BASMATI RICE

Basmati is the Rolls-Royce of rice, a slender, long-grain beauty grown in the foothills of the Himalayas. The rice is aged in storage bins for several years to develop its distinctive nutty-milky flavor. True basmati is recognizable by its slim, slightly curved grains, which taper to sharp points. It also has the unusual property of doubling in length, not width, when cooked. Look for basmati rice in Indian and Pakistani markets, gourmet shops, and natural foods stores. The following method for preparing basmati comes from Indian cooking authority Julie Sahni.

1½ cups basmati rice
3 cups water

1. Wash the rice. Place it in a large bowl with water to cover by 2 inches. Swirl the rice with your fingers to wash it. Pour off the cloudy water. Continue adding water and swirling the rice until the water comes clean. This will take 6 to 8 washings. Drain the rice in a colander, return it to the bowl, and add the 3 cups water. Let the rice soak for 30 minutes.
2. Drain the rice in a colander over a large heavy pot. Bring the soaking water to a boil with the salt.

¾ teaspoon salt

Stir in the rice and bring it to a boil. Reduce the heat and gently simmer the rice, loosely covered, for 10 to 12 minutes, or until the surface is riddled with steamy holes.
3. Reduce the heat to the lowest setting and raise the pan one inch above the burner. (This can be done by placing it on a wok ring.) Tightly cover the pan and let the rice steam for 10 minutes. Fluff the rice with a fork and serve at once.

Serves 4

253 CALORIES PER SERVING: 5 G PROTEIN; 0 G FAT; 56 G CARBOHYDRATE; 409 MG SODIUM; 0 MG CHOLESTEROL

BASIC RECIPE FOR COOKING BEANS

Beans are a mainstay of the vegetarian diet and an important food for anyone who wishes to eat healthily. Low in fat, beans are high in protein, fiber, and complex carbohydrates and, of course, entirely free of cholesterol. There is growing evidence that they have anticarcinogenic properties and perhaps even the power to lower cholesterol.

I much prefer cooking dried beans from scratch to using canned beans: The latter tend to be mushy, and most brands are loaded with sodium. But canned beans certainly are convenient. Below is the basic method for cooking beans, plus a chart for approximate cooking times. If you like your beans on the firmer side, cook them uncovered. If you like them on the softer side, cook covered. Always add the salt or any acidic flavorings, such as wine, vinegar, or tomatoes, at the end: These ingredients cause the skins of the beans to toughen if added at the beginning. **Note**: *Cooking times vary according to the freshness of the beans.*

1 cups dried beans
1 bay leaf
1 small onion, peeled

1 clove
salt

1. Spread the beans on a baking sheet and pick through them, removing any pebbles. Rinse the beans in a colander. Soak the beans for at least 4 hours, preferably overnight, in 8 cups water in a large bowl.

2. Drain the beans. (This rids the beans of some of their flatulence-causing complex starches.) Pin the bay leaf to the onion with a clove. Place the beans and onion in a large heavy pot with 12 cups water. Bring the beans to a boil, reduce the heat, loosely cover the pot, and simmer for the amount of time

shown on page 262. The beans should be tender, even soft, but not mushy. Add water as necessary to keep the beans submerged. Add salt to taste the last 5 minutes. **Note**: The cooking time can be shortened substantially in a pressure cooker.

Makes about 2½ cups cooked beans

Note: To test for doneness, squeeze one between your thumb and forefinger; it should crush easily. There's nothing worse than eating undercooked beans.

159 CALORIES PER SERVING: 10 G PROTEIN; 1 G FAT; 29 G CARBOHYDRATE; 2 MG SODIUM; 0 MG CHOLESTEROL*

Analysis based on 4 servings

*Slight variation among different types of beans

Bean Cooking Times

Presoaked Beans

For beans that have been soaked for at least 4 hours. Add about 1 hour regular cooking time or
10 to 15 minutes pressure-cooking for unsoaked beans.

TYPE OF BEAN	REGULAR COOKING TIME	IN A PRESSURE COOKER
black beans	1½ hours	8 to 10 minutes
black-eyed peas	30 minutes	4 to 6 minutes
chickpeas	1½ to 2 hours	10 to 12 minutes
fava beans	1½ to 2 hours	16 to 18 minutes
Great Northern	1 hour	10 to 12 minutes
kidney beans	1½ hours	10 to 12 minutes
lima beans	50 minutes	6 to 8 minutes
navy or pea beans	1½ hours	6 to 8 minutes
pigeon peas	20 minutes	4 to 6 minutes
pinto beans	1½ to 2 hours	6 to 8 minutes

Beans That Require No Soaking

TYPE OF BEAN	REGULAR COOKING TIME	IN A PRESSURE COOKER
lentils	20 minutes	8 minutes
split peas	30 minutes	15 minutes

Note: The above times are approximate. Check the beans after the indicated amount of time. You may need 15 to 20 minutes additional cooking (2 to 3 minutes in a pressure cooker).

For further information on cooking beans in a pressure cooker, see Lorna Sass's excellent books *Cooking Under Pressure* and *Recipes from an Ecological Kitchen* (both published by William Morrow).

YOGURT CHEESE

Yogurt cheese is made by draining low- or no-fat plain yogurt in a very fine-meshed strainer. What results are fluffy white curds that can be used in place of cottage cheese, cream cheese, or ricotta. The curds have a sourish tang that goes well in dips and cheesecakes. The longer you drain the yogurt, the firmer the cheese will be.

1 quart (2 pounds) plain low-fat or nonfat yogurt

If you have a yogurt strainer (available in cookware shops), place it over a bowl. If not, line a colander with several layers of cheesecloth and place over a bowl. Add the yogurt and let drain, refrigerated, for at least 4 hours and as long as overnight. Discard liquid in bowl.

Note: Four hours will give you soft curds; overnight, firm curds. You don't need to refrigerate the yogurt for shorter periods, but do so when draining it overnight.

Makes 2 cups yogurt cheese

105 CALORIES PER SERVING: 12 G PROTEIN; 0 G FAT; 15 G CARBOHYDRATE; 149 MG SODIUM; 4.5 MG CHOLESTEROL

BOUQUET GARNI

Bouquet garni is a French herb bundle used for flavoring everything from soups to stews to braises. The traditional ingredients are bay leaf, thyme, and parsley, but I like to jazz up the flavor with allspice berries and other spices. It's customary to tie the herbs in cheesecloth. (This facilitates removal, so you don't wind up choking on a bay leaf or peppercorn.) As cheesecloth is hard to find these days, I offer a high-tech alternative!

2 bay leaves
2 sprigs fresh thyme or ½ teaspoon dried thyme
4 sprigs flat-leaf parsley or 12 parsley stems

2 allspice berries
1 clove
10 black peppercorns

Tie the bay leaves, thyme, parsley, allspice berries, clove, and peppercorns in a 5-inch square piece of cheesecloth or wrap them in a piece of foil, which you pierce all over with a fork. Always remember to remove the bouquet garni before serving the dish.

Makes 1 bouquet, enough to flavor a soup or stew for 4 to 6 people

Cook's Notes—A Guide to Ingredients

We live in an age of global shopping and truly international cuisine. Many ethnic and foreign ingredients are naturally high in flavor with little or no fat. Here's a guide to some of the more exotic ingredients that are called for in this book. Mail-order sources for these ingredients are found on page 276.

Agar-Agar

A natural vegetarian jelling agent extracted from sea moss. Granulated agar-agar can be found at natural foods stores and Japanese markets. Dissolve it in boiling water and gently simmer until it melts.

Arborio Rice

A glutinous short-grain rice from the Po Valley in northern Italy. Arborio rice has the ability to absorb up to five times its volume in liquid without becoming mushy. As it cooks, the starches in the rice thicken the broth into a creamy sauce. Arborio rice is sold at Italian markets, gourmet shops, and most supermarkets. Look for the word *superfino* on the label: This indicates the largest-grain rice. The short-grain **Valencia-Style Rice** sold at Latin American markets and most supermarkets makes an acceptable substitute. Never wash Arborio rice: You need the starch to help thicken the broth.

Balsamic Vinegar

A dark, sweet, richly flavored vinegar from Emilia-Romagna in north-central Italy. Unlike most vinegars, balsamic is made from must (fresh or partially fermented grape juice), not wine. This gives it a fruity sweetness beloved by chefs on both sides of the Atlantic. Balsamic vinegar is widely available in the supermarket. Reliable brands include Colavita and Dukes of Modena.

Black Sesame Seeds

A naturally black sesame seed with a delicate nutty flavor. Available at Japanese markets and natural foods stores, black sesame seeds are sometimes sold by their Japanese name: **Gomen**. Their jet-black color makes a striking garnish. If they are unavailable, toast regular sesame seeds in a dry skillet or on a baking sheet in a hot oven until dark golden brown. **Note**: The author manufactures a spice mix based on black sesame seeds called Beijing Blast. The mix is available from Big Flavor Foods, Inc. (See Mail-Order Sources, page 276.)

Cheese

A mainstay of much vegetarian cooking, cheese is quite high in fat, so I make limited use of it in my recipes. When I do use cheese, I pick a sharp-flavored variety, like feta or Romano. This way, a little goes a long way.

• **Buffalo Milk Mozzarella**: A soft, milky, drippingly moist cheese sold at Italian markets and gourmet shops. Buffalo milk mozzarella is a specialty of southern Italy and has a sharper flavor than regular mozzarella. If it's unavailable, use fresh cow milk mozzarella. The waxy vacuum-packed mozzarella sold in the supermarket makes a poor substitute.

• **Low-Fat Cheese**: There are an increasing number of low- and no-fat cheeses on the market. Their quality is mixed. The best-tasting tend to be the Jarlsberg- and cheddar-style cheeses. But in most cases, I'd rather use a smaller quantity of regular cheese.

• **Parmigiano-Reggiano:** Many cheeses are called Parmesan, but there is only one Parmigiano-Reggiano. To bear this name, it must come from a strictly delimited region in Emilia-Romagna in northern Italy. The cheese must be made from partially skimmed milk and aged for at least 18 months. What results is one of the world's greatest grating cheeses, a morsel that is mild and sweet, yet full of flavor.

• **Rennetless Cheese:** Most cheese is made with rennet, a curdling agent found in a calf's stomach. Vegetable curdling agents include lemon juice and artichoke juice. Rennetless cheeses are sold at natural foods stores.

• **Romano:** Italy's other great grating cheese. This one is made from sheep's milk, so it has a sharper flavor.

CHILIES

There's nothing like chilies for electrifying the taste of low-fat cooking. The modern cook has dozens to choose from. **Note:** If you have sensitive skin, it's a good idea to wear rubber gloves when handling chilies. The seeds are the hottest part of a chili, so omit them if you have a tender palate.

• **Ancho:** A dried poblano chili. Three to 4 inches long, 2 to 3 inches wide, and dark red to almost black in color, it is sweet, a little bitter, and moderately hot. There's something about it that reminds me of tobacco and chocolate.

• **Chinese Dried:** A small dried red chili in the cayenne family. A mainstay of Sichuan cooking, it is sold at Asian markets.

• **Chipotle:** A moderately hot smoked jalapeño chili. Chipotles are great for adding the smoky flavor one usually associates with bacon or ham to soups, stews, and chili. The top of the line is the **Chipotle Grande,** made from a giant red jalapeño. Recognizable by the "corking" (tan striations running the length of the chili), the grande is a large (2 to 4 inches long, ½ to 1 inch wide), wrinkled chili, tan to coffee brown in color, with a pungent, earthy flavor that is intensely smoky. Less costly than the grande is the **Chipotle Morita,** a small (1 to 2 inches long), reddish-brown chili with a less pronounced smoke flavor. I prefer the robust flavor of the chipotle grande, but I will use a morita in a pinch. Chipotles are sold in two forms: dried and canned in adobo (sour orange) sauce. When you buy the latter, you generally get grandes. **Note:** The author manufactures a spice mix based on chipotle chilies called Santa Fe Smoke. One teaspoon Santa Fe Smoke can be substituted for 1 whole chipotle chili. The mix is available from Big Flavor Foods, Inc. (See Mail-Order Sources, page 276.)

• **Pasilla:** A long, slender, black dried chili that's wrinkled, like a raisin. (Indeed, "pasa" is the Spanish word for raisin.) Similar in flavor to the ancho chili.

• **Poblano:** A fresh, dark green, triangular-shaped chili that is traditionally used for stuffing. Poblanos are what I'd call baby hot, tasting like turbocharged green peppers. If unavailable, substitute green bell peppers and a little jalapeño or serrano chili for spice.

• **Scotch Bonnet:** This colorful (red, orange, yellow, or lime green), walnut-size chili, with its distinctive dimpled crown, is the world's hottest chili—50 times hotter than a jalapeño! Behind the heat, there's an aromatic, almost smoky flavor that is essential for Caribbean cooking. Scotch bonnets, and their cousins **Habanero Chilies** (the two are interchangeable), can be found at West Indian markets and at an increasing number of supermarkets.

• **Serrano**: A thin, green, bullet-shaped chili smaller and slightly hotter than a jalapeño. I use the two interchangeably.

• **Thai**: A small, slender, green or red chili that belongs to the cayenne family. Sometimes called **Bird Pepper.** Majorly hot!

CHILI PASTE

Used throughout Southeast Asia. The basic ingredients are ground chilies, garlic, and salt. Chinese **Hot Bean Paste** also contains fermented soybeans; Indonesian **Sambal Ulek** is a bright red paste of chilies and garlic; **Thai Chili Paste** often contains fresh basil.

COCONUT MILK

The cream of the tropics. Made by blending freshly grated coconut with boiling water, coconut milk looks and cooks like a dairy product. It's often confused with coconut water (the clear liquid inside a coconut) and coconut cream (a thick grayish product used for making mixed drinks). Traditional coconut milk is quite high in fat, but there's a new **"Lite" Coconut Milk** made by A Taste of Thai that gives you the tropical flavor with acceptable levels of fat.

GARLIC

A sine qua non for high-flavor, low-fat cooking. One clove of fresh garlic makes about 1 teaspoon minced. To peel a clove of garlic easily, lightly pound it with the side of the knife to loosen the skin. To mince garlic, cut the clove widthwise into ¼-inch slices. Lay the slices flat on a cutting board, then pound them with the side of the knife.

GINGER

Not a root, as is commonly believed, but a rhizome (an underground stem). Fresh ginger adds a lively flavor to dishes as varied as Asian, Indian, African, and Caribbean. When buying ginger, look for firm, plump, smooth-skinned, heavy feeling "hands" (as the rhizomes are called in the trade). Avoid ginger that is shriveled or stringy. A 1-inch piece of fresh ginger makes about 1 tablespoon minced.

HOISIN SAUCE

A dark, thick, sweet Chinese sauce made from sugar and soybeans. Available in Asian markets and in the ethnic foods section of most supermarkets.

HOT SAUCES

Guaranteed to give zing to your cooking. There are endless varieties to choose from. Tabasco is a barrel-aged, vinegar-and-cayenne chili-based sauce from Louisiana. **Caribbean-Style** sauces, which include Trinidadian Matouk's and Inner Beauty Hot Sauce, contain the incendiary Scotch bonnet chili. **Thai-Style** hot sauces (typified by the widely available Sriracha brand) have a tangy, garlicky flavor.

LEMONGRASS

This scallion-shaped herb is a defining ingredient in Southeast Asian cooking. Fresh lemongrass has a delicate lemony, herbal flavor that lends zing to any dish to which it is added. To prepare fresh lemongrass, cut off the top ⅔ of the stalk. (The fibrous tops can be used for making teas.) Cut off the root end and strip off the outside leaves surrounding the core. This core is the edible part of the lemongrass, but even it is quite fibrous, so mince it very fine or leave it in large enough pieces for the eater to eat around. A trimmed stalk of lemongrass yields 1 to 2 tablespoons finely chopped.

When buying lemongrass, choose fat, heavy stalks. If you press your fingernail into the core, it should feel moist. Fresh lemongrass can be found at

Asian markets, gourmet shops, and many supermarkets. Dried lemongrass can be found at most natural foods stores. There's no real substitute for lemongrass, but fresh lemon zest (see **Zest** below) is better than nothing. **Note:** The author manufactures a spice mix based on lemongrass called Hanoi Hot. You can substitute 2 teaspoons Hanoi Hot for 1 stalk fresh lemongrass. The mix is available from Big Flavor Foods, Inc. (See Mail-Order Sources, page 276.)

LIQUID SMOKE

A clear, natural, smoke-flavored liquid available at most supermarkets. Use sparingly (a few drops will do) to give stews the smoky flavor one associates with ham or bacon.

MIRIN

Sweet rice wine from Japan. Mirin is sold at Japanese markets, natural foods stores, and gourmet shops. If it is unavailable, substitute white wine sweetened with a little sugar or honey.

MISO

An intensely flavored paste made from salted fermented soybeans and/or other beans or grains. Miso has a rich, tangy flavor; I like to think of it as vegetarian demi-glace. It's best known as the main ingredient in Japanese miso soup, but it's also delicious in sauces and salad dressings. There are many types of miso, including white miso, red miso, rice miso, barley miso, and chickpea miso—each with its own distinct flavor. Look for miso at Japanese markets and natural foods stores and store it in the refrigerator, where it will keep for many months. Like yogurt, miso contains live cultures, which are believed to aid digestion. To get the maximum nutritional value, add miso to a hot but not boiling liquid and never bring it to a boil.

MUSHROOMS

Exotic mushrooms are a great way to add flavor without fat to your cooking. A number of different varieties are called for in this book.

- **Chinese Black**: The Chinese version of a dried shiitake. Chinese black mushrooms have a pungent, almost smoky flavor, which makes them wonderful in soups. Soak the mushrooms in hot water until soft and pliable, 15 to 30 minutes. Cut off and discard the stems. Be sure to save the soaking liquid for soups and stews.

- **Enoki**: A cream-colored mushroom with a tiny cap and long slender stem. Enokis look like overgrown straight pins and are sold in tight clusters. To use them, simply cut off the common base and tease them apart. I like to serve enokis raw in salads. If you do cook them, keep it brief: They overcook easily.

- **Porcini**: Also known as boletus, this is a large brown and tan mushroom with a stout stem and broad cap with holelike pores instead of gills. The flavor is rich and meaty, with a hint of hazelnut. Dried porcini are great for flavoring soups and stews. Soak as described above, under **Chinese Black mushrooms,** and strain the soaking liquid. **Note:** Dried porcini are often very sandy, so wash well in several changes of water before using.

- **Shiitake**: A large, flat, dark brown–capped, tan-gilled mushroom with a pungent woodsy flavor. The mushroom takes its name from the type of tree (the *shii*) on which it's grown in Japan. Domestic shiitakes are widely available. Whether you use the dried or fresh ones, be sure to discard the tough stems.

- **Straw**: A pungent, dark brown, cone-shaped, softly crunchy mushroom used in Chinese cooking. It is virtually always sold canned.

- **Wood Ear**: This thin, wrinkled chip of a fungus is prized for its softly chewy, snappily crisp texture. It doesn't really have a flavor. Wood ears are commonly sold dried at Asian markets. The small ones are the most tender.

OLIVE OIL

Olive oil is my preferred fat for high-flavor, low-fat cooking. Unlike most vegetable oils, it possesses a distinctive flavor that is at once nutty, fruity, and peppery. It's also good for you: As a monounsaturated fat, olive oil is believed to help boost levels of HDLs (high-density lipoproteins—the "good" cholesterol) while reducing LDLs (low-density lipoproteins—the "bad" cholesterol).

There are three grades of olive oil: **Extra-virgin, Virgin,** and **Olive Oil**. Extra-virgin is the best (and the most expensive), with an acidity level of 1 percent or less. This grade has the most flavor and is the one I suggest using for the recipes in this book.

Virgin olive oil (rarely seen in this country) contains 1 to 3 percent acidity. Plain olive oil, sometimes called **Pure Olive Oil,** starts as oil that failed to meet the aforementioned standards. It is industrially refined to remove the excess acidity and sometimes flavored with a little extra-virgin or virgin oil. **"Lite" Olive Oil** falls in this category. Compared with extra-virgin, plain olive oil may seem bland, even tasteless, but it's considerably less expensive, and it does have the health benefits of all monounsaturated oils.

When the oil is used raw (in a salad dressing or stuffing, for example), use the best extra-virgin you can buy. Cooking alters the flavor, so you don't need to use an expensive extra-virgin oil for sautéing.

ONIONS

Unless otherwise stated, when a recipe calls for an onion, I mean a medium-sized onion (8 to 10 ounces), which will yield 1 cup finely chopped.

PICKAPEPPA SAUCE

A sweet-sour, mildly spicy, tamarind-based sauce from Jamaica. I use it in place of Worcestershire sauce, which contains anchovies. If you don't mind using Worcestershire sauce, you'll get a more authentic flavor in dishes like Fishless Caesar Salad (page 60).

RICE NOODLES

A translucent white pasta popular in Southeast Asia and China. Rice noodles are made from rice flour and water and come as thin as angel hair or as thick as pappardelle. Rice paper (see page 15) is nothing more than a giant flat round rice noodle. Rice noodles are sold at Asian markets, gourmet shops, and many supermarkets. Bean threads (mung bean noodles) can be substituted in many recipes.

RICE WINE

A rice-based spirit used in Chinese and Japanese cooking. Chinese rice wine is a brown, unsweetened spirit. Dry sherry makes a good substitute. Japanese rice wine (sake) is clear and slightly sweet. **Mirin** (see separate entry above) is sweetened Japanese rice wine.

ROSE WATER

A perfumed extract of rose petals used in Middle Eastern and Indian cooking. Look for it at Middle Eastern, Indian, and Armenian grocery stores, as well as some pharmacies and cosmetics stores.

SAFFRON

The rust-colored, intensely aromatic stigmas of a crocus grown in southern Spain. Always buy saffron threads, not powder (the latter is easier to adulterate), preferably in small quantities in tiny glass tubes. Tightly sealed and stored in a dark place, saffron will keep for several months. If it lacks an intense aroma when you open the bottle, it's probably past its prime.

SALT

The world's most universal seasoning. I use two kinds of salt in my cooking: kosher salt and sea salt. I like the former for its large-sized crystals, which dissolve more slowly than table salt in slaws and salads. But I also like sea salt, which is rich in minerals, such as iodine and calcium and magnesium chloride—minerals that are lacking in rock salt. Iodine helps prevent some thyroid disorders.

SEAWEED

The Japanese have eaten sea vegetables for centuries. We're just catching on. Seaweed is rich in minerals, including iodine and calcium. Its briny flavor makes a great base for soups, stocks, and stews.

• **Kelp**: A large, flat, olive green leaf known as **kombu** in Japanese. A traditional stock flavoring, kelp can be found at Japanese markets and natural food stores. Its taste is mild and briny. To extract its flavor, simmer it for about 20 minutes. The seaweed itself is seldom eaten.

• **Hijiki**: A slender, jet-black, tube-shaped seaweed that is high in calcium. Hijiki is usually served as a salad. Its flavor is robust, almost fishy.

• **Nori**: Paper-thin, green-black sheets of pressed **laver** seaweed, commonly used as a wrapping for sushi. Nori can also be toasted over an open flame to make a crunchy Korean snack and garnish called *gimgui*.

SESAME OIL

A dark, flavorful oil made from roasted sesame seeds and used extensively in Asian cooking. Look for it at Asian markets and natural foods stores. One good brand is Kadoya from Japan. (Steer clear of domestic sesame oils, most of which lack the intense flavor of the Asian.) Sesame oil is a polyunsaturated oil, which is good for you, but not quite as good as a monounsaturate. Add it as a seasoning at the end of cooking a dish, as heat diminishes its flavor.

SOBA

Japanese buckwheat noodles. Gray-brown in color and square on the ends, soba have an earthy flavor and firm texture that have endeared them to cooks all over the world. Soba can be found at natural foods stores, Asian markets, and most supermarkets.

SOUR CREAM

Who would have ever thought that this rich traditional baked-potato topping would become a mainstay of low-fat cooking? No-fat sour cream is one of the most successful of the low-fat dairy products flooding the market. It looks and tastes pretty close to the real thing. And unlike regular sour cream, it doesn't curdle when you boil it. On the contrary, it actually thickens, so you can use it to thicken sauces. Thanks to the invention of no-fat sour cream, the cream sauces of Europe have returned to my culinary repertory. Land O'Lakes is the brand I like best.

SOY SAUCE

A salty condiment made from fermented soybeans, salt, water, and sometimes wheat. **Shoyu** is a Japanese-style soy sauce made with a wheat and soybean starter, while **Tamari** is a Japanese-style sauce made exclusively with soybean starter. For my money, tamari has the cleanest, tangiest, most elegant flavor of any soy sauce, and I use it whenever soy sauce is called for. (Look for it at natural foods stores and gourmet shops.) **"Lite" Soy Sauce** and **"Lite" Tamari** contain about 33 percent less sodium.

Chinese soy sauces come both **Light** and **Dark**: The latter is enriched with molasses, so it tends to be thicker and sweeter. **Mushroom Soy Sauce** is a thick, pungent Chinese sauce flavored with straw mushrooms. **Kejap Manis** is a very thick, sweet soy sauce from Indonesia. **Note**: It's well worth spending a few extra dollars to buy a quality soy sauce. Quality soy sauce is a naturally fermented product, aged for several months or even years before bottling. Look for it in Asian markets and natural foods stores. Avoid the cheap supermarket soy sauces, which owe their flavor to hydrolized vegetable protein and caramel, not to natural fermentation.

STAR ANISE

A dried, star-shaped spice with a smoky, licoricy flavor. It's used extensively in Chinese, Vietnamese, and Caribbean cooking. Available in Asian and Hispanic markets and gourmet shops.

STOCK

Another of the cornerstones of high-flavor, low-fat cooking. Stock can be used as a flavorful substitute for cream in soups and casseroles, for butter in polenta, and for oil in sauces and salad dressings. On pages 247 to 251, you'll find recipes for different types of vegetable stock.

SUCANAT

Freeze-dried sugar cane juice. It contains the vitamins and minerals removed from sugar during the refining process, and it also has an interesting malty-molassesy flavor. You can use it like sugar, but it tends to clump, so you may need to pulverize it in a food processor. Available in natural foods stores.

TAMARI

See **Soy Sauce.**

TEMPEH

A cultured soybean product. Unlike tofu, which is relatively bland, tempeh has a strong, almost cheesy flavor. It requires equally strong seasonings, especially acids, like lime juice or vinegar. Tempeh is the base of numerous smoked soy "meats," such as Fakin' Bacon.

TOFU

Also known as bean curd, and the dairy metaphor is apt. To make it, fresh soybeans are soaked overnight, finely ground, and cooked with water to make soy milk. The soy milk is then separated into "curds" and "whey," using one of two natural coagulants: nigari (magnesium chloride extracted from seawater) or calcium sulfate (naturally mined gypsum).

Tofu made with the latter is higher in calcium. The curds are then strained and pressed into the familiar cobblestone-shaped cakes.

In East Asia there are literally dozens of types of tofu and tofu by-products, including malodorous fermented tofu and crepelike bean-curd skins. In this country, you'll find four basic types: **Extra-firm, firm, soft,** and **silken.** Extra-firm and firm tofu are designed for grilling, stir-frying, and other preparations in which you want the bean curd to retain its shape. Instructions on pressing tofu are found on page 257.

Soft tofu is great for cheesecakes (see my first book, *Steven Raichlen's High-Flavor, Low-Fat Cooking*), while silken tofu has a custardy consistency well suited to salad dressings and desserts. The Japanese make an **extra-firm silken tofu** that has the characteristic creaminess of silken tofu but holds up fairly well when cooked; one good brand is Mori-Nu Extra Firm Silken Tofu (look for it in a rectangular cardboard container).

Tofu is relatively high in fat (10 grams per 8-ounce serving). As a result, most of the tofu recipes in this book use lots of ingredients. New to the market is a reduced-fat tofu that contains about ⅓ the amount of fat found in regular tofu; one good brand is Tree of Life.

WASABI

Japanese horseradish. (Actually, it's the parsnip-shaped root of the mountain hollyhock.) Outside Japan, wasabi is most readily available in powdered form, sold in tiny cans. To reconstitute dried wasabi, add ½ teaspoon warm water to one heaping teaspoon of powder. Let the paste stand for 5 to 10 minutes to allow the flavor to develop. Wasabi can be found at Japanese and Oriental markets, natural foods stores, and gourmet shops.

YOGURT

Yogurt is, of course, a cultured milk product with a refreshingly sourish tang. Low- and nonfat yogurts are widely available at the supermarket. Instructions for making Yogurt Cheese are found on page 263.

ZEST

The oil-rich outer rind of a citrus fruit. Remove it with a grater or a zester, a tool with a small flat rectangular blade with sharp-edged holes at one end. (To use a zester, drag the holed side of the blade along the surface of the fruit. The holes will remove slender strips of zest.) To make large quantities of grated citrus zest, cut off broad strips of zest with a vegetable peeler. Pulverize them in a spice mill. **Note**: The white flesh beneath the zest is quite bitter and should not be used.

1. Sesame Oil
2. Tamari
3. Rice Wine
4. Agar-Agar
5. Chipotle Chili
6. Black Sesame Seeds
7. Lemongrass
8. Miso

9. Ancho Chili
10. Pasilla Chili
11. Wasabi
12. Sucanat
13. Saffron
14. Scotch Bonnet Chili
15. Star Anise

1. Nori Seaweed
2. Rice Noodles
3. Quinoa
4. Soba Noodles
5. Hijiki Seaweed
6. Dried Black Mushrooms
7. Tempeh

8. Kombu (Kelp)
9. Shiitakes
10. Wood Ears
11. Arborio Rice
12. Straw Mushrooms
13. Porcini
14. Tofu

MAIL-ORDER SOURCES

Adobe Mill Company
P.O. Box 596
Dove Creek, CO 81324
(800) 54-ADOBE
Dried beans, blue cornmeal, spices

American Spoon Foods
P.O. Box 566
Petoskey, MI 49770
(800) 222-5886
*Dried cherries and other fruits,
sugarless preserves*

Arrowhead Mills, Inc.
Box 2059
Hereford, TX 79045
(806) 364-0730
Grains, beans

Aux Délices des Bois
4 Leonard Street
New York, NY 10013
(212) 334-1230.
Fresh and dried mushrooms

Big Flavor Foods, Inc.
P.O. Box 331597
Miami, FL 33233
(800) 352-8670
*Beijing Blast, Hanoi Hot, Santa Fe
Smoke, and other spice mixes*

C.M. International
P.O. Box 60220
Colorado Springs, CO 80960
(719) 390-0505
Stovetop smoker and wood chips

Coyote Café General Store
132 W. Water Street
Santa Fe, NM 87501
(505) 982-2454
*Chilies, spices, Southwestern and
Mexican ingredients*

Dean & Deluca, Inc.
560 Broadway
New York, NY 10012
(800) 221-7714
*Oils, vinegars, beans, Puys lentils,
and other designer beans*

De Wildt Imports, Inc.
RD 3, Fox Gap Road
Bangor, PA 18013
(800) 338-3433
Asian ingredients and cookware

Joyce Chen Unlimited
423 Great Road
Acton, MA 01720
(508) 263–6922
Asian ingredients and cookware

Maine Seaweed Co.
P.O. Box 57
Steuben, ME 04680
(207) 546-2875
Kelp and other seaweed

Monterrey Food Products
3939 Brooklyn Avenue
Los Angeles, CA 90063
(213) 263-2143
*Chilies, spices, Southwestern and
Mexican ingredients*

Old Southwest Trading Company
P.O. Box 7545
Albuquerque, NM 87194
(505) 836-0168
*Chilies, spices, Southwestern and
Mexican ingredients*

Williams-Sonoma
100 North Point Street
San Francisco, CA 94133
(415) 421-4242
*Cookware, oils, vinegars, arborio
rice, grains, and other gourmet
products*